KT-445-811

Screening Novel Women

Screening Novel Women

From British Domestic Fiction to Film

Liora Brosh

palgrave
macmillan

First published in 2008 by
PALGRAVE MACMILLAN
Houndmills, Basingstoke, Hampshire RG21 6XS and
175 Fifth Avenue, New York, N.Y. 10010
Companies and representatives throughout the world.

PALGRAVE MACMILLAN is the global academic imprint of the Palgrave Macmillan division of St. Martin's Press, LLC and of Palgrave Macmillan Ltd. Macmillan® is a registered trademark in the United States, United Kingdom and other countries. Palgrave is a registered trademark in the European Union and other countries.

ISBN-13: 978–0–230–00846–5 hardback
ISBN-10: 0–230–00846–1 hardback

This book is printed on paper suitable for recycling and made from fully managed and sustained forest sources. Logging, pulping and manufacturing processes are expected to conform to the environmental regulations of the country of origin.

A catalogue record for this book is available from the British Library.

Library of Congress Cataloging-in-Publication Data

Brosh, Liora, 1960–
    Screening novel women : from british domestic fiction to film / Liora Brosh
        p. cm.
    Includes bibliographical references and index.
    ISBN 0–230–00846–1 (alk. Paper)
        1. English fiction – 19th century – Film and video adaptations.
    2. Motion pictures and literature. 3. Women in motion pictures.
    4. Femininity in motion pictures. 5. Gender identity in motion pictures.
    6. Feminism and motion pictures. 7. Film adaptations – History and criticism. I. Title.

PR878.M73B76 2007
791.43′6522—dc22   2007022505

10 9 8 7 6 5 4 3 2 1
17 16 15 14 13 12 11 10 09 08

Printed and bound in Great Britain by
CPI Antony Rowe, Chippenham and Eastbourne

Contents

Acknowledgments

I would like to thank John Maynard and Antonia Lant for their helpful suggestions at the early dissertation stages of my research. At Palgrave, I would like to thank the anonymous reviewer for their insightful comments and Jason Pearce for his excellent editing. Special thanks go to my friends and family: to Nancy Glassman, Miriam Davidson, and Ariella Kaye-Hagin, whose valuable assistance made this book possible, and to Oded Brosh, Colin Alfred, and Philip Alan for the many ways in which they provided support. I am also grateful to Nancy Mackin for proofreading the proofs at short notice and to Julie Finton for her encouragement and for designing the jacket. Finally, I would like to thank Taylor & Francis for permission to reproduce an earlier version of part of Chapter 1: "Consuming Women: The Representation of Women in the 1940 Adaptation of *Pride and Prejudice*," *Quarterly Review of Film and Video* 17, no. 2 (2000), 147–59.

Introduction

In 1995 *People* magazine voted Jane Austen one of "the most intriguing personalities of the year."[1] Jane Austen's prominence in a best-selling tabloid almost two hundred years after the publication of her novels reveals how pervasive the British nineteenth-century novel had become in the popular culture of the 1990s. *Pride and Prejudice, Sense and Sensibility, Emma, Mansfield Park, Wuthering Heights, Jane Eyre, The Tenant of Wildfell Hall,* and *The Woman in White* are only a few of the many British nineteenth-century novels that were made into television programs and films between 1995 and 2000. At the time, this flurry of adaptation was characterized by the media as an unusual phenomenon worthy of notice and explanation. However, what appeared unprecedented was really only a new twist in an old cultural tradition.

In the nineteenth century, novels were themselves popular forms of entertainment, not unlike today's television series and films, and were even, like television episodes, published in suspense-enhancing serial magazines and triple-volume installments. More significantly, when they were written, most nineteenth-century novels had lives beyond the written page. Theatrical productions of successful novels, such as *Lady Audley's Secret* and *Oliver Twist,* were common. Dickens adapted his own work in wildly popular public readings, often rewriting scenes to please his audiences. While some of his changes heightened the suspense and drama of the plot, others were politically motivated and removed social criticisms that might have alienated his audience.

Illustrations that translated specific scenes in the novels into a visual medium can also be seen as a form of adaptation, one that made novels more commercially successful. Walter Scott, for example, calculated that illustrating *Waverley* earned him an extra £13,000.[2] However, there was often a lot of tension between authors and their illustrators. Dickens, for example, struggled to maintain control over his illustrators' work, often clashing with Cruikshank,[3] and Thackeray preferred to illustrate his own novels to avoid such conflicts. Even Thackeray's own illustrations, however, "compete and conflict with his prose, rather than merely decorating, supplementing, or supporting it."[4] The relationship between nineteenth-century novels and their adaptations has always been complex, yet it is important to recognize that the nineteenth-century British novel always existed within a broader commercial context that encouraged various forms of visual, dramatic, and/or oral presentation. Most British nineteenth-century novels have always been mediated by other popular cultural forms.

With the birth of cinema, film became the predominant and the most popular mode of adaptation. Early film drew heavily on the British nineteenth-century novel, with *Jane Eyre*, for example, being adapted six times, *Vanity Fair* five times, and *East Lynne* twelve times between 1902 and 1922. Thereafter, adaptations of British nineteenth-century novels were made throughout the twentieth century – at times more frequently, as in the 1930s, 1940s, and 1990s, and at other times, as in the 1960s, quite rarely. Overall, "British Victorian novels and novellas have been more frequently adapted to film than any other body of literature including Shakespearean plays."[5]

This has been explained in terms of formal affinities: film and the nineteenth-century novel have often been seen as contiguous aesthetic forms. Sergei Eisenstein claimed that Dickens and Flaubert, among others, prefigured cinematic techniques such as montage when they shifted back and forth, or cut, from the description of one scene to another.[6] Kamilla Elliott has contested this analysis of montage in novels and refuted the arguments of theorists, such as Christian Metz, who claim that film carries on a realist literary tradition that the novel abandoned. Elliott argues that film is rooted more in a theatrical than a literary tradition. Nevertheless, a literary form that is related to film, according to Elliott, is the illustrated novel. It is the intertwining of illustrations with narrative, and not any nineteenth-century narrative technique, that prefigures cinematic montage.[7] Indeed, according to Elliott, film adaptations displaced the illustration of books. The practice of publishing novels without illustrations began "precisely as film was gaining popular ascendancy in the early decades of the twentieth century."[8] Overall, with its actors, visual imagery, and later sound, the cinema was easily able to supplant nineteenth-century modes of adaptation such as theatrical performances, illustrations, and public readings.

Film and television adaptations of British nineteenth-century novels have been extremely popular. Films such as *Wuthering Heights* (1939), *Jane Eyre* (1944), and *Great Expectations* (1946) and, more recently, television series such as *Pride and Prejudice* (1995) have achieved substantial critical and commercial success. *Wuthering Heights*, for example, was a close runner-up for the Best Picture Oscar, losing only to a rival as critically and commercially formidable as *Gone with the Wind*. Yet the popularity of these adaptations cannot be wholly accounted for by the aesthetic or formal affinities between the nineteenth-century novel and cinema observed by Eisenstein, Metz, Elliott, and others.

There is also something about the content of British nineteenth-century novels that has captivated filmmakers and audiences. Clearly, the ubiquitous marriage plot of nineteenth-century novels is especially amenable to the classic Hollywood version of the marriage plot. Yet the nineteenth-century marriage plot serves a larger purpose: nineteenth-century domestic fiction both constructs and questions cultural ideals that define women in terms of their domestic roles. It is this ideological content that drives the recurring cinematic return to these novels.

What twentieth-century adaptations seem to change most often, and in this sense focus on, is precisely this domestic content, the construction of ideals of femininity, marriage, and home. For example, in Jane Austen's *Mansfield Park*, her protagonist, Fanny, is passive, repressed, and subservient to the uncle on whom she depends for her livelihood. In the 1999 adaptation, in contrast, Fanny is socially conscious and criticizes her uncle for his involvement in the slave trade that underpins and taints his home. In the BBC's 1995 *Pride and Prejudice*, after a spontaneous swim in the lake, Darcy meets Elizabeth with wet clothes clinging revealingly to his body, appealing to Elizabeth in a way that would certainly not suit Jane Austen's sense of decorum. Even more striking is that many "nineteenth-century" female characters flee abusive husbands and comfortably articulate feminist views popular in the 1990s. In the 1990s, film adaptations, like nineteenth-century novels, construct ideals of sexual identity and marriage, but they do so in terms of contemporary discourses about gender, sexuality, race, and feminism.

Adaptations made earlier in the twentieth century also define domestic ideals in terms of contemporary ideologies. In the United States during the Depression, the celluloid heroine of *Pride and Prejudice* is money hungry and loves to shop, yet she is willing to renounce her material desires if her prospective husband cannot afford them. As the

Second World War drew to a close, Charlotte Brontë's feisty female heroine Jane Eyre wants to stay home and look after children. During the Depression in Britain, when national unity was important, an adaptation of *The Mill on the Floss* has Maggie Tulliver sacrifice her own sexual desires so that her brother Tom can learn how to make personal sacrifices for the good of the country. During the Depression and the Second World War, British and American adaptations construct women who renounce their own desires for the good of domestic entities, either the private home or the home nation. In contrast, domestic ideals constructed in the 1990s suggest that women can satisfy all their desires, finding erotic fulfillment, happy marriages, and feminist liberation all at once. Thus, although these adaptations differ in terms of their specific characteristics over time, they all attempt to construct gender ideals in terms of contemporary ideas about women and their relationship to a domestic sphere.

It is often noted that adaptations try to fit the cultural moment, that nineteenth-century novels must be changed in ways that make them accessible to contemporary audiences. Yet the ways this accessibility is achieved at different times, the kinds of changes that are made when nineteenth-century novels become twentieth-century films, has ideological dimensions that have not been studied systematically.

Whether produced in Britain or in Hollywood, in the 1930s or in the 1990s, all adaptations use the British domestic novel to construct domestic ideals that are contemporary. British domestic novels participated in nineteenth-century controversies about women, marriage, and the home in complex and contradictory ways. The marriage plots of British domestic fiction construct ideals of femininity and marriage that in some ways echoed and in other ways questioned culturally dominant views. These ideological complexities have made it possible for the cinema to find, in the novels, disparate ideas about women at different times. Suppressing or emphasizing different aspects of nineteenth-century narratives at different times, film adaptations have been able to construct very dissimilar domestic ideals from the same group of novels. The cinema has been drawn to domestic fiction not only because of its domestic themes and its focus on women and marriage, but also because the novels themselves are rich and complex enough to have enabled an extremely diverse use of these domestic themes over time. It is something about the novels themselves that has enabled film to present these novels as, for example, feminist in the 1990s but home oriented in the 1940s. In addition, it is significant that British nineteenth-century novels, with their emphasis on women and the home, were often popular when the relationship of women to the home had been disrupted – during the Depression and the Second World War, and against the background of the ever-rising divorce rates and increasingly fluid gender identities of the 1990s. Adaptations of the British nineteenth-century novel tend to be popular when style and ideology meet. When commercial film is less interested in experimenting with narrative forms and when conventional gender identities and family structures appear unstable, filmmakers and viewers turn to the classic marriage plots of the nineteenth century. Repeatedly in the twentieth century, the cinema drew on the British nineteenth-century novel to create comforting films that stabilize gender identities, define marriage, and fix the parameters of the domestic sphere.

This book traces some of the different ways in which the British nineteenth-century novel's representation of women has been appropriated by film and, later, television. Concentrating on periods when events or social changes made gender ideals particularly unstable, this book reveals how films have employed British nineteenth-century domestic fiction in the construction of stable domestic ideals that address contemporary cultural anxieties.

Before the late 1990s, the relationship of literary texts to their film versions was studied from a different perspective. Adaptation studies invariably explored questions of fidelity, asking how closely the film reproduced the novel. As Robert Ray has so succinctly phrased it, adaptation studies ultimately asked, "How does the film compare with the book?" and dully concluded, "The book is better."[9] Even cinema studies scholars using more sophisticated theoretical approaches such as structuralism did not depart drastically from questions of fidelity. Influential critics such as Brian McFarlane closely examined how films successfully translate the characteristics of one medium into another. Yet, despite the deeper understanding of the two media such studies exhibited, they were still purely formalist and were ultimately interested in "fidelity," though a fidelity of form not content. As the twentieth century drew to a close, in tandem with the commercial success of many film adaptations, a number of new studies were published that challenged the importance of fidelity.

Theorists argued that, after Jacques Derrida, adaptation studies must acknowledge that the relationship between original and copy is as problematic as the assumption that a literary text has one essential meaning. The question so often asked in adaptation studies about whether one form, a "copy," is "faithful" to the essence of another form, an "original," is theoretically flawed.[10] It is as impossible to find a univocal meaning that can be translated into film as it is to recover an original novel stripped of all its cultural echoes. Robert Self, for example, emphasizes that the fidelity question ignores the richness of discourses that come between a novel and its later film adaptation. "Cinematic adaptations of literature never merely adapt the 'prior whole' of the literary text but a wide array of other cultural texts as well."[11] Between a novel and its film version lie many years of history and cultural change that should not be ignored.

Film Adaptation, a study published in 2000, heralded new directions in the field as it called for adaptation studies to pay less attention "to formal than to economic, cultural and political issues."[12] To a great extent this call has been answered in a variety of ways. Published in the same year, *Adaptations: From Text to Screen, Screen to Text* not only studied the economic, cultural, and political dimensions of adaptation but also broadened the field by examining new forms such as the multiple adaptations of graphic narratives (*Batman*) and a film that was turned into a novel (*The Piano*).[13] With a similarly broad sweep, Michael Dunne explores the cultural and political contexts of *Intertextual Encounters* between American fiction, film, and popular culture. Devoting only a small section of his book to film adaptations, Dunne examines how literary and cinematic texts relate to popular social myths and historical events.[14]

Three broad-ranging books by Robert Stam published in 2004 and 2005 – *A Companion to Film Adaptation, Literature through Film*, and *Literature and Film* – include essays that analyze film adaptations of both realist and nonrealist novels from divergent ideological perspectives.[15] An ideological emphasis also exists in studies that value fidelity and adhere to a traditional literary canon. *The Classic Novel: From Page to Screen*, for example, argues that a novel's textuality cannot extend into the visual medium of film and television and claims that "adaptation becomes a system of difference in relation to which the literary work has become, precisely, literary."[16] Despite its emphasis on fidelity and the literary canon, *The Classic Novel* questions the traditional hierarchical view of a literary work and its adaptation and examines modes of production and other cultural contexts not considered by classic fidelity studies. Overall, the economic, cultural, and political dimensions of adaptation have become more central, and distinctions between "original" and "copy" as well as between "high" and "low" culture have come to be questioned.

Some books on literature and film have focused on one genre or author. An early and insightful work, *Jane Austen in Hollywood*, sometimes situates adaptations culturally but remains rooted in a literary approach to adaptation studies, which is evident, for example, in its use of screenwriters rather than directors to identify films.[17] *Screening the Gothic* describes how gothic literary texts are made less gothic when adapted to film, whereas non-gothic literary texts acquire gothic characteristics through adaptation.[18] This interesting genre-based analysis remains grounded in questions of fidelity and leaves cultural explanations for such changes unexamined.

Overall, then, most recent adaptation studies either focus on one genre or author, but remain rooted in a rather narrow tradition of fidelity studies or, influenced by a more recent interest in cultural studies, examine the ideological dimension of film adaptation but are overly broad in scope, studying films and novels written or produced in different countries in different genres at different times. Partly, this is because, so far, almost every book that has examined the cultural and ideological dimensions of film adaptation has been an edited collection of essays by a number of different critics examining a wide range of unrelated films from a variety of different methodological perspectives.

Screening Novel Women, in contrast, studies film and television adaptations of one literary genre, the British nineteenth-century domestic novel, in terms of one ideological arena, gender. Concentrating on periods when cultural constructions of gender were particularly unstable, the following chapters will examine how film and television attempted to use the British nineteenth-century novel to counter this instability.

This book follows in the methodological footsteps of feminist critics who have studied the nineteenth-century novel so fruitfully. As Mary Poovey has convincingly argued, the nineteenth-century domestic novel participated in its age's ideological work of constructing, contesting, and reconstructing domestic ideals.[19] Film adaptations of these domestic novels undertook a similar kind of ideological work as they constructed ideals of women, marriage, and the home for twentieth-century audiences.

II

To understand why films have been able to appropriate the British nineteenth-century novel in such strikingly different ways during different periods, it is important to appreciate these novels' ideological complexity. Domestic fiction articulated and/or questioned the domestic ideologies of its time. With roots in the latter half of the eighteenth century, nineteenth-century domestic ideals constructed a separation of spheres that insisted the middle-class man work outside the home and the middle-class woman labor within the home. This separation of the private and public spheres, by the mid-Victorian period, had come to mark a sexual division of economic roles and political rights.

Confined to the home, a woman was supposed to display, legitimize, and protect the middle-class status of her husband. The wife's very existence, the fact that her husband could afford to support her, attested to his status: the wife's duty was to display her husband's status by managing her household appropriately. Protected within the home, women were considered to be morally untainted by the capitalist economy in which their husbands competed. Thus, virtue was located within the private sphere, which was depicted as a safe haven from a public sphere ruled by "competition, self interest and economic aggression."[20] Women's work was seen as a locus of virtue in a world no longer considered virtuous. This moral function was represented as emanating naturally from a woman's maternal instincts, as expressed in her selfless care for her husband, family, and home.

This ideal of the middle-class woman and her home, the Victorian "angel in the house," served many functions. One function was to foster an image of the English, with their morally centered monogamous domestic hearth, as morally superior to their imperialized others – an image that was used to legitimize imperial activities and aspirations.[21] Middle-class virtue, emanating from the moral superiority of the middle-class wife, was also used to distinguish the middle classes from the classes above and below them and to legitimize their increasingly powerful political and economic position. The virtuous "nature" of the woman at the center of the middle-class home enabled a representation of the middle classes as superior to the decadent aristocracy, whose women were represented as ostentatious and morally lax, and as superior to the working classes, whose women had to work. Working-class women were considered to be "tainted" by their position in the public sphere of economic and, it was often thought, sexual exchange. However, as Mary Poovey emphasizes in her study of mid-Victorian gender, formulations of this ideology were uneven.

Not only did different writers and thinkers of the period delineate somewhat different domestic ideals, but even within one text or body of work there were many inconsistencies. One major proponent of the role of the "angel in the house" and the separation of spheres was Sarah Ellis. Ellis's guidebooks, such as *The Wives of England* and *The Daughters of England*, offered women advice on how to attain and maintain

Victorian ideals of femininity and an ideal home. However, Ellis, herself supposedly an "angel in the house," became a best-selling writer and thereby violated the separation of spheres by competing in the public world of book sales; she also, one can assume, spent much of her time writing instead of attending to the various household duties on which she so carefully instructs her readers. Her texts, too, reveal contradictions. Though women of her time were assumed to be innately selfless, in *The Daughters of England* Ellis discusses at length how women can cope with feelings of irritation and boredom. Despite its intentions, the text appears to reveal that these roles might not be so inherently fulfilling after all. Indeed, if a life of selfless nurturing were innate, perhaps these guidebooks would not have been necessary in the first place.

Ellis's guidebooks are also full of moments at which the text reveals gaps and contradictions in the ideology it is attempting to reify. Discussing appropriate behavior for a young woman in *The Daughters of England*, Ellis remarks that the right thing for a woman to do if she sees a cat attacking a mouse is to smash the mouse's skull immediately to prevent it from suffering a slow death.[22] This is a strange illustration of the feminine necessity to be sensitive to the feelings of others. The violence this image evokes seems to jar with the sensitive nurturing the guidebook encourages. This indirect expression of aggression in an account of innately selfless behavior reveals that such representations of an ideal "innately" nurturing woman are not seamless.

Formulations of domestic ideologies also differed from one representation to another. At the other end of the cultural spectrum from Ellis's guidebooks, "Of Queens' Gardens" by John Ruskin also defines the ideal woman. Although Ruskin too upholds the importance of the moral role women play, his formulation differs from Ellis's. He emphasizes that women should not constrict their moral activities to the "park walls and garden gates" of their own homes. In asserting that a woman takes her home and moral center with her wherever she goes, he provides women with a "religious and moral sanction for socially significant action" in the public sphere.[23] Thus, Ruskin implicitly contests the separation of the public and private spheres.

More famously, John Stuart Mill, in his impassioned plea in *The Subjection of Women* (1869), or in earlier writing such as *Early Essays on Marriage and Divorce* (published in 1832), is yet another radically dissenting and equally uneven voice in the rich and lively public debates over domestic ideals. Mill and many others questioned the nineteenth-century marriage and property laws that both reified and grew out of

Victorian domestic ideologies. These laws restricted the right of married women to own property independently of their husbands and prevented them from suing for divorce. At mid-century, when Parliament considered slight modifications to these laws in what were to become the Matrimonial Causes Act of 1858 and the Married Women's Property Bill of 1857, a heated public debate was triggered.

Caroline Norton, herself involved in a much publicized divorce case, described nineteenth-century marriage and property laws as

> a grotesque anomaly which ordains that married women shall be "non-existent" in a country governed by a female Sovereign. ... As *her husband* he has a right to all that is hers: as *his wife*, she has no right to anything that is his. As her husband, he may divorce her (if truth of false swearing can do it): as his wife, the utmost "divorce" she could obtain, is permission to reside alone, – married to his name.[24]

Although neither Parliament nor even Caroline Norton intended to change the legal status of married women radically, public discussion surrounding the minor changes that were eventually enacted gave ideas like hers unprecedented public visibility.

The nineteenth-century domestic novel entered into this contested area of public discourse with its own representations of domestic ideals, representations that were themselves complex and uneven. In *Oliver Twist*, for example, Dickens might yearn for a morally pure home protected from the evils of capitalism by an "angel in the house," but he also represents this ideal as flawed and unrealistic. Women writers of the early and mid-nineteenth century had an even more complex relationship to contemporary domestic ideologies; their novels often contest some feminine ideals while adhering to others. Although *Jane Eyre* expresses a sincere yearning for women to be allowed a wider scope of experiences in life, it has its heroine find satisfaction in a small domestic sphere removed from the wider world. Such complexity must be considered in the study of film adaptations; indeed, it may be this very richness or inconsistency of ideas within these novels that enabled films to mine the form in such drastically different ways throughout the twentieth century.

It is therefore important to avoid using simplistic ideological labels to describe novels and their adaptations. In the 1980s, for example, a study of *Jane Eyre* claimed that whereas the novel was "feminist," the 1944 film adaptation was "anti-feminist."[25] More recently, categories such as "radical" and "conservative" have been used to describe adaptations of nineteenth-century novels.[26] Yet such labels assume the existence of coherent meanings and ignore the ideological tensions and inconsistencies inherent in popular art forms such as nineteenth-century novels and twentieth-century films.

The most interesting aspect of the ideological polyphony of these adaptations stems from the fact that as much as films desire to appropriate novels, they cannot always do so completely. Sometimes the novel seems to take its own revenge on a film and undermine much of its ideological work. The 1944 adaptation of *Jane Eyre*, for example, works hard to contain the novel's representation of female sexuality within an idealized representation of women as maternal and home centered, an ideal that became important as the Second World War drew to a close. However, since the novel includes an illegitimate child, Adèle, abandoned by Rochester's French mistress, the film's representation of female sexuality as safely bounded within the confines of home and marriage becomes unstable. This adaptation's attempt to appropriate an inappropriate character is marked by Adèle's excessive cuteness and by the dissonant imagery with which she is associated. Her favorite toy is a music box that is supposed to represent Rochester and Jane but eventually comes to represent Rochester and his French mistress, precisely the kind of sexuality the film tries, but is unable, to excise from its narrative. Often, the British nineteenth-century novel resists seamless appropriation into the ideals of the twentieth century. Significantly, what often becomes most unstable or confused in these adaptations is their representation of sexuality.

III

According to Nancy Armstrong, the eighteenth- and nineteenth-century domestic novel restructures desire in ways that empowered women. She argues that the domestic novel redefines subjectivity in terms of female desire, replacing political and class divisions with divisions based on gender. Using Richardson's *Pamela* as a model, Armstrong contends that the novel displaces distinctions of class between the aristocratic Mr. B and the servant girl Pamela as it represents his growing love for Pamela on the basis of her inner qualities and virtues, a love that is blind to class distinctions. The domestic novel, Armstrong claims, redefines how individuals organized and understood their experiences by giving desire and the relationship between men and women, rather than other class or political distinctions, a central position in the creation of subjectivity.[27]

The central place of desire in domestic fiction intersects with the generic conventions of the costume drama. Costume dramas made by the British studio Gainsborough in the 1940s were extremely popular. These films, according to Sue Harper, provide a vision of history as "a place where only feelings reside, not socio-political conflicts."[28] Gainsborough costume dramas, she claims, represent female protagonists who actively seek sexual pleasure even though the plots ritually excise these characters by having them die or be killed at the end of the film. The mise-en-scène's sensuous and sexually symbolic sets and costumes (such as vulva-shaped fur clothing) cut across the sexually conservative scripts to provide the audience with a permissive subtext. Harper's research into audience responses shows that the costume drama's predominantly female viewers could decode, and enjoyed, these sexual subtexts. Furthermore, Pam Cook, who has explored the relationship between nationalism, femininity, and the costume drama, notes that Gainsborough melodramas have plots that involve foreigners, gypsies, foreign places, and masquerade. This, she claims, enabled audiences to put on and test multiple identities and to explore competing notions of nationality and femininity. Concomitant with the domesticating suburbanization of Britain at this time was "the restless desire to escape the confines of 'home' in search of adventure and exoticism abroad."[29] In their vagrant spirit, these films spoke to female audiences willing to explore alternative notions of place or nation, and alternative versions of femininity. Like Harper, Cook emphasizes that costume dramas enable imaginary travel to a place of greater female sexual expression.

Whereas these nineteenth-century novels are realist and often depict a time almost, if not completely, contemporary with their date of publication, cinematic versions set in the nineteenth century are located in a distant time and, in this sense, a foreign land, a safe place in which to explore female sexuality. Stella Bruzzi has considered how nineteenth-century costumes are themselves erotic. "The power of clothes fetishism is that it exists on the cusp between display and denial, signaling as much a lack as a presence of sexual desire."[30] In their play between sexual desire and restraint, between sexual display and repression, these adaptations harness an erotic discourse central both to nineteenth-century fiction and to the genre of costume drama. As each film works to stabilize ideals of femininity that are changing or controversial in the twentieth century, it also attempts to construct female desire in a way that addresses twentieth-century ideals. Female sexuality is represented differently at different times, yet it is always central to the ideological work each film undertakes.

IV

In general, then, British and American film adaptations of British nineteenth-century novels made in the 1930s, 1940s, and 1990s screen these novels' representations of women through an ideological lens shaped by the anxieties and longings of their own time. As these adaptations negotiate the ideologies of gender that inform the novels, they create, as it were, novel women who differ substantially from those in the novels. At once revealing and concealing dimensions of the novels' own ideologies of gender, the films of the 1930s and 1940s attempt to appropriate them in ways that project comforting domestic ideals for audiences undergoing profound social, economic, and political dislocations as a result of the Depression and the Second World War. In the 1990s, without such major national and economic crises, these films address what was increasingly perceived to be a crisis in intimate relations between men and women. Through the construction of consoling images of women and the home and the representation of these ideals as existing in nineteenth-century novels, ideals of the moment are portrayed as timeless and unchanging. In this way, contemporary ideals of femininity are naturalized as they are projected into a literary heritage. Throughout the twentieth century, the cinema turned to the domestic novel of the previous century to construct a stable domestic vision that was ironically born out of the domestic instabilities of the moment.

This book begins with Depression-era Hollywood adaptations. Chapter 1 examines two American classics that received enormous critical and popular acclaim in their time. The film adaptations of both *Wuthering Heights* (1939) and *Pride and Prejudice* (1940) were conceived, written, and made during the Depression and are marked by its economic and social upheavals. By the 1930s, through an elaborate system of trade agreements and product tie-ins, Hollywood had an economic stake in encouraging its women viewers to buy goods. Representations of female glamour encouraged women to buy the clothes and cosmetics that would make them desirable. Hence, *Wuthering Heights* and *Pride and Prejudice* celebrate a form of consumerism that the novels themselves predate. Yet the Depression had also undermined the capacity of men to support their families or, sometimes, even to marry at all, making women's economic desires seem threatening. In addition, bitter public controversy surrounded the question of whether women should be allowed to work when men often could not. Hence, these films are particularly interesting in that they glamorize and vilify female consumer desire at the same time. While the novels explore the complex relation-ship between sexual and economic desire that existed in a culture that provided women with almost no economic opportunities outside marriage, the films screen this representation through the lens of Depression-era anxieties about money-hungry women. The adaptations not only represent women as economically desirous but also posit an ideal woman who can separate economic from sexual desire. Unlike the novels, both Depression-era adaptations tell a cautionary tale about the need to marry not for money but for love.

Chapter 2 investigates the Hollywood adaptation of *Jane Eyre* made in 1944. Charlotte Brontë explores female sexuality with greater explicitness and in greater depth than most of her contemporaries. The film, in contrast, works to circumscribe the novel's representation of female desire within an idealized construction of motherhood, an ideal circu-lating in American culture toward the end of the Second World War. The film attempts to confine Jane's sexual desires safely within the home. This representation of Brontë's work is shaped by anxieties driving women out of the labor force and into the home as the war seemed to be reaching an end. The adaptation also speaks to a desire for a "return" to a stable, comforting domestic sphere that, it was felt, had been disrupted by the war.

Chapter 3 turns to adaptations made in Britain. Unlike the nation-wide Depression in America, Britain faced an economic depression in the 1930s that was less severe in some regions of the country than in others. Given that some people in Britain suffered greatly during the Depression while others prospered, the 1937 adaptation of *The Mill on the Floss* changes the novel's representation of domestic structures in order to represent an image of a nation united across class and geo-graphic distinctions. George Eliot's representation of the plight of her central female character, Maggie Tulliver, is marginalized as the film foregrounds Eliot's depiction of a family facing economic ruin. Whereas the novel emphasizes Maggie's sexual desires, in the film Maggie renounces her sexuality for the good of others. Unlike the novel, the adaptation represents women as ethereal models of self-sacrifice from whom men learn how to sacrifice their own needs to those of the larger community or nation. Indeed, the film's emphasis on the moral role women play in the national sphere is reminiscent of the very ideals of femininity Ruskin had articulated in the nineteenth century and Eliot questions in her novel.

Chapter 4 explores the postwar British adaptation of *Oliver Twist*. This film departs from the 1930s ideal of the self-sacrificing woman, an image similar to the one Dickens himself relied on in his novel. *Oliver Twist* was made as the British welfare state was coming into being and as the British Empire appeared to be disintegrating. The director, David Lean, uses Dickens's plot to explore and define the parameters of the new postwar Britain. The novel's interest in the private domestic sphere of the home is supplanted by the film's focus on the national domestic sphere of the emerging welfare state. As Lean eliminates the novel's emphasis on the importance of the private realm, his representation of women shifts. Unlike the novel, which yearns for a private home with an angelic woman at its center, the film represents women as a threat to the new national "family." Unlike Dickens, Lean draws an analogy, rather than a contrast, between Fagin and women in order to represent women, like Jews, as an alien threat to the nation.

Chapter 5 turns to the most significant appearance of British nineteenth-century novels in film since the postwar period – the 1990s. As the divorce rate in both the United States and Britain continued to rise steadily, more and more women were unmarried, and a plethora of unconventional domestic configurations were publicly debated in the media; film adaptations turned to the domestic novel of the past to find a utopian vision of heterosexual harmony and stability. At a time when the mainstream culture was incorporating the visual imagery of pornography into advertising and film, adaptations of the British nineteenth-century novel offered an alternative vision of female sexuality. These adaptations combined a resistance to dominant cultural constructs of female sexuality with popular feminist ideas. The adaptations of the 1990s almost always ended in happy marriages between liberated women and sexually respectful idealized men, and thus constructed a utopian space in which erotic fulfillment could merge with feminist triumph. They resisted the increasingly sexually invasive mainstream culture while speaking to the absences and gaps of modern life, and in so doing these films offered their predominantly female viewers an imaginary space in which freedom and sexual fulfillment could coexist in perfect marriages.

This book closes, in Chapter 6, with an analysis of Jane Campion's *The Piano*, a film that does not explicitly represent itself as an adaptation yet adheres closely to the domestic themes of nineteenth-century novels such as *Wuthering Heights* and *Jane Eyre*. *The Piano* both evokes and critiques the classic Brontë adaptations made in 1939 and 1944. Unlike other contemporary adaptations, *The Piano* subtly questions whether feminist triumph can indeed merge harmoniously with sexual liberation. *The Piano* is in many ways a kind of counter-text to the film adaptations of British nineteenth-century novels that preceded and followed it.

Part I

The 1930s and 1940s: Hollywood and Britain

1
Consuming Women: *Pride and Prejudice* and *Wuthering Heights*

As the 1930s drew to a close, two adaptations of British nineteenth-century novels received critical and popular acclaim. Both William Wyler's *Wuthering Heights* (1939) and Robert Z. Leonard's *Pride and Prejudice* (1940) are shaped by the drastic economic and social changes of the 1930s. Produced in the wake of the Depression, these films only marginally address the upheavals overtaking Europe and the war the United States would not join until the end of 1941. Although both adaptations represent England favorably in an attempt to encourage American support for Britain, the most significant aspect of these adaptations is that they remold Brontë's and Austen's novels into Depression-era narratives about the perilous relationship between women, money, and marriage.

Completely transforming both novels' use of clothes as a symbol, these films adhere to Hollywood conventions of glamour but also exhibit tremendous anxiety about female consumerism. Balancing the paradoxical Depression-era goals of encouraging female economic consumption while deflecting anxiety about men's inability to provide for these economic appetites, these films follow a particularly complex ideological trajectory. Leonard's *Pride and Prejudice*, with its explicit references to shopping and economic consumption, makes the ideological content of the film adaptations of this period most explicit. Although *Wuthering Heights* was made in 1939, one year before *Pride and Prejudice*, it is in the later film that the workings of Depression-era anxieties about women are more clearly visible. Leonard's *Pride and Prejudice* provides a clear window on exactly how representations of women at this time were shaped by Depression-era anxieties.

Such anxieties are rooted in the rise of a consumer-oriented economy, a development that had begun in America in the last part of the

19

nineteenth century and continued into the 1920s and 1930s. Largely as a result of Henry Ford's changes in methods of production, the economic market no longer concentrated on increasing production but rather on ensuring that there was enough consumption to absorb the heightened rates of production. The economy and culture shifted drastically. An older Puritan culture, a producer-capitalist culture, was replaced by a "newly emerging culture of abundance";[1] a culture that valued thrift and hard work was replaced by a culture that valued a rising standard of living and the consumption that enabled it.

Surprisingly, statistics show that despite the Depression, the standard of living continued to rise as people spent more on consumer products and more and more new products were introduced into the market. These changes in the economy and the shift to a consumer culture had a tremendous influence on cultural constructions of gender. According to Stuart Ewan, the home had been changing from a site of production into a site of consumption since the nineteenth century, but the change was intensified in the 1920s and 1930s. As a result, women were perceived to be the primary consumers of goods. Housework, done more and more by middle-class women rather than by the rapidly dwindling class of domestic servants, was increasingly seen as a "domestic science" that women could perform well only if they bought a plethora of products. The clothing and cosmetics industries also grew significantly during the 1920s and 1930s. All in all, 80 percent of the goods produced in the market were bought by women.[2] Hence, advertising, which had come to play a major role in the new culture of abundance, directed most of its efforts at female consumers. Advertising encouraged women to buy, buy, and buy, and in doing so represented women as the ultimate consumers.

Hollywood's depiction of glamorous lifestyles contributed to ideals of consumption.

> Frederick Allen, a writer for *Harper*'s during the thirties, observed that Depression America, as portrayed in popular magazine fiction, advertisements, and movies, was a country where everybody was rich or about to become rich, where the ownership of a swimming pool or the employment of a butler (complete with English accent) not only failed to raise embarrassing questions, but seemed accepted as the "normal lot of mankind."[3]

In fact, Hollywood had a direct commercial interest in promoting consumption, particularly among the female members of its audience.

In his essay "The Carole Lombard in Macy's Window," Charles Eckert shows that by the mid-1930s Hollywood was actively marketing products to, mostly female, members of its audience. Rewarded by industries in a variety of ways, films helped sell merchandise through an elaborate system of tie-ins. One way in which films sold merchandise, for example, was that affordable dresses similar to those worn in films were made and then sold at department stores like Macy's. Another marketing ploy was product placement: products already available on the market were introduced into the plot or scenery of films. Often, however, Hollywood's role in advertising was less direct: Hollywood encouraged women to buy clothes and cosmetics by positing glamorous ideals of femininity that could not be emulated except through such purchases.[4]

Mary Ann Doane claims that when a woman goes to a film she buys "an image of herself insofar as the female star is proposed as the ideal of feminine beauty."[5] Women internalize commodified ideals of femininity from films and then shop to emulate the ideals they have absorbed. Thus, on the one hand, observes Doane, women's ability to shop makes them active subjects; on the other hand, because they shop to turn themselves into commodified versions of femininity, they also become objects.

The first scene of the film adaptation of *Pride and Prejudice* embodies Doane's seeming paradox. It opens at a shop where the Bennet girls are gleefully buying material for dresses they will wear at an upcoming ball. This was one of the most challenging parts of the novel to adapt, as shown by repeated revisions to the script. Even though the successful Broadway adaptation[6] of *Pride and Prejudice* was used as a model for the film, the screenwriters abandoned the play's and novel's beginnings, both of which were set at the Bennet home and consisted of a conversation between Mr. and Mrs. Bennet about the future tenant of Netherfield Hall. The fact that this particular scene was revised so often indicates how central the representation of women as consumers is in the film.

In this first scene, unlike in the novel, Elizabeth and Jane do not differ from their mother and Lydia in their interest in clothes and take delight in shopping for materials and in imagining what their dresses will look like. While they are shopping, Elizabeth and Jane see Darcy and Bingley through the window of the shop and, like the other women in the scene, who notice the men's carriages and livery, conclude that Darcy and Bingley are rich. As the women discuss the men and their economic worth, they are joined by Mrs. Phillips as well as Mrs. Lucas and her daughter. Rachel Brownstein claims that in this way, in the adaptation, "[t]he business of marketing is neatly connected with that of marrying as the women look out of the shop widow at the 'exquisite young men.'"[7] But more can be said about the type of marketing depicted here.

This scene embodies Doane's paradox: the women are both objects and subjects in this commercial interaction. Since the women are in the store and are looking at the men from the store side of the display window, they are in the same spatial position as any other item for sale. Moreover, they are buying the clothes that will make them objects of display for the male characters and the camera's gaze. At the same time, they are subjects making choices and shopping as much for materials as for men. The men too are turned into commodities or objects; as subjects women are valuable consumers, but they also consume men. This important opening sequence prefigures the film's multifaceted representation of women.

Partly, the film's representation of women is shaped by the film's desire to counteract American stereotypes of British society. By the time this film was released, Britain was at war, but the United States had officially declared its neutrality and was trying to avoid intervening on Britain's behalf. An influential group of British writers and actors, including Laurence Olivier, Greer Garson, Aldous Huxley, David Niven, and Merle Oberon, all of whom were involved in the production of this adaptation or the previous year's *Wuthering Heights*, advocated American support for Britain. Hence, both films attempt to portray Britain in a way that will appeal to American audiences. To dispel stereotypes of the British as snobbish and represent the United Kingdom in ways that appeal to American egalitarian ideals, the adaptations "recast the novels as images of modernizing England which is learning to reject class and inherited wealth in favour of democracy and love."[8] Unlike in the novel, Darcy's love for Elizabeth brings about an aristocratic embrace of the middle classes, and in this sense Elizabeth is represented as an agent of social change, a catalyst for social progress. At the beginning of Leonard's *Pride and Prejudice*, unlike in the novel, Darcy says that he refuses to dance with Elizabeth because he does not wish to join "the middle classes at play." Hence, his marriage to Elizabeth at the end of the film shows him to have accepted the middle class he had previously rejected. Similarly, Lady Catherine learns to put aside class snobbery, admire Elizabeth, and favor her marriage to Darcy. Thus, the marriages at the end of the film represent the democratization of the upper classes in Britain.[9]

Because Elizabeth, on this level of the film, is the heroine of the middle classes, the woman who democratizes the proud aristocrats, the film represents her as forceful, witty, and strong. At first glance this makes the film seem unambiguously feminist. In one scene that does not exist in the novel, when Darcy teaches Elizabeth archery, he shoots an arrow that misses its target, but Elizabeth shoots three arrows that all land right on target. Darcy apologizes and says, "The next time I talk to a young lady about archery, I won't be so patronizing." To be patronizing in the context of the film is to assume aristocratic prerogatives that Elizabeth reveals to be hollow; Elizabeth teaches Darcy a lesson in democracy, but not, as it initially may seem, in gender politics.

The feminist content of this sequence is later undercut. Although Elizabeth humbles Darcy's masculine pretensions by proving she is more skilled an archer than he, subsequent scenes highlight not Elizabeth's skill at archery as much as her skill at love. Cupid-like, her arrows become associated more with love than with equality. After the archery contest, Elizabeth cries, fearful she has made a fool of herself, and then tearfully admits her love for Darcy, an admission she does not make until a much later stage in the novel. While the socially egalitarian dimension of the plot constructs Elizabeth as powerful in relation to Darcy, aspects of the romantic plot divest her of this power.

The film as a whole, then, portrays Elizabeth as rebellious, unconventional, and occasionally powerful, but the representation of women other than Elizabeth and Jane is very different. In the novel, Elizabeth and Jane's mother and sisters are objects of satire, as are a number of male characters such as their father and Sir William Lucas. In the film, in contrast, the only male character satirized is Collins. In addition, the subtle satire of the novel is translated into a farce that makes the female members of Elizabeth and Jane's family appear grotesque. The women's grotesque qualities are related to the film's representation of their relationship to money and men.

In the novel Jane Austen presents the economic circumstances of her class in great detail. Edward Copeland has identified Austen as belonging to the "pseudo-gentry." These professional families lived in the countryside and were allied by kinship, social ties, and social aspirations to the gentry yet, unlike the gentry, depended on earned income rather than income derived from their land. Moreover, they depended on their income to pay for the goods that gave them their genteel appearance. According to Copeland, then, the "pseudo-gentry" were "a social group that set its boundaries largely through the signifying power of the things it [could] afford to buy."[10] In *Pride and Prejudice* Mr. Collins, who rises in rank through the living given to him by Lady Catherine, is obsessed with goods because these can mark his newly won status. This is why he believes he can make Elizabeth regret refusing his offer of marriage by showing her the furniture, the markers of status, she could have acquired if she had accepted.[11] Clearly, Austen satirizes Collins's interest in consumption: his obsession with consumption is too apparent and his social climbing, therefore, too obvious. An excessive interest in acquiring things is represented as morally tainted in Austen's *Pride and Prejudice*.

Hence, the novel is critical of an excessive interest in clothes. Attitudes to clothes reveal moral character: "In *Pride and Prejudice* ... Mrs. Bennet's obsession with wedding clothes reveals a mind closed to all but appearance."[12] Indeed, Mrs. Bennet's greater interest in Lydia's wedding clothes than the immoral circumstances of her marriage reveals that she is unable to perceive moral distinctions.

In contrast, the opening sequence of the film, showing even the heroines shopping happily for clothes, indicates the extent to which the film values consumption. The visual codes of costume drama and especially Hollywood's commercial stake in consumption cause a transformation in Austen's symbolic use of clothing. This difference contributes to a profound dissimilarity between the novel's and the film's relationship to cultural ideals of femininity.

In the novel, attitudes to dress not only are markers of character and moral discernment but also imply attitudes toward social constructions of class and gender. When Elizabeth gets mud on her clothes because she is impatient to reach her ill sister at Netherfield, she is placing concern for her sister above conduct-book imperatives regarding female dress; she is rebelling against contemporary conventions of ideal femininity. Later in the novel Elizabeth uses her clothing to make another political statement when she refuses to "dress down" for Lady Catherine. Thus, Elizabeth employs clothing to assert her independence from gender constrictions at Netherfield and from class constrictions at Rosings.

In the film, when Elizabeth dresses up at Rosings, it is also depicted as an act of class rebellion, albeit one that is consistent with her representation as a democratizing character, but, unlike in the novel, the film emphasizes that Elizabeth wears the better dress because it pleases her; it is, as she says, so "pretty." As a consumer of "pretty" products, she conforms to rather than rebels against conventional gender ideals. In addition, when Elizabeth arrives at Netherfield covered in mud, the film can only minimally convey her disdain for convention. While the novel asserts the insignificance of feminine dress, the film draws attention to this visual sign of femininity. In the novel the significance of Darcy's attraction to Elizabeth is that it belies conventional notions of femininity and feminine appearance. He is attracted to her despite the mud on her dress, despite her resistance to conventional feminine behavior. In the film, in contrast, the camera lingers on Elizabeth's image, which, though muddy, remains glamorous. Indeed, since this is a costume drama, this nineteenth-century costume is particularly lavish for a twentieth-century spectator, despite the mud. Whereas the novel asserts that physical attraction is not dependent on constructed elements of femininity such as dress, the film relies heavily on clothing to generate glamorous images of ideal femininity. The film, in contrast to the novel, then, constructs rather than deconstructs conventional ideals of femininity. In fact, in light of the opening scene, it is because Elizabeth knows how to shop well and select the right materials that she can make herself look beautiful and glamorous enough to attract Darcy's eye. This relationship between economics and femininity reverses the representation in the novel.

Indeed, in Austen's novel, the economic needs of women are presented not in terms of luxury consumption but in terms of want and necessity. In the early nineteenth century women were severely restricted in their ability to earn an independent income and were barred from inheritance by primogeniture and entailments. Hence, the ability of a woman of the "pseudo-gentry" to maintain the material markers of her status and to continue to live in comfort after her father's death almost always depended on whom she married.[13]

As many critics have noted, Austen was unable to criticize her society's economic oppression of women openly. Austen's account of the restrictions women of her time faced had to be indirect and subtle; she disguises her criticism of the inequitable distribution of power between the sexes. In *Pride and Prejudice*, "just as we are not permitted to feel that men's economic privilege necessitates power, so are we not permitted to feel that women's lack of privilege necessitates powerlessness."[14] Although Elizabeth faces dangerous economic circumstances, we do not experience her as powerless, "for [in *Pride and Prejudice*] there is a disguised expression of discontent with the growing division in money, status, and power between middle-class men and middle-class women."[15] Austen's critique of women's economic status is nevertheless central to the novel. Given the economic dependence of women of the "pseudo-gentry" on marriage, the novel openly presents marriage as a choice that must consider, in addition to other factors, economic interest. "No one, particularly no woman who is economically dependent not *even* Elizabeth, whom we admire, is unmoved by property. We should remember that only the ignorant and imprudent Lydia marries 'for love.'"[16]

In contrast to Lydia, Charlotte marries solely for economic advantage, and the novel's attitude toward her is mostly sympathetic. When Charlotte marries Mr. Collins, she explains her motives to Elizabeth: "I am not romantic you know. I never was. I ask only a comfortable home; and considering Mr. Collins' character, connections, and situation in life, I am convinced that my chance of happiness with him is as fair, as most people can boast on entering the marriage state."[17] Charlotte suggests that most women marry to satisfy their need for economic security.

Critics have disagreed about whether Austen validates Charlotte's perspective. Julia Prewitt Brown, for instance, argues that Austen is critical of Charlotte's economic view of marriage. "Although Charlotte is a far more sympathetic character than Wickham, both are seducers, always a serious sin in Jane Austen, or to be more precise, both engage in a polite form of prostitution."[18] However, Charlotte, unlike Wickham, fulfills all her social obligations, especially toward her family, the Bennets, and even Lady Catherine. Her slightly less dutiful attitude to Collins, finding a room for herself that Mr. Collins would not like to frequent, points to the sadness of being married to someone she would rather avoid. Unlike Wickham, Charlotte is not selfish and is a seducer not by choice but by necessity. Wickham is free to have a profession and avoid getting into debt; Charlotte has no means of support other than through marriage. Austen is critical not of Charlotte but rather of her lack of opportunity. Charlotte's marriage is portrayed as representative of many marriages of necessity. This flawed and unhappy marriage is central to the novel's overall depiction of marriage as an institution marred by the financial dangers women faced. Through her portrayal of Charlotte, Austen emphasizes the unfortunate economic dimension of marriage.

It is significant that the economic motives for Charlotte's marriage are completely omitted from the film adaptation. When Elizabeth asks Charlotte about her marriage to Mr. Collins, Charlotte does not mention his ability to provide her with material comfort:

> *Charlotte*: Happiness, Lizzy. In marriage, happiness is just a matter of chance.
>
> *Elizabeth*: But Charlotte, his defects of character. You know him so little.
>
> *Charlotte*: Where ignorance is bliss, Lizzy, if one's to spend one's life with a person it's best to know as little as possible of his defects. After all, one will find them out soon enough.[19]

There is no indication here that Charlotte marries Mr. Collins because all she asks is a comfortable home. She does not demand much of marriage; however, the film suggests that her options are limited not because she is poor but because she is not attractive. In the opening scene of the film Mrs. Lucas says to her daughter, "You may not have beauty my love, but you have character and some men prefer it." Mrs. Bennet replies, as she gestures toward her daughters, "That is why girls who have both are doubly fortunate." In the adaptation, unlike in the novel, Charlotte's options are limited because she is not ideally beautiful and therefore must settle for a marriage that is also not ideal.

The adaptation's omission of Charlotte's economic motives points to the fact that the film as a whole represents women's economic interests not in terms of necessity and need, as does the novel, but in terms of a consumer desire for luxury products. The women in the film are never depicted as suffering from economic distress or as being in any sort of economic danger or as dependent on marriage economically. In fact, what women hunger for in the film is not economic stability but luxury goods such as livery, carriages, and dresses. Moreover, the omission of Charlotte's economic motives points not only to the film's translation of nineteenth-century economics into twentieth-century consumerism but also to the fact that the film would rather suppress the idea, expressed by Charlotte (and Austen), that women may marry only for money. While Hollywood's stake in the consumer economy led it to valorize women who desire to consume products, Depression-era anxieties about women's relationship to money make the film also critique this desire, often portraying women in terms of feminine threat and excess.

The "crisis of masculinity" that occurred as a result of the Depression shapes the way Austen's novel is adapted. With the rise of the culture of abundance and the changes in the nature of the market, a new social class emerged. "The organizational revolution [that arose with the new market] had its most important consequence in the establishment of a new social class. ... Defined in the simplest ways, it is a class of bureaucrats: managers, professionals, white-collar workers, technicians, mechanics, salespeople, clerks, engineers ... generally people on salary rather than wages."[20] This class of, generally, men lived in a more mechanized, routinized world and came to see their self-worth not so much in terms of what they did as in terms of what they could consume. As Stewart Ewan describes it,

With industry increasingly invading the interstices of social life and with work having become characterized more by a person's ability to keep to a routine than by his or her prowess, there was little about a job which could make a person feel indispensable and little in the way of self-definition that could make a person feel that what he was doing could not be done just as well by someone else. ... Thus while women were cultivated as general purchasing managers for the household, the basic definition of men ... was as breadwinners, wage earners. Man's role was divested of all social authority, except in so far as his wages underwrote family consumption.[21]

When large numbers of men lost their jobs and salaries as a result of the Depression, they also lost a sense of their role, purpose, and self-worth both in society and within the family.

Gender roles were greatly affected by the Depression. Although women were underpaid and severely discriminated against during the Depression, and although they lost the progress they had made in terms of infiltrating higher-status professions, there was still a rise in the number of women who were employed, although not necessarily in satisfying jobs. Even though most women did not work in the 1930s, the rise in the number of employed women in comparison to the significant drop in the number of employed men is noteworthy. Statistics show that in 1930, 24.3 percent of women were working and that in 1940, 25.4 percent were employed. Because women tended to be employed in low-status, low-paying jobs such as nursing or secretarial work, their jobs were less affected by the Depression. In contrast, large numbers of men, who tended to work in private industry, lost their jobs.[22] Although some men attempted to enter traditionally female jobs, their numbers were not significant.[23] As a result of this disparity in (un)employment trends, in many families it was the woman who worked and supported the family while the man stayed at home. Indeed, whether or not the wife was working, "the man who lost his job lost status in the eyes of his family, and he often had to give way to a competent wife who was able to manage the economics of family living under adverse conditions."[24] Moreover, as families faced increasing economic difficulties, they became larger as members of the extended family moved in to share the economic burden. Although the housework remained in practice as well as in theory the realm of women, the family structure became increasingly unstable, and more and more anxiety was generated around notions of femininity, the home, and money.

This anxiety became manifest in intense public debate about women, and particularly married women, working. During the 1930s, the public either ignored or was unaware of the reasons for the relative stability of employment levels among women. The media virulently attacked women, and especially married women, for taking jobs away from men.[25] On the one hand it was believed that women would lose their femininity if they went out to work,[26] and on the other hand their femininity was used to argue for their lack of any real need to work. The widely popular "pin money hypothesis" asserted that married women needed money only to indulge in frivolous feminine desires and that they therefore had no right to take jobs away from men who needed to support their families. Indeed, in some sectors of the economy, there were successful attempts at instituting legislation that made it illegal for women to work.[27]

Alice Kessler-Harris sums up the changes in the position of women as a result of the different ways in which the Depression affected the employment of women and men:

> The ability of women to retain and even expand their job potential played havoc with the cherished set of ideas about home, hearth and women's place in it. It produced crisis and confusion, locking men and women into rigid attitudes, stifling a generation of feminist thought, and intensifying hostility to women wage earners.[28]

In fact, the feminine mystique of the 1950s, so famously described by Betty Friedan, entailed an elevation of hearth and home that had actually emerged earlier during the 1930s. This idealization of the home and its housewife arose in response to changes in family structures precipitated by the Depression and in reaction to the gains suffragists and other feminists had made in earlier decades.

Overall during the Depression, although some people understood the economic need for women to work, most viewed women's relationship to work as a desire for money to consume frivolous items. In the public consciousness, this need constituted a threat to men's work, to men, and to the family. In this historical context, then, it is not surprising that a film adaptation of *Pride and Prejudice*, a novel that represents women's economic interest in great detail, changes the novel's depiction of women's relationship to money. It is precisely because audiences were economically deprived during the Depression that films produced escapist fantasies based on acquiring splendor, riches, and glamour. However, at the same time as *Pride and Prejudice* presents women's fantasies of attaining wealth, it also reflects anxieties surrounding this fantasy. As the "pin money hypothesis" makes clear, women's consumerist desires were perceived, at the time, as trivial and wasteful. Accordingly, the women characters in *Pride and Prejudice* want money only to buy dresses, carriages, and livery, and not because they will be destitute if they do not marry, or marry unwisely, as is the case in the novel. Moreover, the film associates the feminine desire to consume with an excess that seems to overwhelm men, perhaps even to consume them.

The dresses the women make from the material they purchase become a visual manifestation of the film's anxiety about women who consume. After researching nineteenth-century clothing, the filmmakers decided to make costumes similar to the clothes worn about thirty years after the novel was set, when women's clothes were larger. Some of the women characters are made to wear excessive and exaggerated dresses with very loud patterns, extremely large puffed sleeves, and silly large hats. The result is that the women characters appear to fill too much space on the screen. This is especially obvious in the opening sequence, in the shop, and later at the Bennet home, particularly when Lady Catherine visits.

The opening scene includes Mrs. Phillips, three Bennet women, Mrs. Lucas and Charlotte; six female characters wearing enormous dresses clutter a small shop. They seem to swamp the rather small and thin male clerks who work there and appear overwhelmed by this excess of "femininity." Similarly, in shots of the Bennet household, five daughters in huge dresses with exaggeratedly loud patterns loom over the solitary male, Mr. Bennet. Whereas most theatrical adaptations of *Pride and Prejudice* eliminated Mary and Kitty, Leonard's adaptation retains all five daughters. The fact that there are so many daughters adds to the sense of "feminine" excess in the visualization of the Bennet household. Whereas the novel represents Mr. Bennet as a flawed father, the film represents Mr. Bennet as a worthy, sensible man cursed with the presence of too many women. In fact, Elizabeth says to Charlotte at one point in the film, "Oh why is England cursed with having more women than men." This sentiment, which Austen would not have shared, visually saturates the film; visually, there are too many women on the screen. The excess, which is related to the desire to consume, is depicted as overbearing or threatening to men.

Lydia, too, is represented as threatening in her excessive desire to consume. In the novel Lydia's transgression is sexual, but in the film her marriage is presented in terms of a transgression that is as much economic as sexual. This is despite the fact that Lydia is the only character in the novel who marries without any concern for money. In the film, when Lydia returns home with Wickham, she does so in luxurious liveried carriages and brags about all her newly bought possessions to her family. The desire for men is closely linked in the film to the desire for the goods men can buy. Lydia's sexual transgression is equated with excessive economic desire.

In her discussion of *Now, Voyager,* Maria LaPlace claims that women's ability to consume is in some way empowering since the "appeal is to female desire itself, to wants and wishes, to (libidinal) pleasure, sexuality and the erotic, and a species of economic decision and choice."[29] In the *Pride and Prejudice* adaptation, since women's habits of consumption are represented as dependent on men's incomes, they are not shown to be empowering. Yet the desire to consume goods is associated with libidinal desire. Lydia's libidinal and consumer desires are conflated, and the combination is excessive and threatening.

In fact, in the first scene of the film, as discussed, although it is the women who stand in for commodities in the display window, it is the men who are seen *through* the window. The men are as much commodified as the women. Even Elizabeth and Jane's desires are first directed toward the same objects – carriages and livery – Lydia is so proud of possessing as a result of her marriage (which were in fact bought with Darcy's money). Elizabeth, not completely sarcastically, counts Mr. Darcy's horses and livery and concludes, "My word, this Mr. Darcy must also be rich." Elizabeth and Jane's economic interests are potentially as libidinal, excessive, and all consuming as Lydia's. Moreover, after the Bennets leave the shop, the salesman brings the Lucases some material to see, but the Lucas women ignore the material and leave the shop to arrange a meeting with the rich young men "of fashion." The Lucases' interest in the material is rapidly replaced by their interest in Darcy and Bingley. The women's interest in products is soon displaced by an interest in the men who can buy them such products. Stewart Ewan's contention – that men were constructed as wage earners who facilitated female consumption – aptly describes the ideologies that shape this adaptation of *Pride and Prejudice.* Although Darcy and Bingley are not working for salaries, they are represented in terms of their incomes and not, as in the novel, in terms of their property. In fact, the film does not show Netherfield in much detail and omits the scene at Pemberley in which Elizabeth recognizes her love for Darcy while she also admires his property. This is because the film represents the male characters in terms of twentieth-century economics, in terms of salaries or income rather than property, in terms of their power to consume rather than what they already own. Thus, because the novel represents women's interest in men in terms of their economic value, the film does so too, but because men at this time were extremely anxious about their economic capacities, the film also represents women who view men as financial objects as excessive and threatening.

This is why the women who are satirized in the novel become grotesque in their Depression-era representation. The women characters who view men in terms of the money they make are portrayed as monstrous and ridiculous with their loud, vulgar mannerisms and exaggerated clothes. This misogynist representation is a manifestation of the anxieties about women and money that were prevalent during the Depression.

Interestingly, the film was marketed as a film about courtship practices, or dating. "Learn How to Attract Men" reads one advertisement for the film. "Bachelors Beware! Five Gorgeous Beauties Are on a Madcap Manhunt" proclaims another. A promotional blurb for the film says, "Gossip! It [the film] Tells How Pretty Girls T-E-A-S-E-D Men into Marriage."[30] The advertisement sells itself to women by suggesting, however lightly, that it is about how women can snare men. Underlying the advertisements is a male fear of being hunted and trapped. An aggressive woman, particularly one with economic demands, represents a threat.

Indeed, according to research on dating during the Depression years, courtship practices at the time were specifically designed to alleviate men's economic anxieties:

> Even if the national economic marketplace was in disarray, young men could partake in the dating marketplace and have their pick from a bounty of female "goods." Young women who circulated in the dating marketplace and participated in the world of exchange in a passive and nonthreatening manner helped to assuage the crisis in masculinity, reaffirm traditional gender roles, and replenish a sense of abundance. Young men had copious choices of high-quality "goods" at their disposal. Males could conspicuously consume the companionship of females in the public sphere. ... Since marriage was still deemed the ultimate goal in mass-marketed manuals and textbooks, dating a wide variety of people became a method of "window shopping" until prosperity returned and couples could settle down.[31]

In the film, the women characters invert 1930s courtship practices by actively pursuing men. It is the women, as much as the men, who are window-shopping. Indeed, the confusion about who is on which side of the display window in the opening scene raises anxieties that need to be addressed by the end of the film. In part, the film allays the anxieties associated with women actively pursuing men by having women compete with each other for men who are the center of attention.

Moreover, the ... dating system of the mid-1930s to early 1940s encouraged young women to remain in constant competition with one another for male approval. This factor alone positioned males in the center of female attention, making the rating and dating system a means for allaying fears generated by the Depression and the ensuing crisis in masculinity. The mass-marketed manuals indicate that young women focused incredible amounts of energy on competing with their friends and female peers to gain recognition from young men.[32]

In the film, this is clear, for example, in an early scene in which the Lucas and Bennet women participate in a carriage race to see who will reach the newly arrived Darcy and Bingley first. The capitalist struggle between men is replicated in the world of women as a struggle not for goods but for the men who can buy them goods. Elizabeth's comment that England is cursed with too many women also works to enforce the idea that women compete for male attention. However, the competition that takes place between women is satirized, and they are made to look silly. All in all, then, the film works to allay male anxieties both by presenting women's hunger for men as something that makes men the center of attention and by representing this "feminine" competition for men as something farcical and demeaning. More significantly, Leonard's *Pride and Prejudice* works to undercut Austen's suggestion that women value men in terms of their economic worth; the plot is changed so that the heroines are women who learn to separate romantic from economic desire.

Hollywood's need to dissociate money from marriage originates not only in Depression-era anxieties but also in an important aspect of 1930s film history. In the early 1930s in a series of films such as *Blonde Venus* and *Baby Face* women were shown to rise in social status and wealth as a result of extramarital sexual relations. These "fallen woman" films caused so much controversy that they are considered the main reason for the tightening of the Production Code in 1934, which led to stricter self-censorship in the film studios. By the late 1930s, when *Pride and Prejudice* was made, the film industry had developed sophisticated self-regulatory methods aimed at avoiding those characteristics of the fallen woman films that had generated so much controversy. Films of the fallen woman cycle had vividly depicted the heroine's class rise, achieved through sex, by showing her first in excessively meager and then, after the fall, in excessively glamorous surroundings. The fact that in Austen's *Pride and Prejudice* women marry with an awareness of economic gain and rise substantially in wealth and social class through men must have created something of a problem for a 1930s film.

Although there is no direct suggestion of "fallen" women in the adaptation, there are some echoes of the fallen woman plot, because it is men who enable a monetary and class rise and because the women voice their interest in men's money and possessions so openly. In fact, the female hunger for glamour even in itself and unrelated to sexually transgressive relationships was seen as problematic by some groups opposed to its representation in Hollywood. As a result, "particular films began to call attention to and critique spectacles of consumption."[33] The adaptation of *Pride and Prejudice* does just this: it represents glamour in its ostentatious mise-en-scène and costumes, which were so lavish that the film received an Oscar for art direction, and at the same time satirizes those who seek money through marriage. Moreover, in battles over fallen woman films between the Motion Pictures Producers and Distributors Association (MPPDA) – the organization responsible for regulating the content of films – and filmmakers, "while the MPPDA typically advocated the heroine's punishment, the studio preferred the heroine to renounce her riches in favor of true love."[34] *Pride and Prejudice* has its heroine do the latter.

The novel's plot is changed so that Elizabeth renounces Darcy's wealth in a scene that does not exist in the novel. Lady Catherine visits Elizabeth to tell her that she controls Darcy's wealth and will cut off his funds if he marries her. In the novel, Darcy's fortune is completely his own; in the film, a woman is momentarily depicted as having complete power over his fortune. After Elizabeth tells Lady Catherine that she will marry Darcy regardless of how much money he has, Darcy's aunt leaves and meets him outside. Their dialogue makes clear to the audience that she does not really control Darcy's wealth and has only pretended to in order to ascertain whether Elizabeth would marry him if asked. This scene is significant because it raises the specter of women having control over men's finances and then subverts the threat by revealing that women operate only in accordance with men's plans. More significantly, the film adds this scene to insist that Elizabeth marries Darcy, unlike in the novel, regardless of his economic means. The film separates riches from "true love" and reverses the problem established in the opening scene, where women view men as though they are commodities. Elizabeth's visit to Pemberley is eliminated from the film despite all the glamour such a scene would enable the filmmakers to produce. Whereas in the novel Darcy's relationship to his property and Elizabeth's economic interests are integral to her recognition of his worth, the film insists on separating women's interest in men from economic motives.

At the same time, Elizabeth marries a rich Darcy. In fact, the last line of the film is Mrs. Bennet's statement that now Elizabeth will be able to buy all the carriages and clothes she desires. Thus, the film manages to have it both ways; it satisfies the female audience's desire to compensate for Depression-era deprivations while also allaying male anxieties by asserting that women do not really want money, only love. In fact, at a time of great poverty, Leonard's *Pride and Prejudice* raises and then dispels a number of anxieties: it assuages the fear that women measure men in terms of their salaries at a time when men have no assurance that they can earn salaries, it avoids any association with the fallen woman cycle, and it provides female viewers with the fantasy that they can achieve fabulous wealth through marriage.

The anxieties about women and money that shape the adaptation of *Pride and Prejudice* in 1940 had also shaped the adaptation of *Wuthering Heights* one year earlier in 1939. The ideological currents that are more clearly visible in *Pride and Prejudice* are subtly foreshadowed in the previous year's adaptation of *Wuthering Heights*. Since Brontë is less explicitly focused on economic questions than Austen, the adaptation of *Wuthering Heights* employs economic themes more indirectly. Unlike Leonard's *Pride and Prejudice*, Wyler's *Wuthering Heights* does not include scenes in which women go shopping or talk about men in terms of their ability to purchase commodities. Despite its lack of emblematic scenes linking female consumerist and romantic desire, *Wuthering Heights* nevertheless represents women as economically carnivorous. In part because of the different tones of the novels, Wyler's adaptation exhibits an anxiety about women and money that is not mitigated by the type of optimistic fantasy that concludes Leonard's *Pride and Prejudice*. The adaptation of *Wuthering Heights* does not end with a note of hope or a celebratory picture of an idealized egalitarian England. *Wuthering Heights*, unlike *Pride and Prejudice*, represents women's economic hunger as extremely destructive. The more optimistic second half of the novel is eliminated as the adaptation turns the plot into a bleak cautionary tale for women who, unlike Elizabeth, choose money over love.

Like *Pride and Prejudice*, *Wuthering Heights* was a tremendously success-ful and popular film when it was released. Over the years, William Wyler's *Wuthering Heights*, more so than Leonard's *Pride and Prejudice*, has retained its status as a classic film. Most critics who value fidelity have argued that *Wuthering Heights* is a great adaptation because it is faithful to the novel's stormy emotional atmosphere and the extreme passions of its characters. They see the adaptation as faithfully repro-ducing the novel's depiction of characters who are tragically caught between the conflicting forces of nature and culture.[35] Wyler had his scenic designer transplant almost a thousand heather plants onto 450 acres of California's Conejo Hills;[36] his adaptation associates heather with what Nelly calls Cathy's "wild uncontrollable passion for Heathcliff." Heathcliff often gives Cathy heather while they are on the moors, and in one of the more dramatic scenes in the film, Heathcliff and Cathy are shot from a low angle as they stand on the moors kissing amidst heather that glows against the backdrop of a darkening sky. The film in this way represents their passion as natural and rooted in the moors, the heather, and a world beyond the constrictions of culture.

Where the film has been seen as departing from the novel is in how it interprets what culture means. George Bluestone claims that the film forces the novel into a conventional Hollywood mold, "the story of the stable boy and the lady."[37] The socially egalitarian ideal Bluestone sees as unfaithful to the novel is related to the film's attempt to present England in a favorable light.

Even though the war had not yet begun in Europe when this film was made, its imminence was clear to those who wanted to encourage Americans to support the British. Like *Pride and Prejudice*, the adaptation of *Wuthering Heights* also attempts to represent England as a country learning to become more democratic. Lawson-Peebles claims that when the starving Heathcliff is brought to the Heights by Mr. Earnshaw, he tells the children, "[Y]ou must share what you have with those less fortunate than yourselves." Earnshaw subscribes to an egalitarian ideology that Hindley and Linton resist. This is why – unlike in the novel, where it is left vague – it is specifically in America that Heathcliff makes his fortune. America is the egalitarian culture that has enabled Heathcliff to rise.[38] Linton's snide attitude to Heathcliff's social rise makes him all the more a representative of England's restrictive class system.

In Lawson-Peebles's reading of the film, Penistone Crag represents an alternative space to Wuthering Heights and Thrushcross Grange. "Penistone Crag is portrayed as a New World, an imaginative, sacred, protected, and egalitarian space removed from the old worldly decadence of the two houses."[39] It is at Penistone Crag that Heathcliff can be a "lord" and Cathy his "lady"; it is only here, divorced from the social world, that they can be equals.

Penistone Crag does indeed represent a third site in the film. It is particularly associated with natural bonds of passion, since it is a large rock looming over the heather-filled moors to which Cathy and Heathcliff escape whenever they want to be together. However, this site is not ideal. It is undermined by Cathy's disruptive desires. Mapped across the class dynamics of the film is a representation of gender similar to that in *Pride and Prejudice*, a representation shaped by Depression-era anxieties about the relationship of women to money. This adaptation blames Cathy and her consumer desires for failing to create the egalitarian alternative the film idealizes.

Unlike in the novel, it is Cathy rather than Nelly who tells Heathcliff he might be the son of an emperor of China and an Indian queen. In the novel, Nelly tries to console Heathcliff when he feels Cathy's affections for him are being displaced onto Edgar by suggesting that nobility resides not in appearances but within, that though he may look like a servant, perhaps he is in reality noble. Nelly, a servant, might well be indulging in some wishful thinking of her own. In the 1939 adaptation, however, these words are said by Cathy as a young child and indicate that she is already wishing Heathcliff were more noble, or richer, than he is. Cathy tells Heathcliff she has wanted to know someone of "noble birth" and encourages him to take "possession" of Penistone Crag so that he can be like a "prince." Heathcliff "conquers" Penistone Crag because of Cathy's social aspirations.

Cathy's social and economic ambitions are emphasized again in a conversation she and Heathcliff have at Penistone Crag as adults:

Cathy: (*hotly*) I shouldn't talk to you at all. Look at you! You get worse every day. Dirty and unkempt and in rags. Why aren't you a man? Why don't you run away?

Heathcliff: (*in stunned simplicity*) Run away? From you?

Cathy: (*in another world*) You could come back to me rich and take me away! Why aren't you my prince like we said long ago ... Why can't you rescue me? Heathcliff!

Heathcliff: (*swept away*) Come with me now!

Cathy: (*after a pause*) Where?

Heathcliff: (*on fire*) Anywhere.

Cathy: (*slowly shaking her head*) And live in haystacks? And go barefoot in the snow? And steal our food from the marketplaces? No, Heathcliff, that is not what I want.

(*Over the scene the sound of music. She hears but Heathcliff does not.*)

Heathcliff: (*his rage returning*) Oh, you just want to send *me* off. That won't do. I've stayed here and been beaten like a dog, abused and cursed and driven mad. But I *stayed* just to be near you – even as a dog ... and I'll stay to the *end*. I'll live and die under this rock![40]

Unlike Cathy, Heathcliff values love above all else and at any price. He dismisses the significance of material values and feels only what is represented as natural passion.

In general, Heathcliff is a far more sympathetic character in the film than in the novel. In the novel, when Heathcliff and Hindley are both given horses early in their childhood, Heathcliff chooses the best one and, when his goes lame, takes Hindley's horse as well. In the film it is Hindley who takes Heathcliff's horse away from him and hits him with a stone. In contrast to the novel, where Heathcliff is obsessed with acquiring property, in the film Heathcliff is not in himself acquisitive. Heathcliff acquires wealth only to satisfy Cathy's desires. When he returns from America and buys Wuthering Heights, he reminds Cathy of her demand that he be like the son of an emperor and a queen, that he go away and come back to make her rich.

Cathy's desires, however, like those of the women in the adaptation of *Pride and Prejudice*, are disruptively materialistic. She longs for Heathcliff to make her rich and refuses to live with him in poverty. At the end of the dialogue at Penistone Crag, Heathcliff and Cathy hear music. Cathy says, "Music – the Lintons are giving a party. That's what I want. Dancing and singing in the pretty world!" After they follow the music to the Grange, where a lavish ball is taking place, Cathy, looking longingly through the window, says, "Isn't it wonderful? Isn't she beautiful? That's the kind of dress I'll wear and you'll have a red velvet coat and silver buckles on your shoes." After she is attacked by dogs and brought into the Grange, she shouts to Heathcliff as he leaves, "Go on Heathcliff. Run away and bring me back the world." Less explicitly, but as in *Pride and Prejudice*, the first time the heroine sees her future husband, though she barely notices him amidst all the splendid clothes, it is through a window that functions like a display window. In the novel, Cathy wants to belong to a social world appropriate for her class, and not just to a natural world, but in the adaptation Cathy's desires are figured in terms of female consumer desire. In fact, although in the novel Cathy and Linton are of the same class, because of the way in which the film represents glamour and the consumption of goods as indicators of class, the material sparseness of Wuthering Heights and its inhabitants makes it seem as though this is not the case.

Like the adaptation of *Pride and Prejudice*, Wyler's *Wuthering Heights* is situated within a Depression-era consumer culture and uses conventions of Hollywood glamour that the novel predates. Brontë's Cathy desires to embrace culture in a broad sense, in terms of genteel refinement, education, social propriety, and taste, while Wyler confines Cathy's desires to the wish for pretty dresses bought by an equally well-dressed man.

The novel uses clothing to symbolize Cathy's entry into the world of culture and civilization. In Brontë's novel, clothes are not only literal; Cathy's clothes function as a metaphor for the changes she undergoes. Not only does Brontë's Cathy never express a desire for clothes, but as soon as she is dressed as a "lady" she feels constricted. Dressed in the way her culture requires of women, when she returns from Thrushcross Grange, she has to hold up her skirts as she enters the house, cannot approach the dogs freely, and must keep a distance from Nelly because she is covered in flour. Brontë describes Cathy as frustrated by the cultural restrictions that the dress represents. She breaks these bonds when she runs to embrace Heathcliff despite his being dirty. Like Austen, Brontë uses clothing to represent her heroine's resistance to cultural definitions of appropriate feminine behavior. In contrast, in the same scene in 1939, Cathy refuses to embrace Heathcliff because she does not want to dirty her dress. The Hollywood convention of constructing femininity in terms of glamour is unshaken.

Although in one scene in the film Cathy tears off her elegant dress in frustration and runs to the Crag in an old shabby dress to meet Heathcliff, this scene is followed by another in which she admires herself in a mirror in a vain and excessive way. In the midst of Cathy's self-admiring reflective gaze, Nelly says to her, "You are lovely Miss Cathy." Cathy replies, "That's a very silly lie. I'm not lovely. What I am is very brilliant. I have a wonderful brain. ... It enables me to be superior to myself. There's nothing to be gained by just looking pretty – like Isabella." As she recites the speech, she admires herself in the mirror from every angle, performing a narcissistic dance. Her actions belie the words she speaks, making her seem even more vain. Her shiny white dress with its silver decorations indicates that her brilliance resides far more in her looks and sparkling dress than in her mind.

In the same scene, when Heathcliff comes to ask Cathy why she is wearing the dress and is dismissed by her and forbidden to touch her, he retorts,

> Tell the dirty stable-boy to let go of you – he soils your pretty dress. But who soils your heart? Not Heathcliff. Who turns you into a vain cheap worldly fool ... Linton does. You'll let yourself be loved by him because it pleases your stupid greedy vanity to be loved by that milksop.[41]

The film supports Heathcliff's assessment that Linton brings out Cathy's greed and vanity.

Wuthering Heights prefigures the Depression-era paradox seen in *Pride and Prejudice* and also represents the desire to look glamorous as both a natural feminine ideal and a moral flaw that threatens men and marriage. While the camera lingers on Cathy's brilliant dress, encouraging audiences to admire its splendor, Cathy is depicted as vain for admiring it. The producers were so intent on having glamorous costumes that they decided to set the film in the last decades of the eighteenth century because "the Georgian period was marked by fancier dresses for women and Goldwyn was eager to show off Oberon in beautiful costumes."[42] The type of vanity the film criticizes is also what enabled Hollywood to make a profit from its representations of glamour and the attendant marketing of clothes and cosmetics.

Mary Ann Doane discusses the relationship of women to fetishized representations of themselves on the screen and, relying on Freud, describes it as narcissistic: "Having and appearing are closely intertwined in the woman's purportedly narcissistic relation to the commodity. ... The cinematic image for the woman is both shop window and mirror, the one simply a means of access to the other."[43] Women want to buy cosmetics and clothes so that they can become the image they see in the mirror/screen. In Wyler's film, Cathy is made to replicate the female audience's purportedly narcissistic relationship to its own image. Both Cathy and Isabella often stare intently at themselves in mirrors. Even in *Pride and Prejudice*, where there is less emphasis on female narcissism, in the first scene of the film Jane sketches a picture of herself as she will look in her new dress and admires the image. Cathy's consumer-oriented narcissism threatens both Linton and Heathcliff.

Cathy constantly goads Heathcliff to be a "man" and make the money that will enable her to satisfy what he calls her "vain and greedy" desires. Cathy's dialogue with Heathcliff continues:

Cathy: You had your chance to be something else. ...
Cathy: Thief or servant were all you were born to be – or beggar beside a road. Begging for favors. Not earning them, but whimpering for them with your dirty hands.
Heathcliff: That's all I have become to you – a pair of dirty hands ... Well – have them. Then ... (*he slaps her face*) Have them where they belong.[44]

In the novel Heathcliff's violence is never directed toward Cathy, but in the film Cathy is represented as deserving of men's ire. Not only is Cathy excessively hungry for pretty things, but she also goads the man she loves for failing to be enough of a "man" to earn the wealth she desires.

At a time when men's sense of self-worth was often derived from their ability to earn wages to support their families, and when the Depression made this no longer possible or certain, Cathy's castigation of Heathcliff for not being a "man" because he is a bad wage earner has tremendous resonance. It represents the nightmare underlying the Depression-era crisis of masculinity: a beautiful woman refuses the devoted love of a man because he is unable to support her financially.

The film deflects the blame here from the man who cannot make a living to the woman who makes excessive demands of him. Although the film shows Cathy running desperately after Heathcliff on the night he runs away, and close-ups reveal that her acceptance of Linton's offer of marriage is partly reluctant, Cathy is presented as marrying Linton so that she can buy what she desires. Unlike Elizabeth in *Pride and Prejudice*, Cathy does not renounce her consumer desires and does marry for money. Like the women in the fallen woman films, Cathy uses a man for financial gain, and for this she is punished. Because of Brontë's plot, the producers choose the other form of self-censorship not used in *Pride and Prejudice*: the heroine does not renounce wealth but, instead, marries for it and then suffers for her actions.

Blaming Cathy alone for her demise, the adaptation departs from the usual reading of the novel, in which Cathy is interpreted as a character destroyed by her tragic inability to reconcile conflicting polarities. Cathy is seen as torn between storm and calm, between wild passions and tamer emotions, between natural energies and the habits, codes, and manners of civilization, or as split between the spirit and the body.[45] All of these binaries can fall into the nature/culture divide that the film retains, but the adaptation, unlike the novel, represents culture narrowly, in economic terms, as a commodity culture. The adaptation does not represent Cathy as inescapably torn between broader and more profound irreconcilable forces.

Terry Eagleton has described Cathy as torn between the yeoman class of the Earnshaws and Heathcliff (before he becomes a capitalist) and the agrarian capitalists at the Grange. Eagleton claims that Cathy's mistaken decision to marry Linton destroys her as well as Edgar and Heathcliff.[46] If Wyler's critique of consumerism were less gendered and he dealt as severely with Heathcliff once he was a capitalist as he does with Cathy, one could assume that his interpretation of *Wuthering Heights* is as Marxist as Eagleton's. More than Eagleton, however, Wyler's interpretation of *Wuthering Heights* faults Cathy alone for the destruction of her own and all of the other main characters' lives.

Feminist interpretations of the novel have read Cathy far more sympathetically, seeing her as suffering from the gender ideologies of her time.[47] Patsy Stoneman suggests that Cathy seeks a romantic union of souls that does not necessitate conventional monogamy, something Cathy emphasizes when she says she "is" Heathcliff.

> [Cathy's] own words make it plain that it is her belief in her "oneness" with Heathcliff which makes her confident that he will not just tolerate her marriage to Edgar, but "comprehend [it] in his person" – that is, incorporate it into himself. Her argument seems to be, "If I love Edgar and I *am* Heathcliff, then Heathcliff must love Edgar." The actions of the two men, on the other hand, are characterized by "narrow" exclusiveness and the desire for possession.[48]

In this reading, Cathy's assertion that the two men have broken her heart holds true; they have torn her asunder by attempting to possess her exclusively.[49] The adaptation, however, by eliminating Heathcliff's acquisitiveness and heightening Cathy's, lays the blame for Cathy's tragedy on Cathy alone.

Cathy, not Heathcliff or Linton, is to blame for her unhappy marriage. The film represents the married Cathy as trapped in a prison of her own making. When Heathcliff returns, Cathy is obviously pained that she has married the wrong man, but she cannot escape. When Heathcliff leaves the Grange, the camera lingers on an image of Linton wrapping his arm possessively around Cathy's waist. Their backs are toward the camera, and Cathy is stiff in Linton's grasp as the camera tracks backward out of the window through which Cathy had once longingly looked on the prizes Thrushcross Grange had seemed to offer. In the shot of the window enclosing the couple, Cathy is now imprisoned on the wrong side of the display window. Having desired the objects Linton could buy her, she has now become his object. In another window shot as she is dying, Cathy, clutching Heathcliff, looks out of her bedroom window toward Wuthering Heights. Before her death Heathcliff says to her,

> I never broke your heart. You broke it ... greedy for the trifles of living. What right had you to throw love away for the poor fancy thing you felt for him? Misery and death and all the evils that god and man could have handed down would never have parted us. You did that alone! You wandered off like a wanton greedy child to break your heart and mine.[50]

Condensing what Heathcliff says to Cathy in the novel, the film has Heathcliff put more emphasis on Cathy's love of "trifles" and on her "wanton greed." This Cathy has imprisoned herself in a loveless marriage as a result of her own greedy consumer desires and excessive economic demands on Heathcliff.

The novel, too, is filled with images of imprisonment, but they are not prisons of Cathy's own making. Cathy is imprisoned by culture, and, specifically, by nineteenth-century ideals of femininity.[51] Under her sister-in-law's guidance, Cathy is taught how to be a "proper lady" at the Grange. This creates a self-division in Cathy, and she yearns for her previous undivided, ungendered self. Moreover, her marriage to Linton is the socially sanctioned choice, but the novel reveals that a genteel marriage cannot satisfy a woman's desires. Cathy is torn between her childhood self and the social expectations women faced at her time.[52]

In contrast, in Wyler's version of *Wuthering Heights*, not only Cathy but even Isabella dies because of her vain and excessive desires. In some ways Wyler's Isabella is a double for Cathy. Both Isabella and Cathy enjoy staring at themselves in mirrors, both love Heathcliff, and both marry for the wrong reasons. While Cathy marries Linton as a result of excessive economic desire, Isabella marries Heathcliff as a result of her excessive sexual desire. Unlike in the novel, the film simplifies Isabella's motives. Whereas in the novel Heathcliff's sexual potency certainly motivates Isabella to marry him, her motives are not as one-dimensionally sexual as they are in the film. In the novel Isabella is relatively isolated from any male company; in the film she is given choices. Edgar claims that Isabella will not marry for another decade because she is so "particular." Isabella responds, "It's a brother's duty, dear Edgar, to introduce his sister to some other type than fops and pale young poets." Linton then asks, "Oh, you want a dragoon?" "Yes. With a fiery mustache." It is clear she is looking for someone more sexually potent than the men she already knows. Later, when Heathcliff meets her at a ball, she tries repeatedly to find excuses for holding his hand or dancing close with him. In an argument with Cathy, Isabella accuses her sister-in-law of being vain, but Cathy responds by telling Isabella it is she who is vain. The film suggests that both are vain, Cathy for wanting pretty clothes and Isabella for her sexual excesses and her inability to recognize that Heathcliff is immune to her attractions. Thus, female desire, whether sexual or economic, is represented in the film as excessive, destructive, and blind, and both women are punished, by the film, for their desires. Cathy fulfills her economic wishes but dies because she forfeits the "natural love" she could have had with Heathcliff; Isabella's sexual desires for Heathcliff are destructive, forcing her to flee and end up alone.

In the last scene, which Wyler was forced by his producers to add to the film, Heathcliff's and Cathy's ghosts are shown finally united in death at Penistone Crag – achieving, it may seem, their egalitarian ideal. Yet it is only through death that Cathy can transcend her vanity and achieve some form of "natural" union.

Thus, Wyler's adaptation suggests that the egalitarian ideal it valorizes is undermined by women's disruptive desires. Even though Isabella is attracted to Heathcliff largely because he is a "stable boy," a more manly type of man than the men to whom Linton introduces her, her sexual desires and vanity blind her to Heathcliff's real motives. Hence, the marriage of this "lady" to a "stable boy" cannot achieve an egalitarian aim. More centrally, Cathy fails to marry Heathcliff because in her hunger for possessions and goods, for clothes and "pretty things," she denies the natural passions of her heart. The egalitarian, natural, loving, democratic marriage that Elizabeth can achieve in *Pride and Prejudice* is denied to Cathy because she is unable to renounce material desires the way Elizabeth does. These adaptations change the novels in opposite ways, yet they are propelled by the same ideology.

The adaptation of *Wuthering Heights* represents its protagonist as seeking wealth above all else, while *Pride and Prejudice* represents Elizabeth as learning not to care for material benefits. Both films, because of Hollywood's role in the economy and because of its dependence on depicting women as glamorous, change the heroines of the novels into women with the tastes of a consumer culture that the novels long predate. Made at a time when men faced unemployment and working women were criticized for depriving men of the chance to earn wages for their families, these two adaptations project money-hungry women back into the past and represent them in ways that seem to offer contemporary audiences wracked by economic anxieties a form of catharsis. Either economically desirous women suffer terribly, like Cathy, or, like the younger Bennet sisters and their mother, they are ridiculed. In contrast, those women who renounce money for love, as Elizabeth does, gain both money and love. While the marriage plots of nineteenth-century British domestic fiction acknowledge the complex economic, social, and sexual desires of its female characters, Depression-era adaptations create domestic ideals that separate marriage from economics and excessive sexuality. At a time of economic and social disruption, these adaptations represent marriage as a bond that should be removed from the marketplace. Depression-era Hollywood adaptations screen the nineteenth-century domestic novel through the anxieties and dreams of their own moment in time.

2
Maternal Desire: *Jane Eyre*

Four years after the commercial success of *Pride and Prejudice*, and five years after the even more popular reception of *Wuthering Heights*, another British nineteenth-century novel by a woman writer was adapted into film. In 1944 Robert O. Selznick released a production of *Jane Eyre* that was directed by Robert Stevenson, probably with the assistance of Orson Welles. Although aspiring for and achieving similar commercial success, this adaptation differs significantly from its Depression-era predecessors. By 1944 the Second World War had drastically changed American culture. Many men had gone abroad to fight, and the women working in the jobs the men had left behind were receiving a great deal of public attention. Women's wartime work was venerated, and cultural ideas about women changed. Yet the new independence women seemed to have gained triggered anxieties about women abandoning their homes, husbands, and children. Not surprisingly, in this context, the adaptation makes some significant changes to Charlotte Brontë's representation of a woman's quests for independence.

Unlike *Pride and Prejudice* and *Wuthering Heights*, *Jane Eyre* had often been identified as a feminist novel before it was made into a film. Virginia Woolf had drawn attention to the now-famous passage in which Jane asserts that women need wider spheres of experience than baking puddings and embroidering. Elizabeth Bowen, in *English Novelists* (published in 1932 and again in 1942), joins Woolf in quoting Jane's description of women's "silent revolt against their lot" and even concludes that *Jane Eyre* is "the first feminist novel."[1] *The Facts of Fiction* (1932), in a chapter entitled "The Independent Brontës," calls Charlotte Brontë a "womanly anarchist" and claims that she purposely ends the novel with a wife who has an independent fortune in order to assert the importance of women's autonomy from men.[2] In the 1941 *Concise*

Cambridge History of English Literature, George Sampson states that *Jane Eyre* is a novel that "establishes the first independent woman in fiction" as it depicts a character who "is woman herself: confronting man on equal terms."[3]

The novel's sexual content had also been noticed before 1944. In *Early Victorian Novelists: Essays in Revaluation* (1934), David Cecil claims that, despite what he calls the "Puritanism" of the Victorian era, *Jane Eyre* expresses "sexual energy," and he places Brontë in a group of writers that includes D. H. Lawrence.[4] In sum, not only early feminist critics but also readily available popular histories of literature asserted that *Jane Eyre* was feminist and that it explored sexual themes. One can assume that Selznick, who was known for his love of nineteenth-century novels and his interest in literature, was aware of such interpretations. Nevertheless, the 1944 adaptation resists these two central themes in the novel.

The adaptation's erasure of the novel's feminist themes was noticed by feminist critics in the 1980s and early 1990s. Elizabeth Atkins criticizes the adaptation for removing Jane's female role models and editing out her inheritance.[5] E. Ann Kaplan and Kate Ellis claim that the changes the film makes are "a result of a reversion on the part of the two directors to accepted patriarchal structures," that it is "anti-feminist."[6] They particularly fault the film for eliminating Miss Temple – whom they define as a maternal role model who resists patriarchal structures – and replacing her with Dr. Rivers, a character the film invents. This view, as was typical of adaptation studies at the time, overlooks the complexities of both the novel's and the film's representations of gender. The novel is not one-dimensionally feminist, nor is the film simply "anti-feminist."

Since the Dr. Rivers character was actually added to the script at the same time as Bessie,[7] Miss Temple is in fact replaced by two characters. The film's Bessie is also very different from both Bessie and Miss Temple in the novel. In fact, female role models are not simply removed but are reconstructed in accordance with idealized representations of motherhood circulating in the culture during, and especially toward the end of, the Second World War. Brontë's exploration of female desires that are not bound to the home and her critique of Victorian maternal ideals are replaced in the film by an idealized representation of motherhood typical of the period in which the film was made.

Although Adrienne Rich has claimed that in the novel Jane is guided by a series of substitute mother figures, Brontë actually reevaluates her culture's ideals of motherhood by portraying all these substitute mother figures as inadequate or flawed. Miss Temple is too distant and aloof to satisfy Jane's intense emotional needs;[8] Bessie is not consistently nurturing and is sometimes cruel to Jane; Helen Burns is inadequate because of her self-abnegating ideologies and because, though older, she is only a vulnerable child herself.

In addition, the novel's presentation of Mrs. Reed deconstructs Victorian understandings of virtue as naturally emanating from maternal impulses. Mrs. Reed's feelings for her children are represented as a source not of virtue but of immorality and degeneracy; she indulges them to such an extent that they are ultimately ruined. Mrs. Reed's desire to protect and privilege her children leads not to a greater moral generosity, as Victorian maternal ideals would have suggested, but to the immoral and cruel treatment of her husband's orphaned niece, Jane. Brontë questions the Victorian belief that a woman's moral worth has its source in her maternal nature by representing Jane's relationships with all of the maternal figures she encounters as deficient. A perfect, or ideal, mother hovers over the narrative only in the form of Jane's unfulfilled, and unfulfillable, desire. Jane's ambivalent and hostile responses to the painfully inadequate mother substitutes she encounters as a child are mirrored in her attitude to occupying maternal roles herself.

As a child, Jane feeds a hungry robin at her window and nurtures her doll, but these are attempts to be the mother she wishes she had; the doll and bird are projections of her own abandoned, starving self. As an adult, she feels compassion for children only when they remind her of herself; she feels compassion for Adèle only when she learns that she is illegitimate. At other times her attitude to children in her care is grudging, hostile, and resentful. She never gives them more than duty requires. To her pupils at the village school she is cold and distant. Of Adèle, Jane is very critical, and she is jealous of the luxuries Adèle has that were denied to Jane herself. At the end of the novel, Adèle is packed off to school when Jane and Rochester marry, and their new child, mentioned in passing, is described with less interest than any of the other secondary characters described as the novel closes. Brontë's novel, then, undermines her culture's construction of mothers as ideal and morally superior by representing women's relationships to mothers and maternal roles as troubled and complex. Indeed, it is the absence of the mother, or mother figures, in *Jane Eyre* that actually liberates the heroine and enables a radical reconfiguring of gender identities.[9]

The adaptation, in contrast, works hard to resist these more radical dimensions of the novel. The adaptation tries to validate the ideals of motherhood the novel questions and to redefine the independent feminine desires the novel represents in terms of motherhood and the home. To understand this shift between the *Jane Eyre* of 1847 and the

Jane Eyre of 1944, it is important to situate the film in its historical and cultural context.

Written and repeatedly rewritten between 1940 and 1944, Stevenson's *Jane Eyre* was made at a time when women's lives, as well as the way in which they were represented in the media and popular culture, changed drastically. As a result of American involvement in the Second World War, there was an unprecedented demand for women in the work-force.[10] Although initially, "the attitudes of the 1930s prevailed and employers resisted hiring women to fill jobs historically performed by men,"[11] following the attack on Pearl Harbor both industries and the government swiftly abandoned this reluctance,[12] and the female labor force grew by 6.5 million. By 1944, 37 percent of all women were in the labor force on a regular basis and nearly 50 percent had been employed at some period during that year.[13] Many of these women were not new to the labor force. Half the women war workers had already been in the labor force for five years; only a third had actually been housewives before their wartime employment, and even some of these women had worked during the Depression when they could.[14] Still, the overall rise in the number of women employed was significant.

Even more significant, though, was the change in the kind of work women were doing. Because of the war, women were recruited to jobs that had previously been available only to men. Whereas before the war women had been confined to low-paying nonunionized jobs, now women were recruited to better-paying unionized jobs. In munitions plants and aircraft industries, for instance, women earned 40 percent more than in traditionally female jobs. Although they eventually were not allowed to, most women who worked in these higher-paying jobs, 75–80 percent, wanted to keep their jobs when the war was over.[15] Even though not all women had improved opportunities during the war, and union support for women was not as strong as it had been for men, significant numbers of women experienced drastically improved employment opportunities and better economic rewards for their labor than they ever had before. Although they may not have necessarily enjoyed the work itself, as one historian concludes, they discovered new forms of fulfillment:

> The desire for self-expression, personal satisfaction, or escape from the domestic monotony counted little in women's decisions to take jobs. In reality, most of the jobs available to them were arduous and routine and offered few attractions in terms of personal development or expression. Yet, once at work women discovered the nonmaterial

satisfactions of employment. They enjoyed the companionship of fellow workers, the pleasures of mastering a new skill, the opportunity to contribute to a public good, and the gratification of proving their mettle in jobs once thought beyond the powers of women.[16]

Another significant change in the female work force was the increase in the number of married women who worked. "For the first time in the nation's history there were more married women than single in the female labor force." Indeed, "half of all servicemen's wives were in the labor force." Not surprisingly, then, there was also a large increase in the number of women who worked and had children. The number of women who had a child under the age of 10, for example, increased from 7.8 percent in 1940 to 12.1 percent in 1944.[17]

However, public support for married women working was inconsistent. Such women were viewed more positively during the Second World War than during the Depression. More than 80 percent of Americans opposed married women working during the Depression, but in 1942, 71 percent believed that it was necessary.[18] Nevertheless, when it came to working mothers, arrangements made by the government and by industries for child care were usually inadequate. This made work particularly difficult for married women with children, and they had high rates of absenteeism. Moreover, since standards of maternal care had intensified since the 1930s, these domestic values collided with the necessity that women work.[19] Mothers who worked experienced tremendous conflict and anxiety about combining care for their children, which they saw as their most important duty, with their need to work. Public perceptions mirrored these women's conflicted experiences. Despite overall support for recruiting women into the labor force, public opinion and some government policies discouraged mothers with young children from working.[20] The press ran sensational stories of children locked up in basements or infants kept in cars all day while their mothers worked.[21] So, despite the fact that most people believed it was necessary for married women to work, there was tremendous anxiety about what this meant for children and mothers.

All in all, then, women's roles and experiences changed drastically during the war years, but the Office of War Information worked with advertisers, magazines, and other forms of popular entertainment to represent women's wartime labor in terms of traditional gender ideals. Although a significant number of women war workers was actually reentering the workforce and not entering it for the first time, contemporary images of women's war work represented women's labor as something new, a temporary aberration from the normal course of events. Advertisements and stories in magazines also depicted this work in terms that made workers seem "feminine"; the working woman was always, for example, portrayed as sexually attractive to men. In addition, in advertising and propaganda, the woman worker was represented as "a soldier-oriented self-sacrificing martyr," reinforcing her role as a selfless supporter of her husband and children and as someone without personal ambition. In fact, the overarching goal of wartime propaganda was "to discourage individualistic, self-interested attitudes in order to produce a collective spirit of self-sacrifice on the home front."[22] So, although many women had obtained better economic opportunities as a result of the war, this gain was represented as a selfless patriotic sacrifice, a representation that maintained the stability of the earlier domestic ideal of the selfless wife and mother.

Although many advertisements emphasized that women could be good workers for the nation and good mothers to their children at the same time,[23] in 1944, when it appeared that the war might end, these representations subsided and working mothers began to be depicted in ways that suggested they were ignoring the needs of their children. By the spring of 1944, as manufacturers began to shift back from wartime production to a consumer market reliant on female consumers, ads created an intensified attack on working mothers[24] and began dramatizing the unhappiness of their children. The industries that had employed women in wartime production began to suggest women return home to their primary role as mothers and return to consuming household goods produced in peacetime. In one advertisement, for instance, a little girl asks her mother, "Mother, when will you stay home again?" Beneath the child's question is a passage that reads, "some *jubilant* day mother will stay home again doing the jobs she likes best – making a home for you." The passage goes on to explain that when she is back at home, the mother will use the products this company makes in peacetime.[25] The concern about women's maternal roles that was always present during the war years had intensified by 1944 as the economy was about to shift.

Anxieties about the family also escalated as a result of rises in the rates of divorce, juvenile delinquency, and illegitimate births. Although this largely represented the acceleration of trends that had already existed before the war, it drew "heightened attention in a nation already dislocated by war." Often social scientists and welfare workers labeled working mothers as the cause for these changes.[26]

So, at a time when many women were exposed to new opportunities, and despite the many different ways women must have experienced the changes brought on by the Second World War, all of these varied experiences were contained within cultural representations of women's maternal responsibilities: to protect the nation, its soldiers, their husbands, their children, and the family as it once was (or was supposed to have been).

Thus, representations of motherhood at this time were a locus of intense longings and anxieties: a longing for a way of life feared to be lost and a longing for security and protection amidst the dangers and hardships of war. The domestic family with a wife and mother at its center even came to represent the home front that the war was fought to defend.[27]

Charlotte Brontë's questioning of maternal ideals and her emphasis on the importance of female experiences outside the home came into conflict, in 1944, with a culture that was attempting to contain the diverse new experiences of women that were destabilizing traditional domestic ideals. Hence, the adaptation works to dispel anxieties about women venturing beyond their maternal domestic roles and constructs traditional representations of motherhood.

The extremely popular film *Mrs. Miniver* (1942), directed by William Wyler and made two years before *Jane Eyre*, is a striking example of the ways Hollywood employed idealized representations of motherhood even when representing women in nontraditional roles. While her husband rescues British soldiers at Dunkirk and her son, a pilot, has dogfights with the Germans, Mrs. Miniver too captures a German soldier who has sneaked into her house. Mrs. Miniver is as heroic on the home front as men are in battle. Significantly, though, even as she defends her country from the Germans, she maternally worries about the soldier's injured arm, protects him, and insists a doctor treat him.

While Brontë's *Jane Eyre* is a *Bildungsroman* that traces its heroine's complex psychological development as she negotiates a range of desires from sexual desire to the desire for autonomy and adventure, the film represents Jane's development almost entirely in terms of her relationship to mothers and her own maternal roles. All her desires, including her sexual ones, are made to connect somehow with maternal feelings.

The film reinscribes the novel with this new maternal theme by changing two of the novel's characters, Bessie and Mrs. Reed, so that they represent a maternal ideal and its antithesis. Bessie represents a "good mother" that Jane learns to accept and embrace as the film's plot unfolds, and Mrs. Reed is made to represent a "bad mother" from whom Jane must distance herself. Unlike in the novel, where Mrs. Reed's maternal feelings lead her to behave in cruel ways, in the adaptation

Mrs. Reed is dissociated from conventional maternal qualities. With her hard, bony, square face, Mrs. Reed is almost always shot from extremely low angles, accentuating her overpowering harshness toward Jane. After being sent away, the orphaned Jane, who is leaving for Lowood, stands outside the large iron gate of Gateshead Hall. Camera angles and editing make the spectator share Jane's point of view as she looks up to see Mrs. Reed and her son standing side by side behind a window on the top floor of the house. Like a primal scene, this powerful image of Jane's exclusion from a domestic sphere marks the beginning of her journey back to a home. With complex visual imagery and a plot different from the novel's, Jane is represented as able to return securely to the domestic sphere after rejecting the bad mother, Mrs. Reed, and bonding with a good one, Bessie. In the novel, Bessie is far from ideally maternal and is quick tempered, often unfair, harsh, or indifferent toward Jane. In the adaptation, however, Bessie is an older, round, stout, matronly woman, Mrs. Reed's visual, maternal opposite. The actress playing her part, Sara Allgood, was known for playing mothers in other films.[28] This Bessie is never indifferent or unfair and is always kind, patient, nurturing, and wise. While Bessie is associated with home and hearth, Mrs. Reed, the nonmaternal figure, is associated with Lowood, a kind of masculine counter-space to the domestic feminine hearth.

Mrs. Reed sends Jane to Lowood in collusion with Mr. Brocklehurst, with whom she is also visually associated. They share square facial features, and, like her, he is shot almost exclusively from low angles. Unlike in the novel, or in earlier adaptations, the film represents Lowood as a world from which femininity is excluded. This is evident, for example, in the changes the film makes to the way Helen Burns is depicted. Helen is not the martyr-like figure of the novel but a very pretty little girl with feminine curls – Elizabeth Taylor, in fact. In the scene that replaces the point in the novel at which Jane longs to move beyond the stifling confines of Lowood, Jane is depicted as sitting on the edge of a cliff dreaming of going to Spain and traveling around the world. As Jane expresses her desire to explore wider horizons, Helen hangs laundry in the background: Helen is represented as properly feminine, whereas Jane is still somewhat tainted by Mrs. Reed. Brontë uses the scene where Helen's curls are cut off to reveal the class and religious hypocrisies of her society. In Stevenson's adaptation, in contrast, this episode is used to emphasize the masculine ethos of Lowood, an ethos that will not allow Helen to keep her pretty curls. The school is a world in which girls wear ugly clothes, cannot wash, steal each other's food, and have their curls cut off. When Helen is punished on another occasion, it is not, as in the novel, for being messy but for being vain, a far more "feminine" weakness; she is made to walk in circles in the yard in the rain with a board that says "vain" on her back. Jane's board says "rebellious" and marks her as not yet truly feminine. That Helen dies because of this punishment suggests that in killing her femininity, her vanity, and her looks, Lowood has killed her.

Aligned with Lowood's masculine principle is Dr. Rivers, a character the film invents. He replaces several different characters from the novel: he has St John's surname, he is the doctor at Gateshead Hall who suggests that Jane should go away to school, and later he is the doctor who treats the sick girls at Lowood. Like Miss Temple, Dr. Rivers reprimands Brocklehurst for not caring adequately for the health of the girls at the school. Although most critics have seen Dr. Rivers as a role model in the Lowood section of the film, his role is actually ambivalent. He holds to a masculine ethic Jane must learn to reject as she matures into womanhood. Although he argues with Brocklehurst and tries to help the girls at Lowood, he also represents a form of duty that Jane must learn to reshape into feminine forms.

Dr. Rivers often urges Jane to do her "duty." When he finds Jane crying on Helen's grave, he tells her, in the film's attempt to retain something of St John's character, that she must get an education to do God's work in the world. A close-up of Jane's expression shows her to be ambivalent and confused. A somber, darkly lit long shot showing Dr. Rivers leading Jane back to Lowood suggests this direction is a gloomy one. The next time Dr. Rivers asserts the importance of duty is when he burns a longed-for letter from Rochester as he tells Jane that her duty is to stay away from the man she loves. In this scene, he again encourages Jane to return to Lowood, this time to work there as a teacher, a choice Jane never contemplates in the novel. Echoing St John's claim that Jane was "formed for labour, not for love," Rivers is associated with the choice Jane must make between love and labor, between what is represented in the film as work in the masculine realm of Lowood and romance with Rochester in the feminine domestic sphere. This is reinforced by the fact that, unlike in the novel, while Rivers asserts the necessity of Jane's returning to work, he does not ask her to marry him. Significantly for a film made in 1944, Jane's choice here is not between one marriage and another but between work and marriage, between labor and the home, a conflict that had often been faced by women and represented in the media during the Second World War.

In contemporary advertising, work was often represented as something women did to fulfill male notions of duty, or masculine imperatives. In an advertisement for Armco, for example, a woman is shown comforting her son, who is in tears as she leaves for work. "Chin up," she tells him, "just like Daddy said."[29] Work is legitimized in this advertisement by emphasizing that it is something "Daddy" has authorized. Work was portrayed not as something women might desire but as a duty that was not personally fulfilling. The changes the film makes to the dilemma Jane faces in the novel adhere to this kind of construction in which work is represented as a male-authorized, unpleasant duty, but not something that might truly fulfill a woman. When Jane chooses love over labor and returns to Rochester at the end, the film represents this not only as the "right" choice. It also represents this as a choice Jane is capable of making at this point because she has developed and grown as a woman. The adaptation constructs a psychological trajectory that differs from that of Brontë's *Bildungsroman*. Jane's *Bildung* in the adaptation consists of her movement away from the nonfeminine or masculine influences of Lowood and Gateshead Hall toward a fuller "femininity."

Moments of significant transition are often figured in terms of her sleeping and then waking to a new reality. For example, Jane is asleep in the coachman's arms as she is delivered, like a package, to Lowood. She wakes up the next morning to the harsh realities of her new environment. An important transition moment in this trajectory is when Jane first wakes up at Thornfield Hall. Her entry into Thornfield Hall is represented very differently in the film than in the novel. In a series of complex symbolic images that are central to the film's ideological trajectory, Jane wakes up from a long sleep after she arrives.

In this sequence, the first shot shows her asleep in bed surrounded by curtains, but then she is woken by the sound of a music box on which two figures, a female ballet dancer and a soldier, dance. She sees the dancing figures, in a shot/reverse shot sequence, and then sees Adèle part the curtains and appear at the center of the image, between the dancing couple at the right of the frame and Jane at the left. Adèle is pretty and looks very similar to Helen, but, significantly, with her feminine curls uncut. The film then cuts to a close-up of Jane looking euphoric and then to the only double exposure in the film: a frame in which the smiling image of Adèle between the dancing couple and Jane is superimposed over an image of Adèle dancing, turning cartwheels in the air.

This sequence of shots suggests this is a moment of liberation for Jane from the masculine prisons of her previous life. Just as Mrs. Reed shuts Jane in "the red room," which in the film is a small closet, Mr. Brocklehurst imprisons her in other ways at school. When Brocklehurst punishes Jane for being a liar, she is made to stand on a stool. In a noir-style shot, shadows in the shape of long bars fall across Jane. As Selznick writes in one of his memos, "As for little Jane, ... the most logical thing after [the] opening would be to dissolve to an English jail of the period and show a hardened criminal, the result of what the child has gone through."[30] That Jane grows up in a form of jail is made particularly clear in this scene's imagery, but more significant is what liberates her from jail, a feminine influence.

As Jane stands on her stool, Helen descends into the prison-like space and talks to Jane, offering her comfort. The sequences with Helen and with Adèle are related. Helen tries to liberate Jane from Brocklehurst's jail, and Adèle, who looks like Helen, liberates Jane from a mental prison. Even the imagery of the later scene suggests confinement, since Jane is enclosed in a bed surrounded by thick heavy curtains that are then opened by Adèle. Both Helen and Adèle are represented as feminine influences that liberate Jane.

The imagery of the scene depicting Jane's awakening at Thornfield Hall is complex in other ways too. The dancing soldier and ballerina obviously point to a promise of romance in Jane's new home. Yet, at the very moment Jane sees the dancing couple, inserted right between Jane and the emblematic dolls is Adèle, wearing two big bows echoing a bow-shaped brooch Bessie had given Jane earlier in the film. This image of Adèle ties Jane to Bessie as daughter and to Adèle as mother. Romantic love and maternal feeling are evoked in the same sequence of images, emphasizing that they are inextricably linked. Adèle even mentions that the soldier and ballerina are like her parents. Romance is neatly tied to reproductive sexuality. When Adèle turns cartwheels, her celebration is represented as expressing feelings that are Jane's. Jane exclaims, "I have never been so happy in my life." Jane's happiness is symbolically linked not only to the promise of romance but also to a bond with a child. In stark contrast with her lack of patience with Adèle in the novel, in the adaptation Jane says of Adèle, "I lived in the tender warmth of that small and radiant shadow; her laughter became mine. Her joys and sorrows were also mine."

The adaptation diverges from the novel, then, by making the mother/daughter bond – being a mother and identifying with a child – essential to Jane's development. The brooch, echoed visually in Adèle's bows, is a central symbol in the film. In a sentimentalized scene that does not exist in the novel, Bessie gives Jane the brooch as a keepsake when Jane leaves for Lowood. Jane does not wear the brooch in the masculine world of Lowood; she first wears it for her second meeting with Rochester, in an attempt to dress up for him, to be more physically appealing. The brooch is used by the film to connect Jane's awakening sexual feelings for Rochester to her bond with Bessie and Adèle.

That maternal feeling is inextricably linked to sexuality and romantic love is made clear in yet another scene that is not in the novel. Although the film retains the sexual suggestiveness of the scene in which Jane rescues Rochester from his burning bed, this scene is immediately followed in the film by one in which Jane and Rochester rush to Adèle's bedside to see whether she has been harmed. In this sentimentalized domestic tableau, absent from the novel, Rochester mumbles some endearing expressions about the child's welfare. The adaptation frames representations of sexuality with family tableaus that emphasize caring for children. Stevenson's adaptation goes out of its way to keep sexuality safely within the family circle as it repeatedly links Jane's sexual awakening with images of motherhood.

The same is not true of the novel. Literary criticism of *Jane Eyre* has emphasized Brontë's construction of a female subject of desire. In fact, the novel explores the complexities of female desire through a detailed exploration of a girl's development into sexual maturity. Jane must resolve complex psychological conflicts and overcome her fears of the sexually aggressive Rochester.[31] Juliet Mitchell argues that Jane enacts her desire and possesses its language. Although Jane is goaded into doing so by Rochester, she verbally articulates her desire for him in terms that also assert her equality. Jane is a female protagonist who acts on her desires of her own volition.

In addition, claims Mitchell, the power of the male gaze is diminished in *Jane Eyre* because the novel de-eroticizes its female protagonist, emphasizing her plain looks. The gaze is even reversed, since it is Jane who feels acute pleasure in looking at Rochester. *Jane Eyre* also structures desire more in terms of the sense of touch than of sight. While Rochester does very little looking in the novel, he touches Jane often and, at the end, his blindness makes their relationship even more conducive to a tactile rather than visual mode of erotic interaction.[32]

The novel's reversal of the male gaze has interesting implications when it is translated into film. Mary Ann Doane calls *Jane Eyre* a "woman's film," a film made for female audiences that focuses on a central female character who is given access to point-of-view structures. Basing her argument on Laura Mulvey's well-known theory that the classical Hollywood narrative is organized around a male gaze directed at a specularized female body, Doane claims that since women are despecularized in women's films, and since the gaze is female, the woman's gaze has no object and becomes fraught with horror and anxiety. In the adaptation of *Jane Eyre*, Jane's gaze becomes investigative, frantically seeking an object.[33] This is particularly evident in the scenes in which Jane searches for the source of the laugh she often hears.

However, there are also many moments in the film when Jane's gaze does rest on an object of desire, Rochester. Because the novel represents Jane's sexual desire for Rochester, the film cannot avoid doing so as well. If the novel, as Juliet Mitchell claims, eroticizes Rochester's body while de-eroticizing Jane's, so does the film, though perhaps to a lesser extent. The charismatic Orson Welles is constructed more as an object of desire than the plainer Joan Fontaine. The body that is described in greater detail on the page, Rochester's, is also of greater interest on the screen. So, as in the novel, the object of desire in this film is male and the gaze is female.

Since a sexual or controlling gaze potentially empowers the female perspective, the adaptation works to divest the female gaze of its power. Jane's gaze is what Doane elsewhere calls "an imprisoned gaze." Jane often views Rochester through barred windows or banisters and is not allowed access to him. Her gaze is also desexualized and made as innocent as a child's because she is often with Adèle when she views Rochester. Jane is also made less threatening through her depiction as a very passive character, especially in contrast to the charismatic object of her gaze, Orson Welles. Finally, her gaze is also disarmed by being represented as unreliable. Often her vision is dissociated from her understanding.[34] For example, as Doane notes, there is a scene in which Jane goes to help Mason, who has been wounded by Bertha. Jane does not yet know of Bertha's existence, and while she tends to Mason's wounds the door to the attic behind her keeps rattling and banging ominously. Rochester says to her, "What you may see will shock you. Don't try to understand." Though the film allows Jane to gaze on Rochester, she is denied the power of the gaze. Most of all, however, the film divests Jane's desiring gaze of its power by redefining the terms of sexual desire, by rooting female sexuality in maternal bonds.

Feminine sexual desires that strayed from the confines of marriage and the home were a source of tremendous anxiety during the Second World War. Husbands who were fighting far away from home feared their wives would not remain faithful. Many marriages were made hastily, just before the husband left for service abroad and before the relationship felt stable. In addition, men often had extramarital relationships in Europe.[35] The sexual instability in marriages during the Second World War might have been yet another impetus for reframing the novel's representation of the tension between a sexually desiring woman and a married man. The adaptation goes to great lengths to situate sexuality safely within the home and anchor it in maternal relationships.

When Jane returns to Gateshead Hall to witness Mrs. Reed's death, Bessie does not recognize her until she takes off her cloak and reveals the brooch Bessie had given her. This recognition scene is important because it emphasizes that Jane's significant bond is with Bessie, the ideal maternal figure, and not with Mrs. Reed, her antithesis. Bessie's recognition of Jane is a key component of the film's ideological trajectory; it is only after Jane renews her bond with the ideal maternal figure, Bessie, and after Mrs. Reed, the negative mother figure, dies, that Jane can go on to marry Rochester. In other words, Stevenson's film makes Jane's ability to acquire what she desires, her ability to choose love over labor, hinge on her symbolic recognition by and connection with a maternal ideal, and on her symbolic renunciation and killing off of the "bad" mother.

Tania Modleski's psychoanalytic analysis of Hitchcock's *Rebecca* is instructive. Selznick produced *Rebecca* only four years before making *Jane Eyre* and at about the same time as he started thinking about the second film. *Rebecca* is an adaptation of a novel that is itself a literary adaptation of *Jane Eyre*. Hitchcock's films often stage women's pre-Oedipal conflicts, their over-identification with, and their desire to separate from, the mother. With regard to *Rebecca*, Modleski claims that the nameless heroine, threatened and overwhelmed by Mrs. Danvers and the ghost of Rebecca, must develop or mature enough to be able to kill the mother symbolically and forge a separate identity.[36] *Jane Eyre* is very similar in that two evil mother figures threaten the female protagonist.

Jane's desires are thwarted first by Mrs. Reed and then by Bertha, and both are symbolically connected. Bertha's room is shot, like Mrs. Reed herself, from extreme angles, and Mrs. Reed, like Bertha, is almost always situated spatially above Jane. Both women exclude Jane from certain areas of the house. Because of Bertha, Jane must leave Thornfield, just as earlier Mrs. Reed makes Jane leave Gateshead Hall. Other imagery also associates Bertha with Mrs. Reed. The narrative opens with a close-up of a candle held by Bessie as she and the butler approach the red room, where Mrs. Reed has imprisoned Jane. Later, there is another close-up of a candle when Bessie escorts Jane out of Gateshead Hall toward Lowood, taking her from one prison to another. There are no more shots of candles until Jane hears a laugh in the middle of the night and opens her bedroom door to discover a candle left by Bertha at the entrance to her room. This candle is associated with plotlines that emphasize Jane's imprisonment by Mrs. Reed and then by Bertha. Both women are prohibitive mother figures who, by imprisoning and excluding Jane, prevent her from fulfilling her desires.

Nevertheless, she is drawn to both of them. Leaving Gateshead Hall, Jane looks back with mournful longing at Mrs. Reed's window. Later, at Thornfield, Jane persists in trying to discover Bertha on the third floor. She is lured by Bertha's laugh and follows her with a dread fascination that is perhaps also a longing for the mother figure, an inability to separate from the mother. Significantly, the narrative chronology of the film has been changed so that Mrs. Reed dies at the same time as Bertha. Like the main character in *Rebecca*, Jane must symbolically kill off her mother before she can develop her own feminine identity and obtain what she desires. A passage by Raymond Bellure that Modleski uses to describe *Rebecca* applies aptly to *Jane Eyre*:

> For the heroine fulfills the archetypical female dream of marrying the father-figure, who has rescued her from the tyranny of the domineering old woman (i.e. mother). But in doing so she has to confront the rival from the past, the woman who possessed her father first, who can reach out and possess him once again.[37]

In Stevenson's *Jane Eyre*, it is not so much that the father figure has rescued Jane from the mother figure, but, as in the primal scenario Bellure describes, that Jane has to kill off her mothers and renounce her longing for them to gain access to the older, more forceful father figure of Rochester, who has previously been possessed by Bertha. However, unlike in the scenario described above, Jane must also clearly identify with a positive maternal figure.

In her discussion of *Stella Dallas*, Linda Williams argues that classical Hollywood films work to repress and deny the significance of the daughter's bond with the mother so as to affirm the woman's heterosexual place in society. The mother figure idealized in the adaptation of *Jane Eyre* is what psychoanalytic feminist film theorists would consider a symbolic rather than pre-Oedipal mother. While the pre-Oedipal mother, the mother of the Lacanian imaginary order, merges with the daughter, suggesting homosexual bonds, the symbolic mother, constructed in the language of the symbolic order, represses the imaginary merging mother and insists on heterosexual desire and reproduction. Bessie is a maternal figure with the symbolic traits of motherhood; she fits the cultural prescriptions regarding nurturing maternal behavior but is not close enough to Jane to suggest any kind of pre-Oedipal merging. Jane is not Bessie's biological child and is separated from her by class. Jane's bond with Adèle is characterized by similar distances. Jane's bond with Bessie is not too close but is sufficient to enable Jane to fill a maternal role herself toward Adèle and, ultimately, the child she has with Rochester. Unlike in the novel, the end of the adaptation emphasizes Rochester's son, the child Jane and Rochester's sexual relationship has produced.

The adaptation's complex construction of a maternal ideal and its antithesis draws on contemporary anxieties about women and their relationship to motherhood. The 1944 adaptation is particularly invested in representing Mrs. Reed as a bad mother and then clearly exorcising her from the domestic resolution established at the end of the film. Other adaptations often omit most scenes with Mrs. Reed; in the 1997 *Jane Eyre* adaptation, for instance, Mrs. Reed appears only in one brief scene. In Stevenson's 1944 adaptation, like the mothers who were said to lock their children in basements and cars while they worked, Mrs. Reed and her double Bertha neglect and imprison their "daughter" and are associated with the masculine world of Lowood, with the world of labor. Killing them off eases anxieties that were prevalent at the time.

In the 1940s advertisement showing a young girl asking her mother when she will stay home again, the mother straddles a bicycle wearing masculine clothes: dungarees and boots. Her daughter is dressed precisely the same way and stands exactly opposite her, also straddling a bicycle. By having the child mirror her mother in this way, the advertisement suggests not only that the mother is abandoning her daughter but also that the daughter is learning something askew about femininity. This advertisement expresses anxieties about what it is little girls are learning from their wartime working mothers about femininity and their own future roles as mothers. It is important in this context that the film emphasizes the death of the bad maternal role model.

Thus, the film works meticulously, through complex imagery and changes to the novel's plot, to reinscribe the novel within a maternally centered domestic ideology, an ideology the novel goes out of its way to resist. Stevenson's adaptation goes to great lengths to situate female desire within the home and tie it to maternal feelings. Nevertheless, the ideological work of adaptations is never seamless, and aspects of the novel seep into the film and unsettle its representations.

The film's ideological stability starts to unravel at the end of the scene in which Rochester and Jane visit Adèle to see whether she is safe after Bertha has set fire to Rochester's bed. Jane and Rochester stand over Adèle's bed discussing her welfare in a tableau that prefigures the film's idealized domestic resolution. However, as Rochester and Jane leave Adèle's room, Rochester picks up Adèle's dancing slippers and throws them at her music box. He then walks over to the box and, as he strikes each figure dismissively with his hand, mutters, "I was once in love with that and jealous of that." This music box last appeared in the scene in which Jane awoke at Thornfield, a scene that used the dancing couple as a symbol for the romance awaiting her. The soldier and ballet dancer that represented Jane and Rochester in the first scene represent Adèle's parents in this one. Oddly, the child's toy that represents romance and sexuality in one scene comes to represent illicit sexual relations, deceptions, disloyalties, and bastard children in another. Even more interesting, it is actually Jane, not Celine, who is currently having a sexually charged relationship with a married man. Thus, this central symbol of romance and sexuality comes to (pre)figure not only the monogamous married love represented at the end of the film but also the adulterous love that occurs through most of the film. The representation of an ideal homebound reproductive sexuality is undermined at the very moment it is being constructed.

The domestic ideal the film works so hard to represent is unstable because disruptive meanings associated with Rochester's sexual history seep into the film despite its intentions. This instability is caused by the novel itself. The film attempts to represent Jane's sexuality as bound by her maternal feelings, yet these feelings are for a child the novel describes as illegitimate. Somehow the film must account for Adèle's existence, and although the representation of Rochester's sexual past is greatly limited in the film – we hear of only two of his previous sexual encounters: Bertha and Celine Varens – it is still impossible to remove this aspect of the novel from the adaptation. The maternally bound, family-focused sexuality the film tries to represent is overwhelmed here by the sexually transgressive content of the novel. It is almost as though Charlotte Brontë undermines her novel's appropriation by later, different ideologies.

Another interesting ideological slip in the film involves Bertha. In the film, Jane often becomes the object of Bertha's gaze. Several times the audience views Jane, and sometimes Rochester when he is with her, from Bertha's point of view. In a scene in which Jane tries to gain access to the attic, the camera positions the audience in Bertha's point of view as she watches Jane climb up the stairs. Later in the film, the spectator is made to see Jane and Rochester take Mr. Mason back to his carriage from a very high angle, again from Bertha's point of view. When Rochester reveals Bertha to Jane, the camera is situated behind Bertha looking out of her attic at Jane and Rochester. Thus, although Jane spends much of the film seeking and trying to see Bertha, it is Bertha who actually sees Jane. That their gazes are reversed in this way emphasizes the reversibility of Jane and Bertha's positions. The attempt to portray Jane, as Selznick intended, as imprisoned by Mrs. Reed leads to unintended associations with imprisonment. Although Jane is ostensibly portrayed as liberated from imprisonment at Thornfield, there is another woman who is still in prison in Rochester's house. Bertha and Jane are inadvertently represented as occupying parallel disempowered positions.

Indeed, Rochester is in some ways associated with Brocklehurst. When Jane first arrives at Lowood, a page from the "novel" that describes Lowood is shown on screen. In the shaded, dark area of the page there is a reference that in the context of Jane having just arrived at Lowood seems to refer to Brocklehurst: "What sort of man was this master of Thornfield, proud, sardonic and harsh?" This same sentence appears again the next time the "novel" is shown on screen, when Jane is at Thornfield, and then it is clear that it refers to Rochester, not Brocklehurst. Rochester's tyrannical manner when he first meets Jane is reminiscent of Brocklehurst's. It is significant that the film, in its less consciously worked-out areas, associates Rochester with Brocklehurst. The film seems unconsciously to adapt a connection later feminist critics reveal, a similarity between Lowood and Thornfield.

In the classic feminist analysis of this aspect of the novel in *The Madwoman in the Attic*, Gilbert and Gubar claim that *Jane Eyre* is "a story of enclosure and escape."[38] They argue that Jane is imprisoned by the patriarchal culture she inhabits and that Jane's rage, expressed through her double, Bertha, is a response to this imprisonment. Despite the film's attempt to idealize the domestic sphere and Thornfield, it retains the more feminist dimension of the novel that represents Jane and Bertha as doubles. As much as the film tries to idealize marriage, motherhood, and the home, through its portrayal of Bertha it inadvertently retains the novel's representation of the home as a potential prison.

In addition, in the novel, Bertha is described only from Rochester's and Jane's perspectives. That the audience of the film is sutured within Bertha's ominous and anxious gaze, peering uneasily from odd angles out of the confines of a prison, is significant. Women's films were, it has been suggested, so popular with women because they expressed not only their fantasies but also their anxieties.[39] By placing the viewer in not only Jane's but also Bertha's uneasy point of view, the film enables the audience to experience both the fantasy and the fear, the desire and the dread, that are associated with marriage and the home.

While Selznick was making the film, he conducted a survey asking women what the most memorable scenes from the novel were. Most responses mentioned the scene in which Rochester saves Jane from her burning bed and the scene in which Bertha burns down Thornfield.[40] This is interesting since the first scene does not exist in the novel and the second scene is not shown in the novel but is narrated at a distance – Jane narrates what someone else tells her about these events. Yet what women in the early 1940s found memorable in the novel were precisely its more subversive dimensions, the sexuality, represented in these women's memory of Jane – rather than Rochester – lying in a bed of flames, and the rebellious act of Bertha burning down the house. Whatever it is about the novel that made women readers remember Bertha burning down Thornfield seems to infiltrate the film through the strange series of shots that position the spectator within Bertha's point of view, something none of the 1990s film adaptations do despite the attention Bertha has received from feminist critics. In addition, the extremely high and low angles used to represent Bertha's point of view are reminiscent of Orson Welles's style, not only in *Citizen Kane* but also in *A Touch of Evil*. There is disagreement about how much Welles was involved in directing the film, but regardless of who was responsible for these scenes, Bertha's point of view seems to offer a subtle destabilizing counter-perspective on the romantic melodrama shown in the rest of the film. The extreme angles offer the viewer a sardonic wink at the rest of the film in this eerie representation of Bertha's perspective on Rochester and Jane's little domestic world. This part of the film reflects Brontë's more radical vision, a vision that infiltrates and subtly subverts the film's overt ideological trajectory.

The very last scene of the film tries to ensure an ending with an ideal image of marriage and home. It is set, unlike in the novel, amidst the ruins of Thornfield in order to emphasize that it has been destroyed. The fortresses and prisons that Jane must escape have been destroyed, and Jane finds liberation and fulfillment through marriage. The film attempts to avoid the instability of the novel's ending.

The novel's domestic resolution is highly ambiguous. *Jane Eyre* ends not with a description of a conventional Victorian domestic ideal, not with a description of a happy marriage and home, but with Jane's reading of St John's adventures in India, just as it begins with Jane reading

Bewick's book of birds as she contemplates strange far-away places and perhaps flight. One of Jane's favorite books as a child is *Gulliver's Travels*, but she herself does not travel; rather, she ends up secluded at Ferndean thinking about someone else's travels. Is Brontë being ironic about St John's achievements, or is she, as at the end of *Villette*, expressing some doubt about the conventional domestic resolution? Are St John's energies misguided and self-destructive, or are they indeed heroic and Jane's achievements small, mundane, and meaningless in comparison? Is Jane, after ten years of marriage, dwelling on St John's actions and emphasizing his tireless energy because she wonders whether women also "need exercise for their faculties, and a field for their efforts"?[41] Is she here wondering, as she did on the battlements of Thornfield, whether the restlessness of her nature is satisfied with her domestic lot? The ending of Brontë's *Jane Eyre* raises more questions than it answers.

Stevenson's adaptation, in contrast, ends with an unambiguous tableau of a happily married couple with their son. At a time when the war had destabilized traditional gender roles and offered women new opportunities outside the domestic sphere, the adaptation's domestic resolution asserts the importance of marriage, home, and motherhood. In an attempt to contain the multifaceted female desires explored in Charlotte Brontë's *Bildungsroman*, what contemporary critics had identified as its radical, feminist, and sexual contents, the film develops its own trajectory of development for Jane. Using unstable but intricately worked-out visual imagery and psychologically complex character development, Jane is represented as learning to reject one form of motherhood and embrace another. The film works to dispel anxieties about bad mothers while constructing an idealized representation of motherhood that contains female sexuality within the home. When women were encouraged to enter the labor force, only to be encouraged to leave it a few years later, Stevenson's adaptation manipulates a classic nineteenth-century novel in order to construct a stable feminine ideal, not dissimilar to the Victorian ideal Brontë resisted, for viewers living in a time of rapid change.

3
Recovering Victorian Ideals: *The Mill on the Floss*

While Hollywood adaptations of the 1930s and 1940s represented women in terms of their relationship to marriage, British adaptations of this period focused on the relationship of women to British society as a whole. In Hollywood, cultural anxieties about women were expressed and then exorcised through the representation of a romantic ideal culminating in marriage, but in Britain the ideal each film constructed was less individualistic and more collective or nationalist. Rather than heightening and romanticizing the domestic novel's marriage plot, British cinema channeled this literary convention in ways that gave marriage, or its absence, communal significance. Choosing nineteenth-century novels that already had less prominent marriage plots, British adaptations focused more on how female protagonists contributed to Britain's collective character.

British adaptations have generally been viewed as more restrained and more loyal to their sources than Hollywood productions. Brian McFarlane, for instance, has claimed that

> British adaptations have exhibited a decorous, dogged fidelity to their sources, content to render through careful attention to their mise en scène the social values and emotional insight of those sources ... the standard British film version of the novel has been a prime example of those pervasive qualities of "good taste, characterized by restraint, the British cinema's 'negative reactions' to the more dangerously flamboyant and vigorous aspects of Hollywood."[1]

Though the British adaptations of the 1930s and 1940s were indeed more restrained and understated, and certainly less melodramatic and flamboyant than their American counterparts, they were not more faithful to their literary sources. As with all adaptations, British films filtered nineteenth-century novels through a contemporary ideological lens. In part, British adaptations were different because, at the time, British film did not share many of the conventions of classical Hollywood cinema. Intentionally resistant to Hollywood's ideals of glamour, British film represented women less in terms of their desires and desirability than in terms of their social roles. Romantic themes were incorporated into broader social questions. Since Britain faced complex internal class and regional divisions in the 1930s, and it was recovering from the Second World War in the 1940s, most British films of this period project an image of Britain as a society united in the face of internal or external threats. Adapting products of Britain's grand literary heritage heightened this nationalist agenda.

The representation of women in ways that serve this larger ideological goal is particularly striking in the 1937 adaptation of George Eliot's *The Mill on the Floss*. Directed by the prolific director Tim Whelan, this film suppresses the novel's primary interest in the desires of women as it projects an idealized image of Britain united against the economic and social afflictions of the 1930s. Whelan's adaptation foregrounds the plotline that depicts a family facing economic ruin at the expense of the narrative depicting a young girl growing up in a society that thwarts her desires. In the 1930s, as feminist advances were being rolled back and women were increasingly encouraged to move out of the labor force into the home, Eliot's novel is reshaped to represent women as desiring nothing other than what is good for men and society at large. The adaptation represents women as significant only to the extent that they can contribute to alleviating contemporary social tensions. Reinstating Victorian ideals that Eliot questions, the film constructs an ideal of femininity that is naturally self-sacrificing and serves as a moral example for men. The film shows men learning from women how to overcome class and economic conflicts to pull together and serve the needs of the larger community or nation. Despite the dramatic events leading to war on the continent, this adaptation is completely preoccupied with internal social threats to Britain's stability.

The prospect of internal strife loomed over Britain during the economic slump of the 1930s. Britain's economic troubles were very different from those of the United States, since the Depression was not as severe in Britain and its burdens were unevenly distributed. Unemployment and poverty rates were high in some regions in Britain, but in others the economy was actually improving. Since Britain's four major industries – coal, textiles, ship building, and steel – had declined, regions economically dependent on one of these industries were more depressed than areas that were not. For example, in 1932 St. Albans, typical of the towns around London, had only a 3.9 percent unemployment rate, while in Jarrow, in the Northeast, the unemployment rate was 68 percent. The South and West of England even benefited from the slump in the rest of Britain since the Depression lowered market prices but levels of income remained the same. The more prosperous areas of England enjoyed a minor consumer boom as buying power increased and new industries developed to satisfy new consumer demands.[2] This created a significant rift. "It was the sharp division between the 'two Englands' – the England of the South and the Midlands, which were relatively prosperous, and the England of the Depressed Areas in the North, Wales and Scotland – which lent the interwar period its particular complexity."[3]

The 1930s saw a series of hunger marches in which the unemployed from depressed regions in the North marched to London in protest. Such extreme regional differences, and sometimes desperate public actions taken by trade unions, triggered anxieties about social unrest even though events would later prove such anxieties to be unfounded. These anxieties are evident in the way Whelan's *The Mill on the Floss* changes the novel's central narrative so that economic and social tensions are pivotal while women's experiences are marginalized.

The novel, in contrast, explores female desires in great depth. *The Mill on the Floss* has usually been regarded as a *Bildungsroman* because it traces the personal development of two central characters, a girl and a boy, from childhood into maturity. Feminist critics have emphasized how complex it was to portray a female protagonist in a genre that celebrates the social and intellectual development of the individual at a time when avenues for such development were closed to women. Eliot reveals the conflict between the self-determination valorized by the *Bildungsroman* and the ideals of self-sacrifice and renunciation demanded of nineteenth-century women.[4] She creates both a male and a female protagonist in her *Bildungsroman* so that she can expose how a boy is able to find his professional role within nineteenth-century culture while a girl's parallel quest for identity results in her being increasingly excluded from such power structures.[5] Eliot contrasts the opportunities available to men with those unavailable to women and criticizes these socially determined differences.[6] Susan Fraiman has gone so far as to claim that *The Mill on the Floss* interrogates the *Bildungsroman* genre and its values by criticizing the type of development Tom undergoes. She refers to the novel's "repudiation of precisely [the *Bildungsroman*'s] story of self-advancement, its critical if not satirical view of Tom's lonely climb from averted adolescent to competitive businessman, its evident concern to dramatize the moral and narrative deficiency of Tom's story."[7] At the very least, *The Mill on the Floss* questions nineteenth-century ideals of masculine achievement through its assessment of Tom's rise and Maggie's exclusion from opportunities that would have benefited her more than her brother.

In the 1937 adaptation, the exclusion of women is enacted rather than represented. Masculine forms of achievement are foregrounded and valorized, and female characters are pushed to the margins of the plot. Maggie's marginalization is evident even in the film's credits. The opening credits state that Tom is played by James Mason. This credit appears on its own in the frame, indicating Tom's centrality to the plot. The credit for Maggie's character appears later, dwarfed by a long list of other minor parts. Only when the film was released in the United States in 1939, after Geraldine Fitzgerald, who played Maggie, had become a popular actress, were the credits changed to give Fitzgerald double billing with Mason. This change capitalized on the actress's popularity to sell the film across the Atlantic but does not change the film's representation of Maggie as a secondary character. In part, the challenges of the 1930s pushed the economic dimensions of the plot to the center at Maggie's expense; more significantly, a fuller representation of Maggie's desires would have clashed with the domestic ideals of the 1930s.

In some regions of Britain, with the improved economy came changes in family structures and domestic ideals. In the 1930s a housing boom improved the standard of living for women. New, comfortable homes housed families that were smaller than in the past. People no longer lived with their extended families, and despite propaganda encouraging women to have more children, the birth rate dropped significantly. Moreover, since these new homes were built in new locations, traditional community bonds were weakened, and bonds with the immediate family became more significant. Definitions of marriage changed as the institution was increasingly seen in terms of companionship. Men remained at home more often than had men of previous generations, and when they did go out, they usually did so with their wives. Rates of prostitution dropped, and marriage was seen more in sexual terms than it had been during earlier periods. Many sex manuals for married couples were published, and they sold well. Marriage rates rose sharply as marriage came to be seen as more "affectionate and equal."[8] In general, women's standard of living had risen and their position within marriage had improved. Nevertheless, housework, though easier than before, was still difficult, and, as in America, there was a growing cult of domesticity that raised standards for women's work in the home.

This heightened domestic ideology was propagated in the media, which now included a steadily increasing number of women's magazines. Elizabeth, George VI's wife, epitomized the magazines' "idea of womanhood: Petite, charming, motherly, grand-but-accessible, special-but-domestic, and above all, perhaps, she provided vital support for her husband in performing his difficult role."[9] Such powerful media representations worked to keep women in the home and undermined the changes that had opened up many new professions for women. Tremendous cultural force was brought to bear on women to stay in their homes and concentrate on their domestic and child-rearing functions.

Furthermore, women still had no independent property; their comfortable new houses were registered in their husbands' names. In many ways, women faced even greater obstacles in the 1930s than they had in the Edwardian period, despite the favorable laws that had been passed in the wake of their gaining the vote. The number of women entering professions recently made available to them was small. Most working women had badly paid part-time or temporary jobs and faced strong social pressure to work only at jobs "appropriate for women." Therefore, women who worked were a cheap and elastic source of labor, low paid and contingent, and middle-class women lost their jobs when they married. By the 1930s women had effectively been pushed out of the jobs they had acquired during the First World War, as was the case for middle-class women teachers and doctors, for example. The government took measures to ensure that working-class women returned to domestic service after the First World War: anyone who refused to work in domestic service was refused unemployment benefits. Even working-class women who had no choice other than to work were forced to work within a home.[10]

Meanwhile, feminists concentrated on health and welfare issues such as widows' pensions and child allowances. This can be seen as a natural outgrowth of the evangelical strain in feminism that had always focused on improving the conditions of women in the home.[11] This made feminism, too, in a sense, home centered. As the decade progressed, feminism was increasingly dwarfed by the threats of war and fascism.

Feminists of the earlier, more active, era felt that their accomplishments were stagnating, if not receding. In 1929, in "A Room of One's Own," Virginia Woolf described the stringent restrictions placed on women's education and their intellectual development. In 1938, feeling that no progress had been made since 1929, Woolf published another essay on the same topic. In "Three Guineas" Woolf compares the wealth men's colleges possessed with the relative poverty of women's colleges.

Woolf claims that "the colleges of the sisters of educated men are, compared with their brothers' colleges, unbelievably and shamefully poor."[12] Women were not even allowed to put "BA" after their name when they passed their examinations. Woolf concludes that even among the most educated classes, women's education was unequal to men's and that society was unwilling to offer the same status and privileges accorded to educated men to educated women. In fact, "Cambridge did not admit women to full degrees as equals until 1948," and even in 1961 "there were only 593 female undergraduates at Oxford and Cambridge (13 percent)." It was not until the 1970s that Oxford and Cambridge became truly co-educational.[13] Although she could not have known how long it would last, Woolf had a clear sense of how deeply entrenched resistance to equal education for women was in Britain in the 1930s.

Woolf also discusses public opposition to women working. Most people felt that in economically trying times women should give up their jobs to men who needed them more. As a vivid example of this attitude, Woolf quotes a letter to the editor published in *The Daily Telegraph*:

> I am certain I voice the opinion of thousands of young men when I say that if men were doing the work that thousands of young women are now doing the men would be able to keep those same women in decent homes. Homes are the real places of the women who are now compelling men to be idle. It is time the Government insisted upon employers giving work to more men, thus enabling them to marry the women they cannot now approach.[14]

The cultural resistance to women's education and women's labor described by Woolf is evident in the extent to which the adaptation of *The Mill on the Floss* erases these central components of Eliot's novel. In American Depression-era adaptations, even though women characters ultimately renounce their independent desires when they marry, women are represented as desiring money and as being intelligent and somewhat autonomous. British adaptations of the period avoid any reference to women's economic desires. In the novel Maggie works hard to support herself financially, but she does not work in the film. Lacking Hollywood's stake in promoting glamour and female consumerism, the British adaptation can excise Maggie's economic needs and labor from the plot.

More significantly, Tom's and Maggie's attitudes to education, so central in the novel, are represented very differently in the film. Eliot reveals how painful it is for an intelligent and curious girl to grow up in a culture that denies girls the educational opportunities available to boys. Whereas Maggie is intellectually capable and loves studying, Tom hates studying and suffers under the strain of a classical education. It is ironic that Maggie would be more able than Tom to benefit from the education from which she is excluded. It is even more ironic that Tom's education is often described as making him feel like a girl. While education is considered by his teacher and others to belong to the masculine sphere, Tom experiences it as emasculating. Studying undermines Tom's natural active energies. Eliot deconstructs Victorian gender ideals when she represents education as more fitting for little girls than for energetic, playful boys.

Whelan's adaptation suppresses what, for Eliot, is a crucial theme in the novel. The film tries to reify rather than deconstruct ideologies of gender that represent only men as inclined toward education. The novel's education theme is condensed into one short scene in Whelan's adaptation. Maggie goes with Tom to Stelling's school and meets Philip, who draws a portrait of her; Tom then gets jealous because he is not able to draw as well as Philip. Rather than making Tom a boy who hates mathematics, the film represents him as a boy who cannot draw very well, a skill usually seen as "feminine." Maggie is represented not, as in the novel, as easily understanding Tom's mathematics lessons but as someone who sits for a portrait. In the adaptation, Tom has no difficulty with his education, and Maggie never desires one, preferring to be admired for her looks. Conventional notions about women and education are reinforced not questioned. The adaptation omits Eliot's criticism of the unequal forms of intellectual development available to Maggie and Tom. This is a symptom of the adaptation's inversion of Eliot's double *Bildungsroman*.

While George Eliot has Tom die at the end of the novel and thereby "refuses, narratively, to validate his formation and to invest it with significant content,"[15] the film changes the plot so that Tom survives. In the novel Tom's death raises questions about his ability to develop as an individual; in the film Tom's ability to grow morally is emphasized. In a similar change that the film makes, Tom asks Lucy to marry him. Despite Lucy's refusal, this addition to the plot makes Tom into a character capable of romantic feeling. Tom is given an emotional depth and dimension Eliot denies him. Eliot's cold, rigid, stagnant, and even self-destructive male character is very different in Whelan's adaptation.

Maggie is also changed. Eliot's Maggie has active impulses despite the fact that they are thwarted by her culture. She learns to row, attempts to learn Euclid and Latin, and insists on remaining economically independent. The cinematic Maggie does none of these things and is portrayed as only reacting to the men around her. Even the final scene in the film works to maintain Maggie's passivity. In the novel, Maggie uses superhuman strength to row to the mill to save Tom from the flood, and even he recognizes the heroic force of her effort. In the adaptation, it is not Maggie who rows out to rescue Tom in the storm but Philip who tries to rescue a passive and helpless Maggie. Thus, although the film does not reveal much of either Maggie's or Tom's inner worlds, it does represent Tom as an active, energetic character who works, succeeds, pays back his father's debts, and develops morally as a result of Maggie's death. Maggie, in contrast, is passive and peripheral.

Whelan's film also erases the female point of view so central to Eliot's novel. Whereas the American adaptations of the 1930s and 1940s adhere to the conventions of the woman's film and portray conflicts faced by women from the point of view of female characters, the adaptation of *The Mill on the Floss* has almost no female perspective. Marcia Landy has noted that although Britain made some women's films in the 1930s, it made fewer than America. British films, she notes, tended to be preoccupied with "male identity, privilege, and bonding."[16] Hence, they were often more interested in the conflicts men faced. The explanation for this emphasis, she believes, "lies only partially in the fact that the British production has been mainly in the hands of men. ... The explanation lies also in the structure of British middle-class culture, which has been heavily weighted toward segregating the sexes from childhood through young adulthood."[17] Raymond Durgnat concurs, claiming that British films value "the primacy of male allegiance in the public school spirit." Influenced by a culture in which the sexes are separated, whether by all-boy public schools or men's clubs, films of this period emphasize a male sense of community. In fact, they represent growing up as something that occurs "between boys and men, not involving, or only very elliptically, a feminine presence." A recurrent, male-oriented theme of this period was the boy's struggle with a "heavy father" as he attempts to mature.[18] *The Mill on the Floss* is masculinized in all of these ways.

The adaptation focuses on male characters, and especially on the problem of male rivalry, representing it in economic and class terms. Conflicts between men are depicted as rooted in the past, stemming from the feuds of their fathers' generation, and as something the new generation must learn to overcome to progress. The film opens with a pastoral scene in which two oxen pulling a cart cross a pretty bridge over a floss. This bucolic idyll is disrupted by two men arguing about the damaging effect Sir John's dam is having on the water that powers Tulliver's mill. The subsequent sequence shows Tulliver arguing with Sir John's lawyers; a clash rooted in class and economic differences disrupts the community. A couple of scenes later, the film depicts another conflict, this time between two members of the next generation, Tulliver's son Tom and another child, Bob, who fight over a ha'penny.

In the novel, Tom's relationship with Bob is complex. Tom loves playing with Bob because they share a roguish enjoyment of the wild outdoors. When Tom later renounces Bob's friendship because he cheats, Eliot emphasizes that Tom has a very rigid sense of justice. He sacrifices an energetic, life-affirming friendship in the name of abstract principles of justice. Tom's love of play and nature is part of a life force, a vitality, that he will increasingly sacrifice for the sake of earning back the money and status his father loses.

Since the adaptation does not show Tom and Bob's relationship before the fight, their rivalry is situated solely within an economic context, appearing to be only a conflict over a coin. What Whelan criticizes in Tom is his competitive impulse and not, as Eliot does, his rigid lack of compassion. In addition, in the adaptation, Philip walks into the scene as Tom concludes his fight with Bob. The film's sequencing thus places Philip within the network of male rivalries also emphasized by his father's conflict with Tom's father. The younger generation are in this way represented as perpetuating the economic and class-motivated rivalries of their fathers.

The absence of this theme from the novel reveals how important the conflict between the older and newer generations is to the film's ideological work. In the novel, when Tulliver learns that Wakem's son will be in school with Tom, although he tells Tom not to get too close to him, he also feels sympathy for Philip because of his deformity. Tulliver's compassion is contrasted with Tom's disdain for Philip's weakness. Although Eliot's Tom feels some loyalty to Tulliver, he is often also critical of him, and many of Tom's actions are motivated by his desire to erase the shame he feels for what he believes to be his father's flaws. Tom's limitations are not his father's fault in Eliot's novel. In fact, Tulliver is in many ways a sympathetic character. Tulliver's emotional fluctuations and fundamentally compassionate heart suggest that had he known about Maggie's relationship with Philip, he would not necessarily have behaved as cruelly as Tom does when he separates them. It is one of the ironies of the novel that Tom enacts a cold justice in his father's name that would not have fitted his father's more flexible emotional character.

Whelan changes Eliot's representation of Tom's relationship with his father. When Tom discovers that Wakem's son is at his school, Tulliver tells Tom, "Don't get too close with him. I don't like his stock," ordering Tom to continue his own generation's class-based feud into the next. Whelan's Tulliver is blindly vengeful, and Tom follows blindly in his footsteps. By representing Tulliver as more overbearing in the film than he is in the novel, Tom's *Bildung* becomes one in which he must learn to overcome his father's hold on him. The last scene of the film is a shot of Tom erasing the vow Tulliver had written in the Bible never to forgive the Wakems. The film opens with a scene depicting the father in the midst of a conflict with another man and closes with the son erasing his father's vengeful words, now having learned to forgive and forget old rivalries.

The 1937 adaptation of *The Mill on the Floss* represents male social conflict as outmoded and archaic, something that belongs to the generation of the fathers, and posits communal values as ideal for the generation of the moment and the future. Economic differences, the film suggests, should bring people together rather than pull them apart. Changes the adaptation makes in Bob's characterization facilitate this ideology. In the novel, after Tulliver's economic collapse, Bob buys Maggie some books. In the film, in contrast, when Tulliver's household goods are being auctioned, Bob buys some of them and then anonymously leaves them in the home for the Tullivers to use. The more subtle gift of books that acknowledges Maggie's intellect is replaced by a different kind of symbolic act. Since the previous scene in which Bob appeared in the film was the one in which he was struggling with Tom over a ha'penny, Bob is presented as someone who can overcome past economic rivalries through an act of human generosity. He sets aside class differences and makes a personal sacrifice to help someone in need. Bob represents what Tom must learn to become, someone who can sacrifice for the good of others.

Bob, who embodies the self-sacrificing ideal the film valorizes, is also unambiguously depicted as a successful capitalist. He forgoes competition to help those in need but never refrains from competitive economic practices. The film retains the scene in which Bob cheats Aunt Glegg when he sells her a "bit of lace" but omits Maggie's suggestion that Bob "cheats." Bob's business acumen is not criticized but, rather, valued when he is credited with enabling Tom's economic success. The film valorizes both an ethic of "pulling together" in the face of economic hardship and the competitive spirit of capitalism and in this sense too differs from the novel.

Eliot criticizes the new forms of wealth that unsettle the agrarian community she depicts. This is evident in the way Tom's economic rise is paralleled by his increasing moral rigidity and lack of compassion. Furthermore, Tulliver, whose family has owned the mill for almost 150 years, loses his court case to Pivart, a wealthy man who has bought property in the area and is diverting Tulliver's water to fuel the modern irrigation system he is using on his lands. *The Mill on the Floss* explores the tragic dislocations the old agrarian community faces as a new landowning class arrives and introduces modern technologies. Pivart, Wakem, and both generations of the Guests are all dangerous guests, new industrially connected classes who threaten the traditional agrarian community. They are powerful and easily destroy Tulliver and his world.

In contrast, despite its awareness of class conflict, the adaptation criticizes only aristocrats. Tulliver loses his court case not to a new middle-class landowner but to an invented character referred to as "Sir John." In the film it is Wakem and his aristocratic ally who are responsible for Tulliver's fall. The capitalist Guest family is represented sympathetically. Competition is criticized not as an economic practice but as an antiquated personality trait to be overcome by the new generation for the good of the community.

Historians differ with regard to whether Britain was in fact a cohesive society in the 1930s. Some argue that a "consensus" existed; others argue that this was an "imposed consensus." Whether film at this time reflected a cohesion that existed or tried to foster a cohesion that did not, it does repeatedly invoke an ideal cohesive community:

> British cinema had both a "reflective" function, in that it reflected the cohesive society which some historians tell us was in fact prevalent at the time, and a "generative" function, in that it sought to encourage the assumption that society should continue to cohere and unite as it passed through the changing circumstances of the 1930s. To that extent it may be said that the British cinema had a positive and purposeful part to play in shaping the "national life" because it helped (along with many other factors, of course) to achieve that high degree of consensus that seemingly characterized British society during the 1930s.[19]

Whelan's *The Mill on the Floss* valorizes a society that learns to cohere in the face of economic instability.

Allaying contemporary fears of civil strife, the film goes out of its way to represent the haves and have-nots as able to avert conflict and unite.

Whelan's adaptation suggests not only that economic hardships can be overcome with efforts similar to Tom's but also that people can and should pull together to confront misfortune as a unified community. Class conflict is represented as destructive; the film suggests that if Tulliver had not fought Sir John, he would not have fallen. Yet the classes can pull together to help each other only if individuals make the necessary sacrifices. The lower-class Bob, for instance, helps the slightly higher-class Tom rise. Overall, then, the film favors the replacement of individual rivalries with an ethic of self-sacrifice in the name of collective good.

In fact, it has been argued that in relation to British representations of the Depression,

> rather than isolating the unemployed as a forgettable minority, both cinema and literature worked to re-include them in the national family. Cinema's treatment of the issues involved, for instance, tended to concentrate on what the experience of the Depression for a minority seemed to prove about Britain as a whole, thus deftly translating working-class disaster into national valour. Rather than being portrayed as victims, the Depressed Areas were transformed into heroic examples of British fortitude.[20]

The adaptation of *The Mill on the Floss* reframes the novel so that it can perform a similar ideological function; it transforms the novel's representation of one family's ruin in the face of momentous social and economic changes into a story about a community that learns to come together for the greater good of a larger collective, the nation. This ideological trajectory drastically reshapes the representation of women. While the film marginalizes women on one level, it also gives them a central social role absent from the novel.

Since Maggie's intellectual aspirations and frustrations are omitted from the film, the only internal conflicts she experiences are between romantic desire and her duty to other people. Even her desire for men is shaped by this narrowing down of her character. In the novel, for example, Philip offers Maggie intellectual and spiritual companionship, but in the adaptation her attraction to him is represented as the result of her being lonely because no one will visit the Tullivers once they are poor. Economic rather than intellectual isolation binds Maggie to Philip. In addition, although Whelan's Stephen Guest is a sexual and economic temptation for Maggie, the economic aspect of his appeal is muted since Maggie is not represented as working hard to support herself at difficult jobs. The film also eliminates the tremendous internal conflict that Maggie suffers when she decides not to marry Stephen Guest.

The adaptation represents Maggie's renunciation of Stephen Guest as emanating from an innate feminine tendency toward self-sacrifice and therefore as a less agonizing decision. Maggie makes this sacrifice for the sake of others: for the sake of Lucy, to whom Stephen is engaged, and for the sake of Philip, to whom Maggie is engaged. Later in the film Maggie again sacrifices herself for others. After the rupture in Philip and Maggie's relationship subsequent to her journey down the river with Stephen, Maggie agrees to marry Philip even though it is clear that she does not love him. Maggie is represented as naturally self-sacrificing first when she renounces Stephen and then again when she agrees to marry Philip a second time, an event that does not occur in the novel. This plot change enables another one: Maggie's death is represented as a sacrifice that enables Tom to learn from the tragedy, forgive others, and grow morally. Ultimately, in sharp contrast to the novel, Maggie's sacrifices enable Tom to fit in better with his community. Maggie's sacrifices have clear and unambiguous moral motives and ends.

The same is not true in the novel. Although many critics claim that George Eliot validates Maggie's sacrifices,[21] the way Eliot represents them suggests otherwise. Maggie's self-denying impulses are complex. Although Maggie employs notions of self-sacrifice to justify separating from both Philip and Stephen, her motives are not completely selfless. When she decides not to marry Stephen, she remembers Philip's words: "Philip was right when he told her that she knew nothing of renunciation; she had thought it was quiet ecstasy; she saw it face to face now – that sad patient loving strength which holds the clue of life – and saw that the thorns were forever pressing on its brow."[22] Maggie uses the notion of self-renunciation she has read about in Thomas à Kempis to find inner peace, a "quiet ecstasy." Her renunciations of Philip and Stephen serve a quest for martyrdom that has more to do with her own self-image than with either of the men. In addition, when she gives Philip up, she loses intellectual and spiritual companionship, but she also escapes a man she does not desire. She uses Tom as an excuse for escaping Philip's suffocating hold on her but does not really do so only for Tom.

Later, she again rationalizes her renunciation of Stephen Guest in terms of self-sacrifice. Yet, although Stephen is erotically alluring and offers Maggie an economically easier life, she has ambivalent feelings about him. She fears the ways he makes her lose her own will. Maggie desires but also fears the type of loss of will, or loss of self, she experiences when Stephen rows too far in the boat. Just as she uses Tom as an excuse when she tries to escape Philip's control, to a lesser extent she uses Philip and Lucy as excuses to escape Stephen's control. Eliot represents Maggie's sacrifice as psychologically complex; although she does renounce certain sexual and economic desires, her renunciation is also driven by fear and a desire for autonomy. Moreover, as many critics have noticed, Stephen is flawed, flippant, and superficial. By choosing to leave Stephen, Maggie does not give up much. Eliot goes out of her way to avoid representing Maggie's tendency to sacrifice herself as a one-dimensional essential feminine quality.

Indeed, self-renunciation is represented not as natural but as a cultural burden Maggie has internalized. As a child she is taught to make sacrifices. She is often punished for indulging her own desires, for example when Tom is cold to her because she chooses to eat the cake he wants because it has more jam. Eliot also complicates the moral value of Maggie's giving up of Stephen by making it clear that it is completely unnecessary: an elopement would have been accepted by the community, and Philip is injured despite the fact that Maggie refuses to marry Stephen. Even her final sacrifice, her heroic attempt to rescue Tom, is represented as having ambiguous value because it ends in the destruction of both siblings. At the end of the novel Maggie falls to her knees thinking, "Surely there was something being taught her by this experience of great need; and she must be learning a secret of human tenderness and long-suffering." She asks, "Oh God, if my life is to be long, let me live to bless and comfort ..."[23] Her prayer is cut off by the water that will drag her to her death. Eliot's irony here undercuts Maggie's naïve notion of divine purpose. Although Maggie is finally reunited with Tom, both characters die immediately afterwards. Sacrifice, though it has qualities of heroism, is ultimately represented as futile.

Although, as many critics claim, Eliot in some ways respects Maggie's noble actions, she also complicates and questions Victorian ideals of feminine self-sacrifice by revealing women's motives to be psychologically complex and not wholly selfless in origin. Eliot resists Victorian representations of feminine self-sacrifice as natural and critiques such ideals by representing them as tragically wasteful.

In Whelan's adaptation, the Victorian ideals Eliot questions are re-instituted. Since Stephen is clearly attractive and Maggie is not represented as in any way ambivalent toward him, leaving him is depicted as an unambiguous sacrifice. The film also omits Eliot's suggestion that Maggie's sacrifices are futile. In Whelan's adaptation, they all have clear and unambiguously positive results. Maggie's sacrifice of Stephen ensures that neither Philip nor Lucy is injured by Stephen and Maggie's boat trip. Unlike in the novel, Philip will again ask Maggie to marry him, and Lucy is not represented as feeling ill or needing to go away for a time. Most significantly, Tom is not killed in the film and his sister's death brings about his and his community's moral awakening. Maggie's sacrifice benefits everyone.

The community is also figured differently in the film than in the novel. Near the end of the novel, when the community's gossip excludes Maggie because of her "fall," it is specifically described by Eliot as a community of women. In Whelan's adaptation, the community that castigates Maggie is male. Near the end of the film, Wakem gathers a group of male rabble-rousers who are about to go to Maggie's house to punish her for her immoral journey with Stephen Guest. After Maggie's death, the men gather at Tom's house and Lucy reads them a letter Stephen wrote exonerating Maggie of sexual impropriety. This makes the men realize the moral flaws of their attempt at vengeance. The community is figured as male, and it is the women who guard its morality.

With Lucy's help, Maggie's death shocks the community into giving up vengeance and strife in favor of moral understanding and cohesion. At the very moment the film shows the community to be morally cleansed by Maggie's sacrifice, it also asserts Maggie's sexual purity. The women who facilitate the community's moral regeneration embody an ideal of purity and self-sacrifice.

Unlike American adaptations of this period, which represent women in competition with each other, this British adaptation represents women as morally superior to the overly competitive men because they can transcend rivalries and forgive. In a scene heightened by melodramatic music and lighting that makes the characters glow, Lucy comes to visit Maggie to forgive her for going away with Stephen. This scene suggests an idealized alternative community, a cohesive, forgiving, selfless community of women that men must emulate.

This ideal of femininity was not new in British culture. The film's representation of Maggie and Lucy as the guardians of virtue for men tainted by competitiveness is reminiscent of Victorian gender ideals articulated at around the time *The Mill on the Floss* was published. In "Of Queens' Gardens" John Ruskin claims that as a consequence of their innate virtue, women have the moral duty to maintain the purity of men's souls. "It is the type of an eternal truth: that the soul's armour is never well set to the heart unless a woman's hand has braced it."[24] Women have a duty to safeguard men's souls from the corruptions of society. Just as Ruskin claims that women should extend their moral influence beyond their homes into the public sphere, Whelan's adaptation extends women's moral function into the public sphere. Maggie and Lucy reform not only Tom at the end of the film but the whole community; women protect not only the domestic arena of the home but also the domestic arena of the nation. Maggie's and Lucy's sacrifices teach the men how to form a unified community in accordance with the needs of the nation in the 1930s. The national cohesion needed to relieve the social and economic divisiveness of the Depression is found both at the expense of, and through, the sacrifice of women.

This representation of women as both self-sacrificing and more naturally compassionate toward the needs of the poor was characteristic of other films of the time. Alexander Korda's *Victoria the Great*, which was made in the same year as *The Mill on the Floss*, is an interesting example. The film attempts to resolve a dilemma faced during Victoria's reign, the dilemma of representing a political public figure in terms of ideals of femininity that were private and domestic. Korda represents Victoria primarily as a wife. Yet the plight of the poor leads her to forsake her private pleasures and domestic tranquility in order to serve others. In one scene, after reading *Oliver Twist*, which moves her deeply, Victoria passionately complains to Albert that it is terrible to think there could be such poverty in England. She courageously addresses a mob of poor people who have gathered outside the palace to protest the Corn Laws. Subsequently, Victoria institutes reforms that will help the poor. Like the female characters in *The Mill on the Floss*, Victoria, in contrast to Albert, is represented as acutely in tune with the needs of others and is shown making sacrifices for the good of the country.

Overall, then, Whelan's *The Mill on the Floss* displaces Eliot's focus on the plight of women with a focus on the plight of a community in which some segments of the population are facing extreme poverty. However, the film's attempt to contain Eliot's representation of gender within its own ideological trajectory is not seamless. The scene in which Lucy visits Maggie to forgive her for eloping with Stephen is ideologically uneven. Because the scene represents the film's all-important ideal of feminine self-sacrifice, it is presented in a heightened form. The lighting and music it employs, which are intended to convey the idyllic qualities of self-renunciation, are conventionally used in film for romantic love scenes and give the scene an erotic tone that jars with the rest of the film. Unlike in the novel, the women are shown as having no desires other than for men. Coming together to renounce their mutual male object of desire, Stephen, Maggie's and Lucy's desire seems to be redirected toward each other. At the very moment the scene romanticizes and reifies the self-sacrificing woman who renounces her sexual desires, the erotic presentation of the scene seems to deconstruct this ideal as it alludes unconsciously to a feminine, perhaps lesbian, alternative to the homosocial relations given center stage in the rest of the film. The utopian fantasy of female self-renunciation seems to involve a dystopian union of female bodies, an excess of female desire the film is unable to contain. Ultimately, perhaps, this discordant scene is a displacement, a symptom, of the feminine desire the film has repressed in translating a novel about female desires into a film about male social relations.

Another aspect of the novel that seems to disrupt the film's ideological work is the characterization of Philip. In the novel, Philip is clearly feminized. He is physically delicate and his sensitivities are as acute as Maggie's. In the nineteenth century, the deformed Philip is as socially liminal and vulnerable as an intelligent, sensitive girl. Whelan's adaptation struggles with this representation of Philip. On the one hand, it attempts to make Philip more masculine by translating his deformity into nothing but a slight limp, and it eliminates all those parts of the novel that reveal Philip's acute sensitivity. On the other hand, even though, as Wakem's son, Philip stands at the center of the network of male rivalries the film depicts, Philip never acts aggressively toward other men. Despite the film's attempt to masculinize Philip, he remains effeminate in comparison with the other male characters. In this context, it is interesting that the film kills Philip, rather than Tom, at the end. Saving Tom so that he can grow and learn and become part of a cohesive community adheres to the ideological logic of the film. Yet Philip could very well have remained alive for Tom to forgive, and he could have easily been integrated into the new cohesive community. Maggie's death alone would have been enough to convince Tom to forgive his rival. However, it seems that in the newly repaired world of improved male bonds, men with any trace of femininity must be eliminated. Paradoxically, at the very moment the film expels the feminized man from the community, it also reifies his femininity by placing him in the same position as Maggie. Philip drowns with, and like, Maggie. Thus, although the film attempts to construct stable and clearly differentiated gender identities, Philip undermines the neat dichotomies between men, who are represented as active and socially significant, and women, who are represented as passive and self-sacrificing. The novel's interrogation of gender ideals seems to infiltrate and undermine the film's ideological work.

Overall, Whelan's adaptation of *The Mill on the Floss* is profoundly rooted in the Victorian ideologies of feminine self-sacrifice that George

Eliot questioned. No longer a *Bildungsroman* tracing Maggie's thwarted attempt to fulfill her desires, this film turns a fully developed character into an ethereal saint-like woman whose sacrifice enables the really important characters in the film, the men, to reform so that they can overcome their class and economic conflicts to create a unified community or nation. In this way, the film enacts what it represents as it sacrifices George Eliot's female voice to the film's masculine communal ideal. The adaptation employs the novel to posit a new form of domestic ideal, one in which the "angel in the house" becomes a communal angel protecting the morality and harmony of Britain. Informed by the contemporary disapproval of women working and obtaining an advanced education, the adaptation suppresses Maggie's desires and posits a feminine ideal that can encourage social cohesion at a time when social strife threatened domestic stability.

4
Twisted Femininities: *Great Expectations* and *Oliver Twist*

The nationalist impulse that shaped British film adaptations in the 1930s, not surprisingly, continued well into the postwar period of the late 1940s. In response to the Second World War and the ongoing disintegration of its empire and international power, Britain sought to emphasize areas of national achievement. The film industry strove to celebrate Britain's rich cultural heritage and its advanced social policies as it established a welfare state. The by-then renowned director David Lean made two films based on novels by Charles Dickens, *Great Expectations* (1946) and *Oliver Twist* (1948), that appealed to nationalist feeling by honoring, while re-imagining, the work of an author so central to Britain's literary heritage and social conscience.

Great Expectations was admired at the time not only for its superior cinematic qualities but also because it was, according to the *Sunday Express*, "British to the back bone."[1] *Oliver Twist* also celebrates the British character, but less directly. Its less overtly nationalist agenda was misunderstood by contemporary critics. The film reviewer for *The Times*, for instance, castigates the film for its "brutality" and "ugliness" and notes that Lean's elimination of the novel's female protagonist, Rose Maylie, leaves the film devoid of the "lightness and tenderness" he feels is so important in Dickens's *Oliver Twist*.[2] The reviewer underestimates the film's emphasis on Britain's ability to outshine its dark underworld, yet inadvertently does notice that Lean's representation of women is significant.

In both his Dickens adaptations, Lean invokes Britain's social progress but represents single women as threats to this advancement. In *Great Expectations* the female threat is neutralized by a marriage plot that Lean attaches to Dickens's more ambivalent ending; in *Oliver Twist* women are represented as so dangerous that they are almost completely excised from the film's idealized resolution. Not only are the novel's marriage plot and its female protagonist eliminated from the adaptation, but even many of the conventionally feminine traits of characters of both sexes are removed from the adaptation. Like the adaptation of *The Mill on the Floss*, Lean's *Oliver Twist* masculinizes the narrative. However, women are represented not as ideal, as in *The Mill on the Floss*, but as tainted and tainting, as figures who threaten Britain and its social agenda. Departing from Dickens, Lean represents *Oliver Twist*'s main female character, Nancy, as being similar to Fagin. Like the Jewish antagonist, unmarried women are positioned as outsiders and are characterized as treacherous, unreliable, and not quite British.

The need to assert and validate being "British to the backbone" was accentuated by the Second World War and its accompanying influx of foreigners. The arrival of European refugees, European forces, and the GI "invasion" further complicated the social, regional, and class tensions between the Irish, Scottish, Welsh, and English inhabitants of the United Kingdom. During the Second World War, British culture and cinema made an effort "to emphasize that the most important divide was that between Britain and Germany."[3] After the war, the British-German divide continued to influence the way Britishness was represented in film. In 1945, the influential film producer Michael Balcon outlined

> a programmatic schedule for post-war film-making which demon-strates a high level of civic responsibility and patriotic pride. Pointing out that German propaganda had throughout the war depicted the British as "blood soaked imperialists, punch-drunk degenerates, betrayers of our allies, groveling servants of fabulous Jewish pluto-crats," he called for a positive picture in films, what he called a "complete picture of Britain". This he defined as: "Britain as a leader in social reform in the defeat of social injustices and a champion of civil liberties; Britain as patron and parent of great writing, painting and music."[4]

After the war, the film industry tried to construct British identity in ways that countered German stereotypes of Britain and emphasized Britain's rich culture and new, socially progressive character. Both of David Lean's adaptations conform to this program. In addition to giving cinematic life to Britain's great novelist, *Great Expectations*, at least overtly, represents British society as making great strides toward social equality. *Oliver Twist* depicts a society escaping its corrupt past by ridding itself of the types of degenerate influences Balcon says were emphasized by the Germans. Lean's adaptation focuses on prostitutes, gangsters, Jews, those who grovel to Jews, and betrayers of friends in order to represent Britain as liberating itself from these corrupting influences. This indirect representation of Britain's social progress through a depiction of a degenerate past that is overcome is misunderstood by the contemporary *Times* reviewer who was galled by the film's darkness. Modern critics, in contrast, have understood Lean's use of Victorian England.

Referring to Dickens adaptations made in the postwar period, Richard Jeffries has noted that

> wartime experience and post-war reconstruction aimed at building a welfare state focused attention on getting rid of the evils of Victorian England, and the Dickens novels adapted at that time highlighted the evils of the workhouse and the underworld. ... [The films] construct an image of the Victorian era as something dark, fearful, oppressive and about to be eliminated by the Labour Party's new welfare state.[5]

Both adaptations use the Victorian past to highlight Britain's new socially progressive future. Made at a time of austerity as Britain was recovering from the war and building a new society, these adaptations invoke a sense of optimism and hope.

At the same time, both adaptations exhibit tremendous anxiety about the relationship of women to the new state-based family Britain was founding. Both films were made at a time of great social and cultural change as Britain shifted from war into reconstruction and the great social experiment of the welfare state. Women had moved into the workforce during the war, had performed military and other forms of national service, and were then expected to return home. The welfare state, with its intricate public rather than familial support systems, also threatened to undermine traditional gender roles further.

In *Great Expectations* women are represented as threats to Britain's future. Miss Havisham is made to symbolize a force that holds Britain back from advancing socially. Lean uses a Gothic mis-en-scène and eerie lighting to turn Miss Havisham into a grotesque, ominous figure representing resistance to progress. She is stagnant and decadent. In almost every scene in which she appears, Miss Havisham is seated in a chair or wheelchair, immobile. She appears rigidly frozen in the dusty, cobweb-covered clutter of her dark cavernous room where the only movement is that of mice eating a putrid cake. Her clocks, on which the camera often pauses for emphasis, are stopped, and the sunlight that marks the passing of time has been blotted out by thick curtains. Even the tone of her speech is flat and monotonous. Mired in what even she refers to as decay, Miss Havisham represents the attempt to stop time and in this sense becomes the film's emblem of resistance to progress.

The progress Miss Havisham stalls has a social dimension. She and her protégée emphasize Pip's lower-class status. For instance, Estella laughs at him for using the word "jacks" instead of "knaves"; she calls him a "common laboring boy" and later, with a little variation, a "stupid clumsy laboring boy." She also refers to his coarse laborer's hands. At least on its surface, the film represents this kind of snobbery as decadent and outmoded.

More directly than in the novel, however, the stasis at Satis House is represented in the adaptation as the result of Miss Havisham's failure to get married. It is because she has been jilted by her fiancé that Miss Havisham remains in her grave-like room in her unused wedding dress arresting time at the moment when her wedding should have taken place. In one of Miss Havisham's very first lines in the film she refers to her broken heart, and this line is later echoed when Estella describes her own lack of a heart. The film symbolically yokes Miss Havisham's stagnation to spinsterhood and thwarted sexuality. Lean reinforces this connection by having Estella often repeat that she is being brought up to be just like Miss Havisham. Unable to deliver anything new, Miss Havisham can only replicate herself. After Miss Havisham's death, Estella asserts that Satis House will be her "own." As she speaks, she even looks like Miss Havisham, seated in her chair in an identical manner. Moreover, Lean has changed Dickens's plot so that at this point, as Estella is turning into Miss Havisham, she has been rejected by Drummle. Like Miss Havisham, Estella has been jilted and is locking herself up in Satis House trying to avoid life.[6]

However, Pip insists she leave what he calls a "dead house" and dramatically pulls the curtains – reminiscent of the blackout curtains of wartime Britain – off the windows. He has come back, he says, "to let in the sunlight." Pip's love for Estella and his offer of marriage differentiate Estella from the irrevocably jilted Miss Havisham. Pip's offer to take Estella into the sunlight, his offer of marriage, enables Estella's movement forward, away from the dark war years, into the bright future. Romantic love, marriage, and progress are symbolically intertwined in this adaptation in ways they are not in the novel.

In Dickens's novel, the moonlit final scene is highly ambiguous and Estella is described as "broken" and "bent" by an earlier failed marriage, but in the film Estella unambiguously enters the sunlight as she joyfully accepts Pip's offer of love. Lean eliminates Estella's earlier failed marriage to maintain the symbolic connection he makes between marriage and progress. As the film ends, Pip and Estella embrace, laugh joyously, and walk out of the house and through its imprisoning gate. As the happy couple leave the "dead" house, the words "Great Expectations" are superimposed on the image. Pip's great social expectations have now been replaced by the expectations of love, marriage, and a new kind of life offered by Britain's socially egalitarian new world.

Once Pip destroys his aristocratic "mother," Miss Havisham, and acknowledges his real lower-class "fathers," Joe and Magwitch, he is saved from the women's corrupting influence, and his moral or social conscience becomes compatible with the values of the welfare state. Estella, however, is represented as accepting Pip not as a result of having developed a social awareness but because Pip's love helps her recover her "feminine" loving heart. In Lean's film it is only marriage that integrates women into Britain's new society and its noble social goals. Lean's invented ending implies that unmarried women have no place in Britain's new society. It is the man who must pull the reactionary and socially unaware woman along on his noble social journey.

Lean's adaptation of *Oliver Twist* also exhibits anxieties about the relationship of single women to the new Britain. In *Oliver Twist*, Miss Havisham is replaced by a similarly grotesque character whose symbolic function is comparable: Fagin. Visually analogous to Miss Havisham, Fagin is displayed in highly stylized make-up and costumes and presides over dark, stagnant, decaying interior spaces. Like Miss Havisham, Fagin exploits the children under his influence and ensnares the film's main female character, Nancy. In his first Dickens adaptation, Lean constructs Britain's future ideal against a "monstrous spinster"; in his second film, the ideal is constructed against a "monstrous Jew." Both figures have the pivotal symbolic function of representing the past that Britain must reject. Like Miss Havisham's replica, Estella, Nancy is represented as a form of double for Fagin, but, unlike Estella, she is too tainted to be able to escape Fagin's trap, marry, and integrate into Britain's new social order. Indeed, in *Oliver Twist*, the ideal image of Britain constructed against these monstrous "others" is devoid of any significant female presence.

In *Oliver Twist*, which is far more ideologically complex and indirect than *Great Expectations*, the plot is resolved when Brownlow and a community of men rescue Oliver from the clutches of Fagin and his protégés. The film ends not, like the novel, with images of a traditional family at home presided over by the gentle female figure of Rose Maylie but with an image of Brownlow, his middle-aged housekeeper, and Oliver walking toward the Brownlow house. The family and its central female heroine have been replaced by a representation of what Jeffrey Richards has called "the people as hero."[7] Because the film ends with images of the crowd liberating Oliver, it valorizes community effort and displaces Dickens's more private image of a home.

The notion of "home" is no less important in Lean than in Dickens, even though it is defined in different terms. In Britain, after the war, many families were reunited: children returned from wartime evacuations; women returned home from the labor force; and men returned from the front. Aptly, Lean's *Oliver Twist* focuses on homecoming, on bringing Oliver home from his nightmare evacuation to London's underworld. Indeed, by changing the plot so that Oliver is imprisoned by Fagin until the very end of the film rather than, as in the novel, rescued midway through the story, Lean heightens the adaptation's emphasis on homecoming, rescue, and survival – themes that would resonate for war-weary audiences. At the end of *Great Expectations*, too, Lean has Pip repeat the word "home" to Joe as he expresses joy at returning home after recovering from his literal and metaphoric illness. Both films emphasize homecoming, but in the later adaptation there is a noticeable lack of a female presence other than the matronly working-class housekeeper inside the idealized home. On the surface this change seems surprising given the cultural context.

Indeed, postwar Britain and welfare state policies placed an enormous emphasis on the family, motherhood, and the home. No less than in the United States, motherhood and the home were idealized throughout the culture. Images of nurturing, gentle, maternal femininity were invoked to restore a sense of stability, safety, and comfort after the distressing upheavals of war and later postwar austerity. Moreover, there were "gendered notions of the respective contributions of male and female to the nation. Men as workers, women as home-based mothers underpinned social service, health and welfare, and educational provisions."[8] Motherhood was also emphasized because of a postwar panic about a drop in population growth. Social policies were strongly pronatalist, aiming to encourage women to bear at least three or four children, and the culture increasingly emphasized heterosexual monogamous love and sex. However, the increased emphasis on sexuality and reproduction also "threw into greater relief than ever before the 'deviant' nature of both prostitution and male homosexuality."[9] As much as procreation within marriage was emphasized, the fear of transgressive sexual behavior and illegitimate childbearing accompanied such ideals.

Anxieties about "loose" women were also related to wartime fears about women at home sexually betraying their men at the front. *Great Expectations* reins in female sexual danger by marrying Estella off, and *Oliver Twist* – working with a more sexually transgressive plot – excludes sexually "dangerous" women from its resolution. Unlike the novel, the film foregrounds the sexually transgressive qualities of its female characters and aligns these women with Fagin. Sexually transgressive single women, like Jews, are represented as alien and treacherous. The single women who threaten Britain's progress in *Great Expectations* morph, in *Oliver Twist*, into women who are threatening because of their sexual and, by implication, national infidelity. This is a significant change from the novel's domestic themes.

For Dickens the family is central to the solution of the social ills *Oliver Twist* describes. On the overt level of the narrative, Oliver's plight is resolved when he regains his rightful place in an idealized middle-class home consisting of a kind English gentleman, Brownlow, and an angelic woman, Rose Maylie, and her husband. This domestic ideal is constructed by contrasting the Brownlow and Maylie homes with a series of dysfunctional "family" structures such as the workhouse, the Bumble home, the Sowerberry home, and Fagin's gang of criminals. Dickens's ideal family is constructed against lower-class families in which gender identities are not stable. The Bumbles' home is presided over by a woman who has too much "prerogative" and is therefore morally tainted. Neither gently compliant nor virtuous, Mrs. Bumble does not conform to Victorian middle-class feminine ideals. The Sowerberry home represents an older, pre-industrial family where the craftsman still works at home. Trade occurs within the home, and children are made to participate in economic activities. The home is not the refuge from the public sphere of commerce that Victorian domestic ideals favored. The Sowerberry home is also managed by a woman who is miserly, domineering, and selfish rather than maternal and virtuous. In addition, the poorhouse is like a failed family because it is public, not private, and lacks the moral virtues of a family separated from the corrupted public sphere.

Most of the novel, however, describes Fagin's world and not the poorhouse, despite Dickens's interest in the Poor Laws. The novel contrasts the middle-class idyll at the Brownlow and Maylie houses, the world to which Oliver aspires, with the topsy-turvy world of Fagin's den. Indeed, Fagin's den is represented as a parody of the Victorian domestic ideal in which all the boundaries so coveted by conventional Victorian discourses are transgressed. Violating valued Victorian gender boundaries,

Fagin is both paternal and maternal. He is paternal in that he oversees the economic and professional functions of the home's inhabitants; he is also maternal because he is the one who cooks meals, arranges accommodations, and educates and plays with his "pupils." The ambiguous gender positions Fagin occupies combine to suggest sexual perversion and hint at a pedophilia that Fagin exhibits in his "relish of Oliver's pale face and trembling limbs."[10] Both Brownlow and Fagin value Oliver for his looks, and in competing to possess him, they create a kind of homoerotic triangle.

Fagin's gender ambiguities and the allusions to his sexual perversity draw on classic anti-Semitic tropes. Jewish men in the nineteenth century were typically constructed as sexually diseased, perverse, and, most often, effeminate. Hence, Fagin occupies a complex borderline position where he is both masculine and feminine at once. In *Oliver Twist*, Fagin's use of the epithet "my dear" and the indirect ways he achieves his ends, by manipulating and flattering other people to do things for him, constitute both an anti-Semitic and feminized representation. When Fagin sends Nancy to the courts to see what happens to Oliver or when he sends the boys out to rob and pickpocket for him, when he is cunning and manipulative, Fagin occupies a position that is both Jewish and female at once.

The classic anti-Semitic tropes used to represent Fagin also construct him as evil. The medieval stereotype of the Jew as usurer finds obvious traces in Fagin's miserly hoarding of money and valuable objects. Drawing on the medieval dramatic tradition of representing Jews as devils, Dickens portrays Fagin with a red beard and pronged cooking fork, as the devil out to poison the souls of young Christian boys.[11] *Oliver Twist* also echoes medieval blood libels, myths that refer to Jews as killing Christian children so that they can use their blood in Passover rituals. Such associations are particularly obvious in the scene in which Oliver first wakes up in Fagin's house and Fagin threatens him with a knife.

Thus, Fagin's den is an exact opposite of an ideal Victorian family. While many critics have noticed that Rose Maylie and Nancy are foils, they have overlooked the fact that Fagin is also a foil for Rose Maylie. The novel's representation of Rose Maylie as the "angel in the house" is obvious. Reflecting her, however, is the perverse mirror image of the man/woman Jew, Fagin, the devil in the house. Because Fagin is represented as performing domestic functions and as the "mother" in his den, he embodies an inverted Victorian domestic ideal. Just as the mother of the middle-class home is responsible for the moral well-being of its inhabitants, Fagin, the devilish Jew, is responsible for his "children's" moral degeneration. Just as the Victorian mother is the moral center of her household and its inhabitants, Fagin is the immoral center. Fagin even unpicks embroidered handkerchiefs, reversing the embroidery practiced by many middle-class Victorian women. The ideal Victorian domestic space was supposed to keep the public realm of economic competition and strife out of the home. By being both maternal and Jewish at once, however, Fagin undermines the separation of spheres, introducing exploitative economics into the home. Opposite Rose's selfless, self-sacrificing natural desire to care for others stands Fagin's motto of working for "number one." Devilish, ugly, and immoral, Fagin is an inverted double to beautiful, angelic, self-sacrificing, and Christian, Rose Maylie.

Fagin is also represented as uncivilized and unevolved. His ugliness is described in a striking passage in the novel:

> The mud lay thick upon the stones, and a black mist hung over the streets; the rain fell sluggishly down, and everything felt cold and clammy to the touch. It seemed just the night when it befitted such a being as the Jew to be abroad. As he glided stealthily alone, creeping beneath the shelter of the walls and doorways, the hideous old man seemed like some loathsome reptile, engendered in the slime and darkness through which he moved: crawling forth, by night, in search of some rich offal for a meal.[12]

Crawling through the slime, the reptilian Fagin is represented as parasitical in his hunger for offal and morally degenerate. In Dickens, Fagin's animalistic uncivilized filthiness is used to highlight Rose Maylie's angelic, civilized nature.

Using an "other" to reify and define a domestic ideal is common in Victorian literature – *Jane Eyre*'s use of Bertha from the West Indies is a well-known example. Through classic anti-Semitic tropes, Fagin is constructed as an "other" to reinforce the normative value of a domestic ideal that is the direct inverse of Fagin's den. However, the use of a Jewish character as an "other" is complex.

The Jew has an ambivalent position in English literature as both "racial other" and part of a supposedly common Judeo-Christian culture. Overtly, the plot works to expel the Jewish character from its resolution. However, a character associated with Dickens's cultural-religious origins is not so simply exorcised from the conclusion of a novel about the recovery of origins and identity. As in later Victorian novels that construct domestic ideals against racial others, the ideal is unstable. Fagin's force, energy, and anarchic appeal, like those of the later Heathcliff or in some ways even Bertha, make the Victorian family seem tepid, fragile, and, perhaps, even unappealing.

Hence, the domestic resolution of *Oliver Twist* is not as conventional as it may seem on the surface. The family that is constituted at the end is partially fragmented, since Oliver will spend his life shuttling back and forth between the home of his adoptive father, Brownlow, and the Maylies. Both of these families have been shown to be vulnerable to Fagin's infiltration. Brownlow is unable to keep Oliver at home, proving to be an irresponsible parent who sends his "son" to the streets of the criminal underworld to win a bet with a friend. What Dickens would see as Brownlow's innately male competitive impulse, the desire to win a bet, supersedes his conscious plan to nurture and care for Oliver. Rose Maylie never loses Oliver and is a more effective parent in this sense. However, she is too weak and fragile to protect the space over which she presides from being infiltrated by Monks and Fagin. It is not clear whether the scene in which Fagin and Monks stand outside the Maylie window and stare at Oliver is Oliver's dream or a reality. When Harry Maylie looks for Fagin's and Monks's footprints, they are no longer there. Either, as devils, they leave no footprints, or this is Oliver's dream. Cruikshank illustrates Fagin and Monk staring at Oliver, increasing the significance of this dream/event. Whether real or imagined, the Maylies' paradise is proven not to be impervious to Fagin's dark influence. The domestic refuge the Maylies and Brownlow ultimately create seems fragile and perhaps unreal.

The whole concluding chapter is narrated in the unreal conditional tense:

> And now, the hand that traces these words, falters, as it approaches the conclusion of its task; and would weave, for a little longer space, the thread of these adventures.
>
> I would fain linger yet with a few of those among whom I have so long moved, and share their happiness by endeavoring to depict it. I would show Rose Maylie in all her bloom and grace of early womanhood, shedding on her secluded path in life soft and gentle light, that fell on all who trod it with her, and shone into their hearts.[13]

The self-reflexive narrative technique and the unreal tense give this domestic ideal a fantastic or fairly tale–like quality that makes it seem less "real" than the rest of the novel. The domestic ideal is represented more as an ideal fantasy than as a real possibility.

Even the fantastic ideal has dark shadows. In the penultimate chapter of *Oliver Twist*, Fagin is left in his cell awaiting death, still hoping Oliver will find the papers that will rescue him. Unconverted by Oliver's plea that he get on his knees and pray, Fagin is left to die. The Cruikshank illustration of Fagin in his darkened, foreboding cell is considered by many to be the most powerful illustration in the novel. The novel's image of Fagin awaiting his death seems to haunt the following, final, chapter of the novel, which describes Oliver's recovery of his origins and family.

There is something death-like about the domestic ideal that Dickens depicts. Rose Maylie is described as never hungry, her lack of hunger pointing perhaps to a lack of desire and sexual repression. In Fagin's den, the inhabitants eat more than in any other home in the novel. Even at Brownlow's house, Oliver is given a controlled diet of broth. The devil in the house is in some ways more nourishing, or nurturing, than the angel in the house. Hence, Fagin represents a carnivalesque expression of Oliver's own hungers as well as the hunger and vitality that are repressed in the middle classes.[14] Just as Bertha embodies the emotions Jane Eyre represses, Fagin expresses desires Rose Maylie denies. The quiet, neat, tidy world of the Maylies, which the narrator compares to Heaven, lacks the vital energies of Fagin's den. It is a deathly paradise. This association is reinforced by the fact that the very last scene in the novel, and the very last illustration, are of Oliver and Rose standing over Oliver's dead mother at Agnes's empty tomb.

Complicating this stagnant deathly atmosphere described at the end of the novel and the fact that the novel ends with a description of Agnes's grave is the fact that the previous chapter points toward the future hanging of Fagin, a death that, unlike Sikes's, is not represented but anticipated. Strangely, it is Agnes's death that is represented. If Fagin represents the repressed desires of the middle classes, the last line of the novel, referring to Agnes's sexual transgressions, again evokes Fagin and his anarchic, uncontrolled desires. As the novel closes with Oliver's visit to his erring mother's tomb in a church, Fagin's more recently dead, differently erring, invertedly maternal ghost hovers uneasily over the scene. The devil haunts the angel's tomb. The family idyll with which *Oliver Twist* ends is very ambiguous, constructing, but at the same time questioning, the limits and possibilities of the Victorian domestic ideal. Fagin thus functions to construct, but also to subvert, Victorian ideals of home and gender.

The adaptation also constructs its ideals against the figure of the "other," Fagin, but both Fagin and the domestic ideal are different in

Lean's film. In a departure from the novel, Lean's ideal is less about the private domestic sphere and more about Britain's collective domestic identity. Aptly, the world against which this ideal is constructed, Fagin's world, is marked less by ambiguous gender identities than by ambiguous national identities. If "[n]ationalism is about drawing boundaries, about marking an inside and an outside,"[15] Lean's *Oliver Twist* is obsessed with those characters who subvert national boundaries. Both Fagin and the prostitute Nancy are represented as untrustworthy and not reliably British. Both are corrupting influences who by the end of the film are removed from the sunny collective British ideal the film ultimately valorizes. Because Oliver is imprisoned by Fagin for most of the film, and the Maylie subplot has been eliminated, Lean actually spends relatively more time depicting Fagin's world than Dickens does. Fagin's sphere is darker in Lean than in Dickens, both metaphorically and literally. Dark noir-style lighting and ominous silhouettes dominate the visual land-scape of Fagin's underworld, whereas the Brownlow home is almost always bathed in sunlight. Fagin's dark underworld, the relief against which Brownlow's Britain glows, is darker, more violent, more dangerous and less British than in the novel. Most significantly, unlike in Dickens, sexually transgressive women are more firmly positioned within Fagin's darker, other, nationally liminal world.

Fagin is more violent and masculine than in the novel; the film invents a much more macho Fagin. Despite cooking in one scene, usu-ally Fagin is not shown performing the household duties he undertakes in the novel. Although Fagin is still obsequious and manipulative and still uses the epithet "my dear," these qualities do not seem effeminate given Fagin's rough mannerisms and large physical size. Fagin is dressed in long robes that, rather than feminize him, make him appear physi-cally large and ominous. Even though Lean is said to have relied on Cruikshank for his film, unlike in the illustrations, Fagin is not small and lanky. In fact, when Alec Guiness asked Lean to cast him as Fagin, Lean and his producer, Ronald Neame, hesitated because they feared that Guiness would be "too soft, too small."[16] In the illustrations Cruikshank drew for the novel, Fagin is thinner, smaller, and shorter than any other adult character, especially Sikes. In the film, in contrast, his costumes make Fagin appear larger even than Sikes. While Cruikshank's Sikes is large, muscular, and square shaped, in Lean's adaptation Sikes is shorter and smaller than Fagin and has a large-eyed naïve-looking face and a soft, rounded build. In the 1922 film version of *Oliver Twist*, directed by Frank Lloyd, as in the novel and its illustrations,

Fagin is a shriveled, bent little old man who is weak, shivering, and cowardly. The 1922 adaptation includes the scene in which Sikes shoots Oliver at Chertsey, a scene that Lean omits. Overall, Lean makes Sikes less violent and less physically threatening than he is in the novel, its illustrations, or the 1922 adaptation to heighten his representation of Fagin as violent.

Although Lean's film is more violent than the novel in general, it is Fagin who is most changed in this respect. When the Artful Dodger returns to Fagin's den to tell him Oliver has been captured, Fagin hits the Dodger violently. The effect of this scene is very different from that of the novel's humorous description of Fagin "seizing the Dodger tightly by his collar." In a later scene, when Oliver is returned, Fagin tries to beat Oliver with a club. In addition, unlike Dickens, Lean goes out of his way to implicate Fagin in Nancy's murder. The club Fagin uses to try to beat Oliver is identical to the club Sikes will later use to kill Nancy. Lean establishes a visual link between the two acts of violence. In the same scene, when Nancy tries to hit Fagin, he shoves her away, making her fall, through Sikes's arms, onto the floor, where she lies looking as she will later after Sikes has murdered her. Again, Lean visually associates Fagin with Nancy's murder. In terms of the plot, Lean has Fagin goad Sikes into killing Nancy. Later, unlike in the novel, Fagin gives Sikes the idea that he use Oliver in a robbery, and Fagin manipulatively suggests it would be good if Oliver were killed. Overall, then, Fagin is more masculine and more dangerous in this adaptation than in the novel or in any earlier adaptation. Unlike in the novel, Lean makes Nancy fall victim as much to Fagin as to Sikes.

In part, Fagin is made more masculine as a result of the general masculinizing tendencies of British adaptations at this time, but Fagin's more threatening violent characterization is also related to the film's historical and cultural contexts. This film was released in 1948 and was made when the Second World War was a recent and vivid memory, the British Empire was disintegrating, and Jews were fighting the British to establish an independent Jewish state. On an almost daily basis, British newspapers covered not only the problems in India but also violence between Jews and British soldiers in the British Mandate of Palestine, a dimension of the crumbling empire that was more directly related to Dickens's Jewish character. These new historical contexts changed the conventional trope of the cowardly feminized Jew represented in Dickens.

In the novel, although Fagin speaks the criminal language of his peers, and even though Charlie Bates and the Artful Dodger have accents appropriate to their class, Fagin, like Oliver, has a middle-class accent. The only aspects of Fagin's speech that seem unique are its obsequious character and his use of the term "my dear." To the extent that Fagin's language is unique in the novel, it is feminized but not foreign. Only Toby Crackit, a minor character, has an accent that marks his Jewishness. In the film, in contrast, Fagin has a strong East European Jewish accent and speaks very differently from any other character. Fagin's difference is clearly marked as nationally alien. In response to the accusation that the film was anti-Semitic, Alec Guiness said that Fagin "is not a Jew as far as I am concerned, just some curious Middle Eastern character in the East End."[17] This statement clearly indicates the crew's concept of Fagin as foreign and the extent to which events in the Middle East were influencing their work. In the novel, Fagin's gender identity is unstable; in the film it is his national identity that is unstable.

Even Lean's use of Dickens's classic anti-Semitic tropes, by 1948, had associations with national threat. During the war the medieval representation of the Jew as usurer metamorphosed into more contemporary wartime constructions of the Jew as black-market racketeer, "foreign, dark and 'evil-faced' and an internal threat to Britain."[18] Fagin's devilish lust for lucre is faithfully replicated in the film in, for instance, the scene in which Oliver wakes up to see Fagin lovingly handling his hidden treasure chest of jewels, a scene eliminated from the 1922 adaptation. As this sequence closes Fagin even jokingly tells Oliver that some people call him a "miser." By 1947 such references would have had a resonance with contemporary representations of Jews as hoarding money illegally during the war.

When the Motion Pictures Producers and Distributors Association (MPPDA) banned *Oliver Twist* in the United States because of its anti-Semitic content, in an attempt to avoid having the film cut, Lean offered to shoot a new scene in which a "representative Jewish leader would offer the services of his community to hunt down Fagin."[19] This change would have retained the construction of the Jew as violent, even if for the right reasons; more significantly, it reveals Lean's view of British Jews as a separate community, separate from the community already represented as hunting Fagin down. Lean's representation of the "people as hero" does not include British Jews.

During and after the Second World War, it was not uncommon for Jews to be represented as suspect aliens not loyal to Britain. Jewish refugees living in England during the war, for example, were often suspected of spying for, or being secretly loyal to, Germany. During the war, spy novels in which the German spy was ultimately revealed to be

Jewish were popular.[20] Foreign Jews had also traditionally been linked with prostitution. The first Aliens Act, attempting to limit Jewish immigration into Britain, for example, had specific clauses dealing with Jewish immigrants "soliciting, living on the proceeds of prostitution or keeping immoral houses."[21] Lean draws on the association, equating Nancy and Fagin in ways the novel does not.

Although in Dickens's novel, Nancy is morally corrupted by Fagin, she is not in any way similar to him. Lean, in contrast, goes out of his way to yoke these two characters together symbolically. After Sikes murders Nancy, there is a sequence that does not exist in the novel in which Sikes has a vision of Nancy and Fagin. In the sequence, following an extreme close-up of Sikes, the film cuts to an extreme close-up of Nancy, positioned opposite where Sikes had been in the previous frame. She whispers to Sikes that Fagin lied. "He deceived you; he deceived you; he deceived you," she repeats. After cutting back to an extreme close-up of Sikes, the film then cuts to a close-up of Fagin, who is positioned in the frame in the same place as Nancy. He tells Sikes that Nancy "told" on him to all her friends and then, echoing Nancy by repeating it three times, he says, "She did; she did; she did." Subsequently, Sikes imagines killing Fagin with a club, in exactly the same way he has just killed Nancy. Fagin falls to the floor dead and his imagined body lies in exactly the same position as Nancy's real body. Images of Nancy's and Fagin's bodies are superimposed before Sikes flees the scene, his dog's howls filling the soundtrack.

The visual symmetry and the echoes in the dialogue make Fagin and Nancy doubles. Significantly, the characteristic they share is that they are both unreadable and deceptive. This sequence, in strong contrast to the novel, depicts Sikes as a victim of Nancy and Fagin's treachery. Sikes is represented as a not-too-bright bumbler caught up in the clever machinations of a far more cunning prostitute and Jew.

Dickens emphasizes Sikes's guilt by giving Nancy a role in punishing him for her murder. Sikes is haunted not by Fagin but only by Nancy's ghost. In Dickens, Nancy accuses Sikes, not Fagin, of the crime. Aptly, as he tries to escape along a rooftop, an apparition of Nancy's accusing eyes makes Sikes lose his footing and fall off the roof into the noose he is carrying. In the film, the only apparition Sikes has of Nancy is the one in which she tells him Fagin betrayed him; it is an image that emphasizes not Sikes's guilt but his confusion. He cannot decide who really betrayed him, Nancy or Fagin. Sikes is represented as helplessly trapped by the slippery unreadable loyalties of the prostitute and the Jew as the film visually and thematically fuses the figures of the threatening foreigner or Jew and the sexually transgressive woman.

In the novel, Dickens takes pains to emphasize Nancy's loyalty to Fagin and Sikes. When Rose Maylie and Brownlow offer to rescue Nancy from her life of prostitution and protect her from her criminal associates, Nancy refuses and asserts that she would never betray Fagin and Sikes. Her loyalty to Sikes reaffirms what Dickens represents as Nancy's innately feminine impulses – her self-sacrificing loyalty to the child Oliver and also to the man she loves, Sikes. When Sikes kills Nancy, her loyalty accentuates the brutality of his act. The novel represents Nancy as innately good and unambiguously loyal despite the fact that she is a prostitute.

Although Nancy is mostly sympathetic, the adaptation also undercuts her positive attributes and very subtly presents her as disloyal. Both Nancy and Oliver's mother are represented as naturally maternal. Oliver's mother reaches out to her baby before dying, and Nancy regrets having helped Fagin recapture Oliver and later tries to help the child escape. However, in Lean's version both women's transgressive sexuality is evoked as soon as their maternal impulses are represented. Oliver's mother is represented sympathetically as a victim, especially in the opening scenes in which the pregnant woman struggles against the storm to reach a place to give birth. However, not long after her death the doctor who attends her says, "It's the old story. No wedding ring I see." In Dickens Agnes's sexual transgression is muted by the fact that Oliver's father was planning to marry her before he died. In the film, Oliver's father is never mentioned. Moreover, as her name suggests, the novel represents Oliver's mother as angelic despite the fact that she is also "weak and erring." The adaptation does not soften the sexual transgression that causes Oliver's plight. Similarly, when Nancy behaves maternally toward Oliver and tries to help him escape, Sikes reminds her of her profession by telling her she's "a pretty subject for the boy to make a friend of." Nancy responds by blaming Fagin for her condition, claiming he had her "thieving" for him when she was younger than Oliver. "The cold wet dirty streets are my own," she screams, hysterically. While blaming Fagin for her fallen state, the film nevertheless, in code, reminds the viewer of Nancy's streetwalking. She is also not represented as being as conventionally feminine or as vulnerable as Dickens's far younger Nancy. Haggard, tough, and worn out, Lean's Nancy is more prostitute-like than the character in Dickens. She is morally more tainted by Fagin in the film than in the novel.

The fact that Lean never explicitly identifies Nancy as a prostitute but makes her profession clear in scenes such as this one points to the degree to which the culture of the time stigmatized transgressive sexuality.

These coded references to her profession also often fuse Nancy's role as prostitute with her deceitfulness. This is emphasized in an important scene that is very different in the novel and in the adaptation. In the novel, Nancy inadvertently catches sight of Monks meeting with Fagin and then eavesdrops on their meeting. In keeping with Victorian ideals of femininity, Nancy is passive and eavesdrops on Fagin almost by accident. In Lean's adaptation, in contrast, Nancy has guile and is assertive. In the adaptation's eavesdropping scene, Nancy makes an elaborate effort to follow Monks and Fagin until she sees that they have entered a small room. From outside the room, Nancy spies on Monks and Fagin through a hole that passes through a painting and the wall on which it hangs. An image of Nancy's face as it watches Fagin is merged into the painting that surrounds it, symbolically tying together Nancy's function as a "painted lady" with her spying.

In a related scene, Sikes looks nostalgically around his and Nancy's room after he has murdered her. In a series of shot/reverse shots the viewer is given Sikes's perspective. In sequence, the film cuts from a close-up of Sikes to a close-up of Nancy's dresser to a close-up of Sikes followed by a shot of their bed and then another close-up of Sikes. On the surface this sequence shows Sikes looking with regret and guilt on his past life with Nancy before he flees London. But these images also refer to the tools of Nancy's trade, the bed and the make-up and perfume on her dresser. Nancy's loyalty and disloyalty to Sikes are evoked together in the same series of images as her role as performing painted prostitute undercuts her role as Sikes's nostalgically viewed intimate lover.

In the eavesdropping scene, the suspect nature of Nancy's loyalties is further emphasized by having an as-yet-unidentified male character watch and follow her. The complex series of shots in which the unknown man in a coat and hat secretly spies on Nancy as she spies on Fagin, together with the use of lighting characteristic of film noir, makes this sequence resemble a Second World War spy film. When her spying is complete, Nancy goes back to her table and leans across it, pretending to be drunk. The fact that Nancy performs so often, earlier at the court and then again in this scene, foregrounds her duplicity.

Antonia Lant has analyzed Second World War films and propaganda posters to identify the ways in which female sexuality and national identity were represented. In one poster she describes, a beautiful, heavily made-up woman reclines seductively on a sofa surrounded by three talkative admiring men. The poster states, "Keep Mum, She's not so Dumb. Careless Talk Costs Lives." Wartime posters suggest that whether through careless gossip or active collaboration, overly sexual women could convey military secrets to the enemy. Lant notes that underlying these representations is the "intimation that female sexuality was threatening to wartime security." As Lant concludes from her examination of films and posters of the time, "women are always potentially marked as collaborators, despite the representational upheavals that work to circumvent the inference. For while British wartime propaganda demands patriotism in women, the message that women, especially young single women, are a national risk is never far below the surface."[22] This association between female sexuality and national unreliability or collaboration is echoed in David Lean's postwar representation of Nancy.

Although Nancy is spying for the right side – she is trying to help Brownlow and Oliver – the film situates her actions at the center of a web of deception that paints Nancy as a more ominous character than she is in the novel. While Dickens has the unsympathetic Noah Claypole spy on Nancy, in the film the Artful Dodger is made to spy on her. The Dodger is younger than Noah and sympathetic. After being bribed by Fagin to follow Nancy, the Dodger is shown, in a sequence of eerie noir shots reminiscent of spy films, following Nancy down dark deserted streets in the rain and listening to her as the camera lingers on her large looming shadow. The spying done, the next shot is of the Artful Dodger, who, bereft of his baggy coat, looks more child-like than usual, lying asleep with a silver coin in his open hand. It is an obvious image of innocence betrayed. He is brutally woken by Fagin, who goads and manipulates the semiconscious child into telling Sikes about Nancy, into telling him things the Dodger is not even sure Nancy said. Fagin here not only deceives Sikes but also implicates and corrupts the Artful Dodger by making him indirectly complicit in Nancy's murder, something that does not happen in the novel. In Lean's version of the plot, it is even the Dodger who finds Nancy's murdered body. Although Fagin is clearly the villain, Nancy's slippery allegiances are foregrounded and represented as precipitating this larger web of deception, betrayal, and guilt. Nancy corrupts the Dodger as much as Fagin does. When the Artful Dodger wakes up, he is racked by guilt, so much so that, unlike in the novel, he will be the one who shouts out of the window to the police to come and capture Fagin and Sikes. Although the Dodger collaborates with the police here, his betrayal of Fagin is represented positively, as enabling justice and leading to Oliver's rescue. Nancy's betrayal of Fagin, in contrast, is represented far more ambiguously: it is tainted by being visually associated with prostitution and spying, it does not directly help rescue Oliver, and it precipitates a whole series of subsequent deceptions and betrayals, including her own murder.

Other British films of the period represent women in similar ways. Nancy is played by Kay Walsh, who also played the role of Queenie in Lean's *This Happy Breed*, released in 1944. The earlier film starts with a voiceover stating that the family it is about to show is "the symbol of a nation." In the plot, Queenie betrays the family/nation by falling in love with a married man and going to live with him abroad, in France. Even though Nancy's tainted national affiliations are far less explicitly represented than in other British films of the Second World War period, like *This Happy Breed* and *I See a Dark Stranger* (1946), where the central female character is a spy, *Oliver Twist*'s subtle evocation of Nancy's machinations references cultural constructs of nationally ambiguous femininity current at the time. Making Nancy similar to Fagin accentuates her marginal and slippery national affiliations. As a sexually transgressive, deceitful woman, Nancy, though portrayed sympathetically in some ways, is also portrayed as an outsider, an unreadable liminal character whose shaky sense of loyalty threatens the community.

Overall, then, without Rose Maylie and her kind aunt, all the female characters in the film are represented as either sexually transgressive and destructive women, like Oliver's mother and Nancy, or old hags who are cruel and dominating, like Mrs. Bumble and Mrs. Sowerberry. The elimination of the novel's more appealing female characters, like the erasure of feminine desires in the adaptation of *The Mill on the Floss*, inadvertently creates a dissonant representation of sexuality. As in the adaptations of *Jane Eyre* and *The Mill on the Floss*, the suppression of feminine desires and attributes represented in the novel undermines the adaptation's ideological trajectory. In an attempt to erase the novel's depictions of femininity and expunge transgressive female sexuality from his concluding domestic ideal, David Lean inadvertently ends up representing other forms of transgressive desire in his film.

Although Fagin is not represented as effeminate, the film does retain a slight suggestion of Fagin as sexually perverse. In one scene, for example, when the Artful Dodger first brings Oliver to Fagin, his words, different from the novel's, are "Do you want him Fagin?" The film then cuts to a close-up of Fagin and his perversely large nose as he eyes Oliver. Staring him up and down, Fagin leeringly states, "I do." In a later image, Fagin gazes at Oliver while he is curled up in bed sleeping, uncovered and with his back to Fagin. The composition foregrounds Oliver's backside and the shot/reverse shot positions the spectator within Fagin's homoerotic point of view.

As the film, unlike the novel, is devoid of female erotic objects, Oliver becomes its only eroticized object. In Dickens, although Oliver is sometimes described as similar to Rose Maylie, he is also often contrasted with her and in this way made less effeminate. The film, however, has no women who are represented as unproblematically sexually desirable. All of the women in the film are either extremely old, or extremely harsh, or sexually tainted by prostitution. Despite her sexual profession, Nancy's representation is de-eroticized. She has a harsh lower-class accent and in most of the scenes is shouting in a shrill voice or fighting. Oliver's mother appears very briefly in the film at an advanced stage of pregnancy and then dies. Without Rose Maylie, Oliver becomes the most feminized character in the film. Although Dickens fought against Cruikshank's desire to draw Oliver as a "pretty boy," Lean's boy is "pretty." In the 1922 *Oliver Twist*, Oliver is a round-faced, chubby little boy who appears to be about six years old, but Howard Davies, the actor playing Oliver in Lean's film, is made to appear prepubescent. He is also more feminine and frail looking than Pip in Lean's *Great Expectations*. Moreover, since the adaptation focuses on rescuing Oliver from Fagin's clutches rather than, as in the novel, on discovering Oliver's origins, the film makes Oliver into something of a helpless damsel in distress.

Even when Oliver is first shown in the film, his sexual identity is not clear. In the first image of Oliver as a child, he is filmed from behind, his backside at the center of the frame, as he scrubs the floor on his hands and knees. It is unclear whether the Cinderella-like child scrubbing the floor is a girl or a boy until the camera reveals his face. In the novel Fagin's transgressive desires are distanced from the heterosexual resolution of the plot. In the adaptation, however, the absence of representations of femininity leaves the homoerotic desire unbalanced by any other form of eroticism. In the film, unlike in the novel, it is not so much Fagin who seems to hover over the resolution and make it ambiguous as Fagin's transgressive desire.

Lean's elimination of the Maylie plot is typically seen as an excision of Dickens's excessive sentimentality, a quality conventionally associated with the feminine. Interestingly, though, the novel seems to subvert its own masculine adaptation. By eliminating all forms of femininity, whether Fagin's more effeminate sides, Nancy's softer qualities, or the Rose Maylie character, Lean inadvertently feminizes Oliver. The "softness and lightness" the *Times* critic missed so much in the film travels to the boy. Just as the masculinization of George Eliot's novel shifts representations of desire, channeling them in nonheterosexual directions, so too in this masculinized version of Dickens's text, the omitted representations of femininity leave a homoerotic trace. As the film works to exclude transgressive female desire, it inadvertently ends up representing homoerotic desire.

Great Expectations is also ideologically unstable, but less in terms of gender than in terms of class. A film that critiques Miss Havisham and Estella's class snobbery also asserts the importance of "knowing one's place." Pip must learn not to aspire too far above his class and to accept his true class origins, as must Estella. Analogous to this class ideology, the film's representation of gender insists on men and women knowing their place – which is with each other – in clearly defined, different roles. Biddy, who marries Joe much earlier in the film than in the novel, provides a brief but clear emblem of femininity. In every scene she is either nurturingly advising Pip about his life or hanging washing as she blissfully fulfills her domestic roles. The film represents clear gendered identities and heterosexual marriage as integral to Britain's social progress. Pip's overreaching class aspirations stem from the twisted attitudes of single women, but marriage, the film suggests, corrects gender and class transgressions by making social relations orderly and stable. Marriage lets Britain be a sunnier, better place.

In *Oliver Twist* Lean posits a similar sunny ideal. The later adaptation's allusion to the welfare state is more direct in the sense that the film's resolution is rooted in the public sphere. The suspense-filled scenes of the British crowd rescuing Oliver from Fagin are shown in the penultimate sequence of the film. These closing images of the heroic people capturing Fagin and victoriously leading the poor orphan to safety emphasize the importance of communal effort in social improvement. The police, Mr. Brownlow, and the community work together to apprehend and punish villains such as Monks, Mr. Bumble, and Fagin. The novel's questioning of whether society is itself unjust is omitted from the adaptation. Oliver's visit to Fagin in jail, a chapter that evokes sympathy for Fagin and points to Victorian social injustices, is absent. In conformity with Lean's darker representation of Fagin, no sympathy is ever evoked for "the Jew," leaving the community that imprisons and hangs him with no moral taint. In the novel, when Fagin says, "What right have you to butcher me?" his words have some validity. In the film, in contrast, and despite the recent history of the Holocaust, when Fagin utters this question, his perspective is not validated. Dickens, on the other hand, questions the justice system's moral authority by, for example, naming the judge who almost imprisons Oliver Fang, a name reminiscent of Fagin's that points to the venom in the system. Whereas Dickens questions the authority of the state by making Fang and Fagin doubles, Lean authorizes the authorities that bring order and expunge

Fagin at the end of the film. Furthermore, Dickens has the Artful Dodger, after his arrest, playfully mimic the legal system, using parody to expose its class hypocrisies and injustices. In the film, in contrast, the Dodger tells the police where Fagin is, collaborating with rather than critiquing the justice system. Overall, while the novel never vindicates Victorian society and posits only the family as a source of hope, Lean ends with a more optimistic vision of the British people coming together heroically in the cause of justice. Lean's resolution represents a just society cleansing itself of corruption. The locus of corruption is not, as in Dickens, in British society itself; for Lean it is rooted amongst the film's "others," its murderers, Jews, and prostitutes.

Even more explicitly than in *Great Expectations*, Lean's ideal is also middle class. In the film's closing image, Oliver, Mr. Brownlow, and the housekeeper walk toward the Brownlow house, which is obviously opulent. Oliver's class status is even emphasized in a scene in which Mr. Brownlow looks at the picture of Oliver's well-dressed, obviously well-born mother as he swings in the sunlit garden. Like *Great Expectations*, despite its critique of social injustices, the film still valorizes the middle-class home, and like *Great Expectations*, it also excludes single women.

The clean, clear sunlight that shines on the Brownlow home is symbolically associated with a kind of purity. Following Nancy's murder, Lean cuts to a panoramic shot of London rooftops. The light dims and then, after a shot of a street light being turned off, the rooftops gradually get lighter as a new day starts and sunlight floods the city. The film then cuts to an image of bright sunlight shining through the windows of a church, and an image of a woman opening a window to let in the sun's rays. On the surface these images simply indicate that night has passed and a new day has arrived, but there is also a suggestion that the sun is purifying the city after Nancy's murder. Lean uses sunlight at the Brownlow house and also in *Great Expectations* to refer to renewal and purification. Nancy's brutal death is made to represent a form of cathartic cleansing that will purify the whole community.

Women who are in any way sexualized are purged from the film's resolution. The "family" at the end of the film has a kindly middle-aged married housekeeper who even wears a wedding ring. Mrs. Bedwin is maternal, de-eroticized, and working class. Paid labour is represented as in no way less capable of fulfilling Oliver's needs than his female blood relatives in the novel. While the novel, at the end, pauses on and reminds the reader of Oliver's mother's erring ways, the film omits female desire completely. The more public collective that provides a safe haven for Oliver at the end of the film is very different from the novel's, albeit ambiguous, family. In this new world of collective protection, the family is less relevant and single women are dangerous. In this adaptation, sexually uncontrolled women and foreigners represent a significant threat to British social order and well-being. The marginal groups who have most often been labeled as drains on the welfare state, sexually active single women and immigrants, are evoked and then excised from the film's optimistic, seemingly progressive resolution. As in other British and American adaptations made in the 1930s and 1940s, female desire is contained, erased, and expunged. Fifty years later, in the mid-1990s, desiring women would return to this genre of film with a vengeance.

Part II
The 1990s: Convergences

5
Violence, Liberation, and Desire

Catherine is a wealthy, successful writer with a degree in literature and psychology from Berkeley. She also likes to fuck men she does not necessarily like, wears no underwear, and exposes her vagina to five police detectives she has just met during an interview. The spectator sees Sharon Stone's body from the voyeuristic point of view of the middle-aged male detectives and the protagonist, Nick. *Basic Instinct* (1992), with its classic shot/reverse shot sequences, constructs the type of male gaze Laura Mulvey had discussed two decades earlier. An international blockbuster at the time, this film is remarkably lacking in female point-of-view shots; it sutures the spectator into a male heterosexual viewing position, and the narrative reinforces a male heterosexual construction of sexuality. After an explicit, semi-violent scene in which he forces his girlfriend, Christine, to have sex, Nick criticizes her for not being able to "get off." Even though the scene does not indicate that Nick makes any effort to satisfy Christine sexually, the plot represents her failure to achieve orgasm as completely her own. Indeed, despite the sexual deficiencies of this relationship, and despite the fact that Nick betrays his girlfriend by having sex with another woman (who orgasms very easily), when Christine is accidentally murdered by Nick at the end of the film, she still manages to whisper "I love you" with her dying breath.

Representing sexuality from a male heterosexual perspective was of course not unfamiliar in film before 1992. What was new in the 1990s, however, was that films such as *Basic Instinct* had become part of a broader cultural trend that legitimized soft porn. From Victoria's Secret catalogs to the *Sports Illustrated* swimsuit issue, which by the end of the 1990s included no articles about sports, pornographic imagery had become increasingly legitimate in mainstream culture and pervaded American advertising, magazines, popular music, and film.

What was also new was that feminist critiques that identified these representations as oppressive to women had broad cultural appeal. Susan Faludi's bestseller *Backlash* – popular enough to be featured on a *Time* magazine cover – argued that women's economic achievements were accompanied by an undermining onslaught of sexualized media representations. Naomi Wolf's bestseller *The Beauty Myth*, which also received a great deal of attention in Britain, asserted that the media was constructing an unnatural ideal of female beauty and sexuality that made women insecure about their bodies and detached from their sexuality, regardless of how successful they were in their careers. Other writers and filmmakers, such as Susan Douglas and Jean Kilbourne, also showed how media representations of women constituted a backlash against feminist success. Although some feminists, including Camille Paglia, argued that representations of female sexuality such as those in *Basic Instinct* were empowering to women, feminist critiques of these new pornographic cultural trends were sold by mainstream publishing houses and had become international bestsellers. It seems that the popularity of this type of feminism was noticed by the international conglomerates with film and publishing interests.

By the mid-1990s a new genre of film had become commercially successful. Adaptations of British nineteenth-century novels, usually novels by women authors, proliferated. Alongside Sharon Stone's naked flashes and the striptease of popular actresses such as Demi Moore, cinemas pictured the fully clothed women characters of the Victorian and Edwardian eras. Victorian clothing was not new on screen, but in the 1990s it took on a different meaning within the more undressed context of popular visual imagery and the increased attention feminism was giving to the way female bodies were represented. Popular films like *Sense and Sensibility* (1995) and *Pride and Prejudice* (1995) represented female sexuality in a way that resisted trends in the broader culture. At the same time that films such as *Basic Instinct* provided mass audiences with *Playboy*-style images of sex – naked female bodies filtered through soft lenses, explicit yet aesthetically sanitized copulation – other films were turning back to the nineteenth century to construct an alternative sexuality. The automatically orgasmic women who had walked off *Playboy*'s pages into movie theaters and advertisements across America now existed side by side with women whose erotic needs were more subtle. Like the British Gainsborough costume dramas of the 1940s, 1990s adaptations of the British nineteenth-century novel aspired to represent female sexual desire, and they did so in a way that reacted to contemporary trends in mainstream culture. Even more significant, many of these adaptations fused this more female-oriented representation of sexuality with popular feminist discourses.

Most of these adaptations constructed a utopian space in which women could have it all. In merging the eroticism of costume drama with a new feminist triumphalism, these adaptations differed significantly from those made during the Depression and the war years. After a long absence, the nineteenth-century novel had returned to the cinema in yet another guise.

During the more home-oriented 1950s, there was less cultural interest in finding domestic models of stability in nineteenth-century literary plots. Adaptations made at this time did not enjoy as much commercial success or receive as much media attention as films like *Wuthering Heights* (1939), *Jane Eyre* (1944), and *Great Expectations* (1946). During the more experimental periods of filmmaking in the 1960s and 1970s, there had been relatively less cinematic impetus to translate nineteenth-century novels for the screen, despite noticeable, but relatively rare, adaptations such as *Far from the Madding Crowd* (1967) and *Tess* (1979). In the 1980s and early 1990s, the cinema turned from Thomas Hardy to the Edwardian novelist E. M. Forster; adaptations of *A Passage to India* (1984), *A Room with a View* (1985), *Where Angels Fear to Tread* (1991), and *Howard's End* (1992) met with critical acclaim and substantial success at the box office. This cycle of adaptations of novels by the same author set a commercial precedent followed during the 1990s.

Mostly, however, from the 1960s through the 1980s, the early and mid-nineteenth-century domestic novel had traveled into the home. Adaptations of British domestic novels were primarily shown as television series, which, with their many episodes, could retain much of the narrative detail of the original. Unrelated to the cinema, this cycle of television adaptations is outside the scope of this book. In the 1990s, however, television adaptations became intimately related to the cinema. New modes of production and distribution brought television and the cinema closer.

In the 1980s and 1990s major changes in the economic organization of the culture industry coincided with a series of media innovations. In the United States, changes in Federal Communications Commission (FCC) regulations, the introduction of cable television, the arrival of new networks such as Fox, and increased household ownership of VCRs and later DVDs created what many at the time called "the new media." To maximize profits, distribution companies release each film in a number of exhibition windows. In the United States a film is released first in movie theaters, then on videocassette and DVD, then on pay-per-view cable, pay cable, basic cable, and broadcast network television, and then through syndication to local stations.[1] Thus, each film made from a nineteenth-century novel in the 1990s appeared and reappeared at multiple sites, enabling the nineteenth-century novel to exist in an endlessly replicating world of shifting cultural forms. In a related change, the ownership of media outlets was consolidated. In the past, production companies made a film and then exerted vertical control over its profits through their ownership of distribution companies and movie theater chains; in the 1990s the media were organized horizontally. A small number of large conglomerates owned, in addition to distribution and production companies, television stations, video stores, and publishing houses. Hence, a single conglomerate could profit from sales of a film adaptation, the videocassette, television adaptations of the same novel, the original novel, a published screenplay, books about the making of the film, magazines in which the film was discussed, and even Jane Austen T-shirts and mugs.

In addition, these modes of distribution blurred national boundaries. Already in the 1930s and 1940s British- and American-made adaptations were related because many British and American individuals were involved in each other's productions, and British films have always aspired to sell well across the Atlantic. Since the 1980s, however, the international character of "British" costume drama has increased significantly. As Claire Monk has succinctly put it, British adaptations, a subcategory of what she calls the "period film," "are repeatedly made by non-British personnel with non-British money, and measured in terms of their reception and commercial success abroad."[2] They are "one of British cinema's most reliable exports."[3] By the 1990s British film was increasingly researching and concentrating on the American market. Even though most period films make significant profits internationally, the large American market has been the most lucrative. For example, the Australian production of *The Piano* made 7 million dollars in Australia, 16 million in France, and 6.5 million in Britain, but in the United States it made 40 million dollars, more than in these other countries combined. *Sense and Sensibility* made 43 million dollars in the United States, not counting revenues from video, television, and cable networks.[4] The fact that the primary market for adaptations of British nineteenth-century novels made during the 1990s was American contributed to the blurring of these adaptations' cultural affinities.

The three successive versions of Jane Austen's *Emma* made during the 1990s exemplify such international exchanges. In 1995, Paramount released *Clueless*, an American comedy based on *Emma* set in Beverly Hills. The New York–based company Miramax capitalized on the international commercial success of *Clueless* when it produced a more literal adaptation of *Emma* in 1996 starring the American actress Gwyneth Paltrow. This British/American coproduction, released in movie theaters, was soon followed by a British adaptation of the novel made for television. The British adaptation, however, was largely funded by the American-owned Arts and Entertainment network, A&E. In February 1997, it was shown on American A&E cable channels, and the video was later distributed by them. Both A&E and Miramax, however, were owned by the same corporation, Disney. The British television adaptation has simple, unglamorous sets, understated witty dialogue, and a British cast and was written by Andrew Davies, who had also written the BBC adaptation of *Pride and Prejudice* in 1995. In contrast, the British/American Miramax film looks more "American" with its simple, direct dialogues, abundant use of nondiegetic music, and sentimental crescendos. Despite their apparent differences, the television adaptation worked to increase videotape sales of the earlier Miramax adaptation. The very appearance of difference between a British television adaptation of *Emma* and a British/American film adaptation enabled one corporation, Disney, to profit from two adaptations of the same novel. The "Britishness" of certain adaptations is to a large extent part of a marketing package that employs styles and codes that have become identified as "British."

Unlike films of the 1930s and 1940s, British productions of the 1990s were often shaped by market research conducted in America. The ability to appeal to the American market was also enhanced in the 1990s by the rapid merging of cultural discourses enabled by new technologies and the global economy. With the Internet, international programming on cable television, and large international publishing houses, the zeitgeist of the American market was readily accessible and familiar to any non-American producers of adaptations. Given the extent to which American funding, American markets, American personnel, and American culture influenced the production of British adaptations in the 1990s, it would be inaccurate to view these adaptations as solely or even primarily British cultural products.

In general, at least on the surface, adaptations constructed as "British" tend to seem more overtly feminist than "American" adaptations. The Miramax film adaptation of *Emma*, directed and written by Douglas McGrath, for example, seems to be less feminist than its subsequent

"British" adaptation. McGrath's *Emma* retains Austen's actual language for much of its dialogue, but it also omits and changes much of the novel. The film invents a scene depicting Knightley and Emma engaged in an archery contest. This scene clearly refers back to the archery competition in the 1940 adaptation of *Pride and Prejudice*. Interestingly, in the 1940 archery sequence Elizabeth shoots her arrow straight on target, humbling the patronizing Darcy, who misses his target. In the 1996 reworking of the same scene, for an adaptation of a different novel, Emma is unable to shoot her arrows on target; in fact, she is so inept that one arrow almost kills Knightley's dog. Emma's flighty incapacity in this scene makes her appear less formidable than either Emma in the novel or Elizabeth in the *Pride and Prejudice* adaptation made 56 years earlier.

Emma's limitations are further exaggerated because McGrath makes Knightley, acted by Jeremy Northam, almost the same age as Emma, despite his being much older in the novel. In the novel, Emma's shortcomings are contrasted with the wisdom Knightley has acquired with age. In McGrath's adaptation, in contrast, there is no excuse for Emma's lesser intellectual capacities. Indeed, the age difference in the novel also accounts for Emma's slow realization of Knightley's worth, whereas in the film Emma comes across as especially dense for taking so long to choose the handsome Jeremy Northam, who often plays romantic leads in other films, as her mate. The dumbing down of Jane Austen's female protagonist and the trivializing of her character flaws turn Emma into a goofy, silly female character reminiscent of the conventional "dumb blonde" clichés of commercial American cinema. Thus, usually, films that employ American mainstream codes tend to be less interested in feminism. Occasionally, however, this is also true of some "British"-seeming films, such as Franco Zeffirelli's *Jane Eyre* (1996), where Jane is extremely passive.

Most adaptations of the 1990s, however, defied mainstream Hollywood representations of women. Just as British adaptations in the 1930s and 1940s were resistant to Hollywood glamour, so too British-seeming adaptations of the 1990s avoided mainstream constructions of female beauty. This was evident already in 1980s BBC adaptations such as *Mansfield Park* (1983), but it was now used in parallel with an ostensibly feminist narrative trajectory. By employing Hollywood-style romance while resisting mainstream representations of women and adding a feminist spin, these adaptations became immensely successful in their primary market, the United States.

Just as at previous times when adaptations of domestic novels were successful, the nineteenth-century marriage plot became extremely popular in the last decade of the twentieth century, when ideas about gender, marriage, and family were culturally contested and appeared extremely unstable. Domestic living arrangements were changing so much in the United States that in the mid-1990s "family values" were a matter of political controversy discussed in elections. A variety of domestic arrangements different from the nuclear family gained legitimacy in some segments of the culture and were resisted by others. Divorce rates continued to climb, the number of single women rose significantly, and couples were getting married at later and later ages.[5] Although it was usually women who initiated divorces, they often did so because they felt they had no choice, and, at least economically, women paid a high price for divorce. Whether what some called "the culture of divorce" was more liberating or distressing for women was debated widely among researchers.[6]

In Britain, too, the divorce rate had risen significantly, with about 40 percent of marriages ending in divorce in the 1990s. Twenty percent of all families were headed by a lone mother, and the marriage rate had also fallen "by about half between 1971 and 1991." In addition, "it was estimated that 21 percent of all women born in 1965 would remain childless."[7]

In America these types of instability gave rise to a series of popular books and television programs obsessed with preserving marriage and stabilizing gender identities. Two enormous bestsellers of the 1990s reveal a popular desire to rediscover essential heterosexual identities. *Iron John: A Book about Men* asserted that men needed to get in touch with "the magnetic field of the deep masculine" and recover their "Wild man energy," an energy that "leads to forceful action undertaken ... with resolve."[8] In Britain a similar book, *No More Sex War*, appealed to what was called a "men's movement" and attacked feminism explicitly. *Iron John*, the book central to the American "men's movement," had a female corollary. Clarissa Pinkola Estes's *Women Who Run with the Wolves* drew on Jungian psychoanalysis to assert the importance of "the Wild Woman archetype" through which "we are able to discern the ways and means of woman's deepest nature." Women, claims Estes, are like wolves: they are "relational by nature, inquiring, possessed of great endurance and strength. They are deeply intuitive, intensely concerned with their young, their mate, and their pack." She calls on women to rediscover this wild woman within.[9] As constructions of gender shifted drastically, these books sought essential stable gender identities.

Outselling both these books was *Men Are from Mars, Women Are from Venus*, a phenomenal commercial success in non-fiction publishing.

According to *Publishers Weekly*, it was one of the top-ten bestselling books in the United States every year from 1993 through 1997.[10] It was also a significant bestseller in Britain. The *Venus and Mars* book offered consumers a clearly delineated list of male and female characteristics and provided suggestions on how these two different types of people could get along. All these books suggested that gender differences could be neatly defined and that once these essential differences were understood and respected, heterosexual bliss could follow. If only we could all remember that men were like rubber bands and women were like waves, marriages would thrive.

Like these self-help books, the booming talk show scene on American television also appealed to an audience seeking stable gender ideals and clear definitions of "healthy" heterosexual relationships. From the more bizarre to the sentimental, such television programs had a common agenda. Jerry Springer and others used representations of sexual deviance to enforce normative heterosexuality. Parading a freak show of sexually "aberrant" behaviors – such as men who slept with their girlfriends' mothers or women who had slept with so many men they did not know who their children's fathers were – Springer drew clear boundaries of horror around implied normative behaviors. At the other end of the talk show spectrum, using less spectacle and more pop-psychology, Oprah Winfrey, with the help of Dr. Phil from 1998, counseled married couples in front of millions of viewers. Regardless of their strategies, such talk shows aspired to define normative heterosexual relations and prescribe or imply the shape they should take.

Clearly, then, American culture in the 1990s emphasized how troubled relationships between men and women were by shining a light into every nook and cranny of interpersonal difficulty. At the same time, books and television programs suggested that marriages could and should be perfectly satisfying and conflict free. The film adaptations of the 1990s drew on these cultural trends – trends that were not alien to British film producers, who lived in a culture in which marriage was also destabilized.

As the cinema had done during the Depression and the Second World War, in the mid-1990s film turned to the domestic novel of the previous century to construct its domestic ideals, ideals born of the perceived deficiencies, anxieties, and hopes of the moment. Even visually, in a culture filled with boyish models such as Kate Moss and sexually ambiguous advertisements for Calvin Klein, a cinema of women in elaborate dresses and men in jodhpurs made heterosexual identity visibly clear and unambiguous. This nostalgic turn to the nineteenth century enabled an idealized construction of marriage between clearly gendered individuals that addressed contemporary anxieties and fears.

Critics differ about whether such an agenda can be seen as feminist. Janice Doane and Devon Hodges claim that nostalgic films "resist feminism by fixing sexual difference"; Devoney Looser retorts by claiming that Austen films reveal "progressive, feminist elements at work in popular culture." Whereas Doane and Hodges argue that feminists should leave "definitions of masculinity and femininity in play rather than in place,"[11] Looser contends that what matters is not whether gender identities are fixed but rather what those fixed identities are.[12] In her view, Austen adaptations are feminist because the women are active and bond with communities of women and because men learn the importance of expressing and understanding their emotions. Men are also represented as closely bound to the domestic sphere and the women they admire. From a different perspective, Kristin Flieger Samuelian argues that Austen adaptations such as *Sense and Sensibility* are postfeminist, by which she means that in the name of feminism they discount its goals. Emma Thompson's script for *Sense and Sensibility*, for instance, "registers protest through the speeches of her female characters and then quiets it by means of a courtship plot that obviates the conditions protested against." This dynamic, Samuelian asserts, erases the implicit feminism of the novel:

> In demonstrating that feminist protest is both tolerated and satisfactorily answered by courtship, Thompson links such protest to the institutions – marriage, the family, compulsory heterosexuality – that feminism engaged in critiquing. Hence, in appearing sympathetic to the goals of feminism, her film ends by undermining them.[13]

It is significant that what underlies the controversy over whether or not these films are feminist is actually a disagreement about what makes a film feminist. Feminist perspectives differ on whether, or how, a film should fix gender identities. There is also an implicit debate about whether a marriage plot can be feminist. Thus, more important than labeling these films as "feminist," "antifeminist," or "postfeminist" is understanding that these films were popular in a culture in which feminist goals themselves had become unclear. These films incorporate multiple contradictory feminist discourses and speak to a growing fragmentation within feminist and, particularly, popular feminist ideals.

Hillary Clinton was an apt emblem of the internal contradiction in 1990s feminism. In the early part of the decade, the president's wife was controversial, an ambitious career woman who openly asserted her feminist identity and even publicly stated that she would not be baking cookies at the White House. Although she was perceived to be a feminist, a future senator, and maybe even a future president, her political career depended on that of her husband. By the end of the decade she had become a feminist who stood by her man when it became known that he had had oral sex with a 22-year-old White House intern. Indeed, confusion among feminists about how to view Bill Clinton's sexual behavior was yet another indication of the increasingly apparent contradictions within feminist thought.

In Britain the icon of feminist paradoxes was Margaret Thatcher, a woman in a highly powerful position who disavowed feminist causes. There were relatively few female members of parliament while she was in office, a situation that changed with the election of the Labour government in 1997. In Britain, as in America, feminism was increasingly perceived as fragmented and lacking a clear agenda.[14]

There was also a divergence between feminism within academia and feminists published by mainstream publishing houses. For instance, the third wave of academic feminism is "a movement that contains elements of second wave critique of beauty culture, sexual abuse, and power structures while it also acknowledges and makes use of the pleasure, danger, and defining power of those structures." This view emphasizes "the multiple, constantly shifting bases of oppression in relation to the multiple, interpenetrating axis of identity."[15] Steeped in Foucault and postmodern theoretical models, these feminists identified themselves in opposition to the more culturally visible, and intellectually accessible, feminists who were publishing bestsellers. Yet even popular writers who identified as feminists held divergent views. Writers such as Naomi Wolf, Katie Roiphe, Camille Paglia, and Christina Hoff Sommers disagree about date rape, sexual harassment, the need to resist pornographic images of women, whether feminism has become "victim feminism," and whether it is important to assert women's power and what that means. Interestingly, Sommers identifies two main directions in feminism, one that emphasizes female empowerment and one that emphasizes women's status as victims.[16] Although this distinction is disputed by some feminists, it is useful for identifying the two main feminist discourses that inform film adaptations of British nineteenth-century novels. Most of the adaptations made between 1995 and 2000 represent women both as victims and as empowered. To enhance their commercial viability, these films draw on different, contradictory forms of feminism that were already commercially successful in publishing.

Another contentious subject for feminists at the time was female sexuality and its representation in culture. There was controversy about the nature of female heterosexual desire and how it could or should be represented within a male-oriented culture. Camille Paglia celebrated Madonna for representing female sexuality as it reveled in its power to enthrall the opposite sex, but other feminists resisted the idea of women defining their sexuality in terms of their desirability to men and did not believe that this type of sexual display was empowering. Controversy over date rape and sexual harassment added yet another twist to feminist discourses about female sexuality. Katie Roiphe, for instance, believed that women's sensitivity to every male sexual advance was turning them into the sorts of "prudes" their mothers' generation had been.[17]

Others saw certain forms of sexual "prudery" as empowering. At the end of *Promiscuities*, a book that explores the sexual histories and desires of individual women, Naomi Wolf discusses why women like to wear Victorian-style white dresses at their weddings:

> On our wedding days, we tend towards the imagery of the Victorian Age ... precisely because of our time's denigration of female sexuality and desire ... there is a terrible spiritual and emotional hunger among many women, including myself, for social behavior and ritual that respect and even worship female sexuality and reproductive power. ... In Brideland, today, unlike in the "real world" with our boyfriends at the beach, we are hard to unbutton, to get at – even to feel through the stiff corsetry. We are made into treasure again. In white we retrieve our virginity, which symbolizes that sexual access to us is special again.[18]

Although Wolf has been criticized for her facile leaps from personal experience to generalizations about all women, it is interesting that in seeking to explore female desire she finds her ideal in Victorian imagery. Wolf's ideas are echoed in the commercial success of films such as *Sense and Sensiblity* and *Pride and Prejudice*, which emphasize courtly behavior and ritual. In the 1990s there was a significant market among female consumers for representations of female sexuality as special, treasured, corseted, and more respected than it was in films such as *Basic Instinct*.

The British nineteenth-century novel was adapted to construct female heterosexual desire in a way that suggests these films were reacting to what Wolf describes as a "denigration of female sexuality." Unlike much of popular culture, these films were populated by women wearing clothes that concealed, rather than revealed, their bodies, as the viewer's gaze shifted from the female body to the face. In some films, such as *Mansfield Park* (1999), the clothing was often so ornate that it drew the spectator's attention away from the body. In contrast, in films such as *Basic Instinct*, women wore costumes in monochromatic colors that were plain, tight, and scant, revealing and accentuating the body. In the context of the surgically altered silicone-breasted striptease of much of the decade's visual imagery, adaptations of nineteenth-century novels provided a visual correlative for the domestic novel's emphasis on the value of a woman's inner qualities over her appearance.

Whereas the female body was deemphasized in such ways, the male body was emphasized. Departing radically from contemporary representations of male heterosexual desire, these films constructed an alternative female heterosexual gaze. In one scene in *Pride and Prejudice*, lit in soft golden tones, the spectator views Darcy stripping for a bath. In another sequence, also absent from the novel, an underwater camera enables the viewer to gaze at Darcy's athletic body as he swims through a lake. Elizabeth then meets him by surprise, in a shot/reverse shot sequence, enabling the spectator to gaze at him, dripping wet, clothes clinging to his body in a reversed "wet T-shirt" scene. As many critics have noted, the representation of the male form as an explicit object of desire for a carefully constructed female gaze recurs, in different ways and with varying degrees of subtlety, in other adaptations.[19]

Heterosexual female desire was also expressed in voiceovers coordinated with female point-of-view shots. In the television adaptation of *Jane Eyre* (1997), for example, Jane often verbally expresses her desire for Rochester, and the film is suffused with images of the couple touching, holding hands, and standing very close together, always visibly yearning for contact. Shots of tantalizingly close physical proximity between the characters are often intercut with close-ups of Jane that position the spectator within her longing point of view. This 1997 television production is the only adaptation of *Jane Eyre* that retains the novel's descriptions of tactile sexual tensions – for example, its many descriptions of Rochester touching or grabbing Jane's hand. Yet the male objects of desire these films construct diverge significantly from their counterparts in the novels. The difference stems from the ways the films translate the novels' depiction of the social, economic, and ideological forces constraining the lives of nineteenth-century women. *The Tenant of Wildfell Hall* (1996) and *The Woman in White* (1997) are salient examples of the way adaptations represent women as being oppressed less by broad cultural forces than by individually evil men. Some male characters are represented more negatively in the films than in the novels; others are represented far more positively, and, through this contrast, the adaptations construct a masculine ideal absent from the novels that changes or erases the novel's social criticism.

In Mike Barker's adaptation of *The Tenant of Wildfell Hall*, for instance, Huntingdon is an even more villainous character than he is in the novel. In Anne Brontë's novel, a young woman, Helen, marries a handsome young rake called Huntingdon against her own better judgment, and, as his name suggests, he indeed turns out to be coarse and predatory. Huntingdon drinks excessively, disappears from home for long periods, has an affair with an opera singer, and later brings one of his mistresses home to be the governess of his young son. In its detailed depiction of Helen's painful marriage, the novel reveals how severely women suffered from their culture's domestic ideals, their lack of economic independence, and their inability to sue for divorce.

However, Huntingdon's flaws are mitigated by the novel's critique of Victorian culture as a whole. The novel emphasizes that the Victorian ideal of a wife's moral role in marriage is flawed. For example, Helen knows how evil her future husband is before she marries him. He openly boasts of his decadent, selfish exploits. Helen marries him nevertheless, not only because of his physical attractiveness but also because she has internalized Victorian domestic ideologies that insist women have the moral power to redeem their husbands.[20] When Huntingdon's mistress suggests that Helen's moral beliefs are destructive to her marriage, Brontë's novel supports this judgment. Helen's constant preaching about how Huntingdon should behave aggravates his fall into alcoholism. Even Helen's return to her husband's bedside when he is dying is represented as a form of revenge in which Helen can assert her moral superiority over Huntingdon.[21] Overall, the novel suggests that the Victorian ideal of the "angel in the house" works to further Helen's delusions about her capacity to reform Huntingdon, and, in her attempt to enact the moral superiority attributed to women at the time, she contributes more to the marriage's demise than to its rescue. Helen's angelic ambitions are in fact destructive and sometimes morally tainted.

Brontë's novel also criticizes Victorian marriage and property laws. While Lowborough is easily able to divorce his wife when he discovers she is Huntingdon's mistress, Helen, because she is a woman, has no right to sue for divorce and cannot be economically independent.

The visually stunning, thematically rich television adaptation of *The Tenant of Wildfell Hall* remains remarkably faithful to Brontë's rendition of the Victorian home as a prison, yet it blames this prison-like quality on something different. Although the film retains the suggestion that

Helen is partially trapped by her sense of duty, it also represents Huntindgon as violently oppressive in ways he is not in the novel.

The home is represented as a prison through an extended visual analogy linking Helen with tortured and caged birds. In an early scene, Helen's son Arthur taunts a crow. Later, when Helen's voiceover states that she was "a slave and a prisoner" in Huntingdon's home, the camera pans to a caged budgerigar. Helen and the caged bird are equated. Most significant, a disturbing recurring image in the film is a bird's-eye-view shot of Arthur spinning around victoriously, stretching the bloody wings of a dead bird above his head. Later the film reveals that Arthur has killed his budgerigar because Huntingdon trained him to hunt and kill, trained him in a masculine ethos of male brutality. The film thus draws a parallel between Arthur's murder of his caged pet and Huntingdon's hunting of Helen. In fact, Huntingdon's first dance with Helen is shot from an identical bird's-eye-view angle that shows the couple spinning around while Helen spreads her arms out wide like the wings of the murdered bird held by her spinning son in the analogous images. Later, when Huntingdon physically attacks and almost rapes Helen, she dangles in the air, held by the throat, like a helpless bird. Although the image of mutilated birds actually comes from Brontë's *Agnes Grey*, it is used in Barker's *The Tenant of Wildfell Hall* to represent Helen as hunted and caged.

Even though the telefilm retains some of the novel's broad social critique, it reshapes it in ways that are significant. As in the novel, the representation of Huntingdon training his son to be brutal critiques learned masculine behavior. The film's early dialogue, taken directly from the novel, in which Helen attacks the way men are taught to behave makes this criticism obvious. However, the film deletes many of the novel's descriptions of the excesses of Huntingdon's male friends and omits Brontë's criticism of Markham, Helen's second husband. By making Huntingdon the only villainous male character in the story, the adaptation undermines Brontë's attack on a culturally broad masculine ethos from which no men, in the novel, are exempt. Even more important, the adaptation's invention of an attempted rape, a graphic scene absent from the novel, leads to a representation of Huntingdon as physically dangerous, thereby significantly shifting the novel's representation of the forces that endanger women. The visual symbolism of the film, accompanied by the dramatic representation of Huntingdon's physical violence, lays the responsibility for Helen's predicament more on the vicious actions of an evil individual than on the broader social, economic, legal, and ideological forces the novel exposes.

Tim Fywell's adaptation of Wilkie Collins's *The Woman in White* works in a similar way. Like other sensation novels of its time, *The Woman in White* explores the darker sides of Victorian marriage and gender ideals. Because of a promise she made to her father on his deathbed, Laura Fairlie marries Sir Percival Glyde even though she has fallen in love with another man, Hartright. Laura's internalized Victorian ideals of duty and self-sacrifice make it impossible for her to escape her engagement. Even after she understands that Glyde wants only her money, Victorian marriage and property laws prevent Laura from escaping her husband. However, despite the atmosphere of potential physical danger and Glyde's incarceration of Laura in an asylum at one point, the novel never represents Glyde and his ally Fosco as themselves physically violent. Indeed, the novel shows that men do not need to be violent to have control over women. Glyde's power rests on a web of legal, social, and cultural forces that make violence unnecessary. For example, Glyde's power over Laura is initially largely emotional and depends on her acceptance of contemporary ideals of proper female behavior. Glyde is able to manipulate Laura because he knows she feels guilty about her undutiful love for Hartright. Glyde can also rely on social institutions such as the lunatic asylum to keep Laura under control. Indeed, Collins makes the lunatic asylum serve as a metaphor for marriage and the position of women in Victorian society. In Fywell's adaptation, in contrast, Laura's doctor lets her leave the asylum as soon as her identity is known. It is significant that the power of the asylum is so easily undermined in the 1997 television version of the novel. The all-pervasive oppressive cultural forces that the barely escapable asylum symbolizes in the novel are no longer a central thematic concern in the telefilm.

A major indication of this thematic shift can be seen in the way the adaptation changes the novel's secret. Like many sensation novels, *The Woman in White* finally reveals a secret, in this case that Glyde is illegitimate. Collins expresses his unease with the marriage laws of his time by laying some of the blame for Glyde's vicious personality on his obsessive need to hide his illegitimacy. However, in the television series, Glyde's secret is that he sexually abused Anne Catherick when she was a child.

Like the television version of *The Tenant of Wildfell Hall*, this adaptation represents the oppression of women in terms of violent male abuse. When Marian visits Laura after her honeymoon, she notices bruises on

Laura's neck. Laura explains, "I never knew men could enjoy the act even in hatred." Unlike in Collins's novel, Glyde abuses Laura both physically and sexually. In another change the film makes, Glyde and Fosco are shown throwing Anne Catherick off the roof to her death; in the novel, Anne, although she is kidnapped, dies of natural causes. The social, economic, legal, and ideological structures that oppress the women of the novel are transformed, on television, into a contemporary representation of sexual and domestic abuse.

American audiences had already been eagerly consuming stories about sexual harassment and abuse since the beginning of the decade. The early 1990s saw the Clarence Thomas Supreme Court hearings, in which the future judge was accused of sexually harassing a former female employee. Questions of race (both were African-American) were intermingled with intense public controversy about sexual harassment and its significance. Date rape also became a hot topic in the media, and feminist organizations such as the National Organization for Women worked to draw greater attention to the problem of domestic abuse, which was referred to as a major national issue by Bill Clinton in a radio address. Although feminists disagreed about the extent and significance of what some called "victim feminism," the media did report often on domestic and sexual abuse. The much more subtle oppressions implicit in nineteenth-century novels were translated for audiences unfamiliar with the marriage and property laws of the time into a visual language of sexual violence, which had become more familiar. This representation not only made the sensation novel more sensational in contemporary terms but also enabled optimistic resolutions that involved women marrying men who were not abusive.

Although it is understandable that informing a contemporary film audience about nineteenth-century culture, law, and economics is a challenge, there are ideological ramifications to restricting feminist critique to abusive individual men rather than, as in the novels, broader social forces. By representing the oppression of women in clear-cut terms of domestic and sexual abuse, the adaptations suggest that the difficulties women faced were easy to identify, obvious, and, most of all, escapable. Melding a feminist agenda that represents women as the victims of male violence with an agenda that emphasizes female empowerment, these films offer far more optimistic resolutions than do the novels. Legal, social, economic, and ideological changes are difficult to accomplish, but evil individual men can be replaced by better ones. The ambiguities evoked by nineteenth-century writers disappear and women are offered more choices in the adaptations of the 1990s. In the adaptations of both *The Woman in White* and *The Tenant of Wildfell Hall* women escape abusive husbands and marry ideal ones.

Against their portrayal of sexually and physically abusive men, many 1990s adaptations constructed an alternative ideal of masculinity that offered their heroines erotic opportunities unavailable to their counterparts in the novels. In Fywell's adaptation of *The Tenant of Wildfell Hall*, for example, Helen's sexual relationship with Huntingdon is visually contrasted with the one she has with Markham. Huntingdon's sexuality is dangerous; Markham's is not. The red-toned lighting used for Helen's sexual encounters with Huntingdon culminates in the red-toned candlelit image in which Helen, dressed in her mourning veil, sits staring vacantly at Huntingdon's coffin. The lighting and imagery suggest that Helen and Huntingdon have been consumed in the fires of a destructive sexuality. Although Helen is represented as enjoying sex with Huntingdon, he is a destructive sexual choice. His sexuality is unrestrained, not monogamous, and violent; it also objectifies Helen. He values Helen solely for her looks and ignores her other attributes, even complimenting her on the texture of her skin and stating that he wants her just for himself in his "museum." In the terms of 1990s popular feminism, Huntingdon views Helen predominantly as a sexual object, one he can possess and control. Moreover, his sexual desire lacks discernment; he desires Annabela Wilmont (whom the film portrays as particularly unattractive) as much as, if not more than, Helen.

Brontë's novel has often been criticized for making Helen's second husband, Markham, so unappealing. At the beginning, "he is conceited and condescending towards women." Markham is an overindulged son and is drawn toward the superficial Eliza Milwood.[22] Later, he attacks Helen's brother, Lawrence, because he mistakenly thinks him to be her lover. After beating him brutally, Markham leaves Lawrence to die in the pouring rain on the side of a road.

In Barker's adaptation, Markham's flaws are diminished, and, more importantly, he is not violent. The opening sequence of the film shows Markham shooting a rifle but then cuts to a scene in which he rescues Arthur, who is falling from a tree. Later, there is an ominous sequence of images in which Markham cleans his rifle and then goes to attack Lawrence. Yet here, in contrast to the novel, after beating Lawrence, Markham quickly recognizes his mistake, apologizes, and shows concern for Lawrence's well-being. It is interesting that Markham is so often shown with a rifle yet, unlike Huntingdon, never uses it to kill. Markham is sexual, but his sexuality is restrained, nonviolent, and safe in contrast with Huntingdon's.

To develop the contrast between these two forms of masculinity further, Barker's *The Tenant of Wildfell Hall* invents a scene that does not exist in the novel. In Brontë's narrative, after Helen leaves Wildfell Hall to go back to Grassdale and look after Huntingdon, who is dying, Markham is restrained and waits in silence while Helen fulfills her wifely duties. In Barker's plot, Markam heroically races to rescue Helen from her abusive husband. Markham's ride to Grassdale is importantly positioned in the film's narrative trajectory. The film cuts back and forth between three plot lines: Markham's ride to Grassdale, Helen's tale of the brutal last period of her marriage, and Helen's nursing of Huntingdon. This narrative structure repeatedly juxtaposes Markham and Huntingdon, highlighting their differences. Shots of Huntingdon's brutality and blindness to Helen's suffering are intercut with scenes in which Markham reads Helen's diary as he dashes to her rescue. Images of abuse are intercut with images of a man learning about a woman's inner heart. At Grassdale the two men meet (something that never happens in the novel), creating a vivid visual contrast between the inadequacies of one form of masculinity and the superiority of the other. Images of Huntingdon's wasted, sickly body are contrasted with images of Markham's physical strength and health.

Markham is represented as masculine, nurturing, sexual, and sexually restrained all at once. He is visually striking, muscular, and tall. He is often filmed in the midst of vigorous, healthy physical activity, walking across farmland or climbing cliffs. There are many close-ups of his boots and strong legs as they make large strides across the harsh landscape. Yet this physical strength is balanced by a nurturing personality. He saves the little boy, Arthur, twice, brings him a puppy, and in general loves children and dogs. In another scene that the adaptation invents, Markham even helps a lamb give birth. Nurturing, rugged, and strong, he is also sensitive and respectful of women.

The erotic scenes between Markham and Helen are made to look different from those between Helen and Huntingdon. Filmed in gray rather than fiery red tones, these scenes are marked by male sexual restraint rather than excess. In the scene in which Helen and Markham first kiss, he leaves almost immediately afterward. His is an eroticism of subtle gestures and small movements, of a masculinity that is desirable and desiring but in which sexual action is restrained. In the adaptations of the 1990s, a decade that explored the dangers of date rape and sexual harassment, nineteenth-century heroes were represented as knowing when "no" meant "no."

Like many adaptations of the 1990s, Barker's telefilm combines an extreme critique of male brutality with a highly eroticized romantic hero who can save the heroine in the end. With a female narrator telling the story of her resilience in the face of male oppression and in its optimistic erotic ending the television version of *The Tenant of Wildfell Hall* offers a compelling utopian vision that binds feminist empowerment with erotic fulfillment.

Fywell's adaptation of *The Woman in White* functions in a similar way. Collins's novel depicts characters who occupy ambiguous gender positions. Hartright is hysterical, weak, and ineffectual most of the time. Marian is described as having masculine traits, most notably in the passage in which Hartright first sees her and discovers that she is ugly and even has a moustache. Only Laura fits neatly into Victorian notions of gender identities. Laura is angelic and feminine in conventional terms, but Collins deconstructs this ideal by representing her as emotionally deficient and childlike. As Hartright reiterates, she is "wanting" and not much different from her emotionally unbalanced double, Anne Catherick. The many ways in which Collins complicates the gender identities of his characters work to expose the flaws and contradictions in Victorian gender ideals.

In the television adaptation, in contrast, Hartright is far less effeminate, and Marian is attractive, has no moustache, and is conventionally "feminine." By softening Marian's hard, assertive edges, the film can make Hartright more heroic and masculine. In the novel, Marian is highly efficient; it is Marian who discovers Laura in the insane asylum and Marian alone who daringly rescues her. In Fywell's adaptation, in contrast, Hartright is with Marian when they find Laura, and they rescue her together.

Mirroring contemporary preoccupations with sexual harassment, the film invents a subplot in which Hartright is accused of sexually harassing a maid. Later it is revealed that the maid is Glyde's mistress and the harassment has been staged to discredit Hartright. This episode is important because when Hartright is eventually exonerated, it is emphasized that he is different from sexually abusive men. This contributes to the film's representation of some men, notably Fosco and Glyde, as unambiguously evil and abusive, and others, specifically Hartright, as unambiguously good and desirable.

Therefore, when Laura marries Hartright, the telefilm ends far more optimistically than the novel. In the last section of the novel, Hartright is portrayed far from sympathetically. He does not allow

Marian or Laura to leave their home when he goes out into the world to legitimize not only Laura's but also his own class position. His actions, including burning Glyde alive, are morally tainted. Hence, the domestic tableau with which the novel closes is ominous. As Laura notices, Hartright is deeply drawn to Marian as well as to herself, resulting in a strange ménage à trois in which the two women fulfill different functions in Hartright's new home. In the closing passages of the novel it is Marian who is referred to by Hartright as an angel. Since she is not his wife, however, and does not wish to conform to angelic ideals, the novel's domestic resolution is ambivalent.

In the adaptation, Laura is indeed said to carry the wounds of her abuse, and reference is made to the abuse Anne Catherick suffered as a child; however, as Fywell's *The Woman in White* idealizes Hartright and emphasizes that he is not abusive, his marriage to Laura is represented more positively. Laura's second marriage is represented as a feminist triumph, one in which a female character has escaped from an abusive marriage into a better one with a respectful, heroic husband. Indeed, Hartright and Laura even have a daughter, rather than the son they have in the novel. In a seemingly feminist twist, the suggestion is made that this marriage engenders a more female-friendly environment and that the daughters of the future will live in a better world than earlier generations of women. The ideal domestic tableau is similar in *The Tenant of Wildfell Hall* because Markham can offer Helen the sort of perfect marriage that is absent from the novel.

All in all, then, many 1990s film adaptations of domestic novels represent the oppression women faced in the nineteenth century in modern terms of domestic and sexual abuse. By idealizing men who are not abusive, they also offer their women characters erotic alternatives. In this way, the adaptations suggest that the difficulties women faced were easy to identify, obvious, and, most of all, escapable in happy second marriages with better men. Melding a feminist agenda that represents women as the victims of male violence and sexual threat with an emphasis on female empowerment, liberation, and erotic fulfillment, these films offer their contemporary audiences more optimistic resolutions than the novels do. Although they evoke the oppressive dimensions of women's lives represented in the novels through their discourses of sexual danger, these films also insist that women are ultimately able to free themselves.

Lady Audley's Secret (2000) is an extreme example of this trend. Mary Elizabeth Braddon's novel depicts, in great detail, the distressing economic circumstances that force Lady Audley to marry for money. Later, suspecting her of a murder she did not actually commit, her husband's nephew, Robert, hunts her down and imprisons her in an insane asylum. The novel suggests that Robert's obsessive need to punish Lady Audley emanates from his extreme misogyny and homoerotic desire for his allegedly murdered friend George. Braddon's chilling description of Robert's incarceration of Lady Audley in an obscure Belgian asylum, in a chapter appropriately entitled "Buried Alive," is a central metaphor for the position of women in Victorian society.

The novel's concluding chapter describes the marriages that have taken place since Lady Audley's incarceration. Although the novel appears to end with a number of happy marriages, Braddon subtly suggests otherwise. Robert marries not a woman he loves but the sister of the man he loves because "she is so much like George." Lady Audley's stepdaughter, Alicia, is hungry for the male attention that will validate her and marries someone she does not love out of a sense of duty to her father. In the middle of this chapter news arrives that Lady Audley has died in the asylum. Lady Audley's incarceration and destruction lie at the symbolic center of the novel's troubling domestic conclusion.

In the television adaptation, which typically erases the ambiguous gender identities of the novel, Robert is unambiguously heterosexual and erotically obsessed with Lady Audley. As in other adaptations, he represents a heterosexual male threat. Even more striking, at the end Alicia liberates Lady Audley from the asylum. Drawing on feminist ideas about the power of women's communities, the film shows women collaborating to escape their oppression by men. The film's empowerment of Alicia and Lady Audley in this way undercuts the novel's representation of the inescapable nature of the restrictions that bore upon Victorian women's lives.

Empowered women characters are prevalent in film adaptations made between 1995 and 2000. Many have a female character narrate the plot, making nineteenth-century novels appear as though they are stories told by women about their escape from oppression into freedom. This gives the plots a sort of feminist narrative trajectory that is more characteristic of late twentieth-century than of early or mid-nineteenth-century discourses. A female narrator is used even for adaptations of novels without central female narrators. *Wuthering Heights* (1992), for example, is narrated not by Lockwood, a man through whom Nelly can tell her story only in a mediated form, but rather by Emily Brontë, a character seen walking across the moors as she describes the events of *Wuthering Heights*. In Anne Brontë's *The Tenant of Wildfell Hall*, Helen's narrative is framed by Markham's narrative, in which he relates their story to his male friend. In Barker's version, only Helen's narrative remains, in the form of a voiceover. The change to a female perspective is even more significant in the adaptation of *The Woman in White*. The multiple male and female narrators of the novel, in which women narrators can be brutally cut off by men, are replaced by one narrative perspective, the voiceover of Marian, the most assertive and active female character from the novel. These shifts enable the films to make the novels into first-person tales of feminine triumph.

In the novels, women's stories, their voices, are constantly invaded and usurped. For instance, in Brontë's *The Tenant of Wildfell Hall*, Helen's husband reads her diary without permission and then forbids her to write or paint. In *The Woman in White*, Marian's diary is read by the dangerous Count Fosco. Collins structures his narrative in such a way that the novel's reader unknowingly reads Marian's diary together with the character Fosco. The reader is thus implicated in what both novels represent as a form of rape, an invasion of a woman's private self. Both novels depict female self-expression as besieged.

Most of all, the embedded and/or shifting narrators of many nineteenth-century novels indicate how difficult it is for women to express themselves and be heard as they wish to be. Female self-expression is represented as tenuous, difficult, and dangerous. When the cinematic versions of these books offer female viewers an uncomplicated site of identification with a female narrative point of view, they undercut an important theme in the novels. The adaptations of the 1990s give women characters a dominant, empowered narrative voice at the expense of the sort of feminist critique women's voicelessness enabled in the novels. The films suggest that women are not really silenced.

Feminist content is drastically reshaped in film adaptations of the 1990s in other ways. Adaptations of *Jane Eyre* provide a clear example. Although there is disagreement among critics about how feminist *Jane Eyre* is, some parts of the novel, such as the speech Jane delivers on Thornfield's battlements, provide unambiguous moments of feminist expression. Jane asserts that one day women will revolt against their lot and seek wider spheres of experience than baking puddings and embroidering. A British play produced in 1997 by the Shared Experience Theatre Company strongly emphasizes the feminist dimensions of the novel. However, the explicitly feminist sections of the novel are eliminated from both the 1996 and 1997 film adaptations.

In Zeffirelli's *Jane Eyre* (1996) at the point in the plot where Brontë has Jane pacing the battlements of Thornfield expressing feminist frustrations, Zeffirelli has Jane look wistfully at a picture of Rochester as a young man. Zeffirelli translates the wider sphere of experiences Brontë's Jane craves in her feminist moments into a romantic discourse. Indeed, Zeffirelli's Jane is remarkably passive, and the film retains relatively little of the novel's depiction of her relationship with Rochester as enmeshed in unequal economic and gender power positions. Both the characters' rougher edges are smoothed over and muted. Rochester is soft-spoken and restrained. William Hurt, often cast as a "sensitive" man in other commercial films, is a meek, not masterful, Rochester. Hence, the film's representation of Jane's need to assert her equality with this man is not emphatic. Although Zeffirelli tries to cash in on the popularity of the nineteenth-century novel in the 1990s, his film remains largely oblivious to the feminist discourses incorporated into other contemporary adaptations.

In contrast, Hugo Young's television adaptation of *Jane Eyre* is more typical of contemporary adaptations that merge feminist ideas with a highly erotic plot. In this version, the point in the novel at which Jane makes her feminist speech on the battlements of Thornfield is replaced by the statement "I felt restless and stifled. I felt sure there must be more to life than this." Jane's sense of dissatisfaction is immediately eased in the following sexually charged scene when Rochester arrives. The scene is filmed in shot/reverse shot sequences and from an extremely low angle, as the viewer and Jane see Rochester loom large as he rides his straining horse through a moist mist and then violently falls, with Jane, into a pool of dark water. The novel's reference to the discontent of women in general is translated here into a personal discontent that can be assuaged by an erotic awakening. The political is personal, and erotic. The novel's exploration of the unequal power positions of men and women is maintained in the television adaptation, but only within the narrow context of Jane's relationship with Rochester.

Young focuses even more exclusively on the novel's romantic plot than Zeffirelli, eliminating large sections of the novel not set at Thornfield. Yet, unlike in Zeffirelli's adaptation, the romance is represented as a struggle for mastery and control. Rochester, though less distant, is characterized as far more boorish and brutal than in previous adaptations; he is even rougher than the formidable Orson Welles of the 1944 adaptation. Ciaran Hinds's Rochester is sharp, gruff, curt, domineering, and rough. He has a drive for mastery that Jane must resist, and this struggle, unlike in any other adaptation, is explicitly articulated in terms of class and power differences.

Jane:　　Certain facets of your character are somewhat unpleasant.
Rochester:　I am listening

Jane:	You ask by way of command.
Rochester:	Do I?
Jane:	Yes.
Rochester:	That is because I have had a lifetime of saying, "do this" and it is done. What else is wrong with my character?
Jane:	That is all.
	...
Rochester:	And do you expect me to change my manner because of one little governess? (*Jane pauses*)
Rochester:	(*roughly*) Well?
Jane:	I expect nothing sir, you asked a question and I merely answered it.
Rochester:	As you understand, I have the right to be masterful in my own house.[23]

Unlike previous adaptations, Young's *Jane Eyre* foregrounds class-based patriarchal power, emphasizing the economic gap between Rochester and Jane and making frequent references to her salary. Nevertheless, Rochester does eventually change because of "one little governess." By the end of the film, Jane is represented as having quietly, in Rochester's words, "outmaneuvered" him.

Indeed, the end of Young's adaptation is strikingly different from earlier versions of *Jane Eyre* in the extent to which Rochester has changed. In the Zeffirelli film, since Rochester is so passive throughout, at the end his energies hardly seem reduced by his injuries. In the 1944 adaptation, Orson Welles, surly and powerful throughout the film, does not look particularly changed in the final scene. In fact, he barely seems injured at all; despite being blind, he walks authoritatively around the ruins of Thornfield. In Young's 1997 adaptation, in contrast, when Jane first finds Rochester at Ferndean, he is seated, immobile, and vulnerable, rather than standing or walking. Later in the scene he weeps watery tears that Jane wipes away – in an explicit reversal of their previous power positions, and in opposition to more conventional representations of relations between men and women – as she reassures him that she will indeed marry him. More masterful at the beginning of this adaptation, Rochester is far more tamed at its end.

In keeping with the notion that "every woman's fantasy is to change a man," executive producer Sally Head emphasizes the power Jane has to effect such a transformation in Rochester. Indeed, despite the film's emphasis on the economic gap between Rochester and Jane, Jane does not receive her inheritance. In an interview posted at the time on the

A&E *Jane Eyre* website, Head describes this change as a feminist move: "[S]he doesn't need the money."[24] Jane is powerful enough to outmaneuver Rochester without the help of an inheritance. The seemingly feminist representation of Jane as more powerful than in the novel actually undermines, again, the novel's feminist emphasis on women's need for material bases of power, for economic autonomy. In addition, like the adaptations *The Tenant of Wildfell Hall* and *The Woman in White*, Young's *Jane Eyre* offers its protagonists an ideal husband at the end; in this case, however, he is not a different, better man than the villainous abusive male character but a man Jane is powerful enough to have reformed.

It is also significant that this adaptation evokes images of the classic 1944 adaptation to replace that film's representation of Jane's maternal impulses with an emphasis on erotic desire. For instance, in the 1997 film Rochester buys Jane a music box that is not described in the novel but is similar to the one Adèle brings Jane in the 1944 adaptation. In both films a shot of the dancing couple on the music box is superimposed on another image: in 1944 the figure in the background of this romantic image of the music box is the dancing child; in 1997 it is Rochester and Jane who dance in the background image. The 1997 adaptation works to separate Jane's desire for Rochester from the classic adaptation's merging of Jane's love of children with her love for Rochester. The film even replaces the "cute" Adèle of the 1944 adaptation with an older, unappealing child. Consciously working against its classic predecessor, this film divorces maternal from sexual desire as it makes Jane's erotic quest for Rochester the center of the narrative and represents her relationship with Adèle as unfulfilling. Female sexual desire is central.

Brontë's novel ends ambiguously, with Jane musing – perhaps longingly, perhaps critically – not on hearth and home but on all the energy and activity St John finds in India. Young's adaptation, in contrast, ends with a blissful, unambiguous domestic tableau. Indeed, when the film eliminates her inheritance, it even reduces the novel's emphasis on Jane's need to enter into her marriage from a more equal economic standing. In the telefilm Jane achieves her equality with Rochester in erotic not political, economic, or social terms. It is Rochester's desire for her and her ability to manipulate it to her advantage, not her inheritance, that empower Jane within their relationship. Jane is empowered because she can reform a masterful man and make him into a satisfying and unthreatening erotic object. The novel's broader ideological critique of the narrow social and economic opportunities women had in the nineteenth century is subsumed within the libidinal thrust of the film.

Like other television adaptations of the late 1990s, then, this *Jane Eyre* is less a broad social critique than a depiction of a woman's quest for power and fulfillment within a heterosexual relationship. Feminist liberation, as defined by these films, consists of finding erotic fulfillment in a relationship with a man who is tamed, respectful, sexually desirable, and unthreatening. Moreover, as in *The Woman in White*, after marriage the Rochesters have not a son, as in the novel, but a daughter. The optimistic vision of a world in which empowered women can manipulate their environment to fulfill their emotional needs is projected into the future by ending on the image of a female child. Similar codes operate in Patricia Rozema's more experimental *Mansfield Park* (1999).

Despite its broader social and economic palette, this film relies on many of the conventions of its immediate predecessors. In a new twist on the representation of male violence and control, it develops an explicit analogy between the domination of colonized others and of women. In one of the first scenes in the film, not present in the novel, Fanny hears the cries of slaves referred to as "human cargo" from a ship docked below a cliff. Later, the analogy between slave women and Fanny is made explicit in a pivotal scene in the film. Sir Thomas Bertram mentions how attractive one of his mulatto slaves is and suggests bringing a slave to England. In response, Fanny politely criticizes the slave trade. Sir Thomas then turns the conversation into a discussion of Fanny's looks and form. An imperial discourse is represented as easily slipping into one about women. In the ensuing conversation, while Edmund asserts that Fanny's strengths reside in the quality of her mind, Sir Thomas insists on emphasizing her physical attributes. He then suggests to Henry Crawford that Fanny be shown off at a ball to attract a suitor. Sir Thomas refers to Fanny as a commodity in a manner similar to the way he talks about his female slaves. While the men having this conversation gaze at Fanny, she appears extremely uncomfortable. Fanny flees the house and later tells Edmund, "I will not be sold off like one of your father's slaves." The analogy is explicit.

Later, near Tom's sickbed, Fanny finds sketches of Sir Thomas torturing and raping slaves. Unlike in the novel, Tom's decadence and illness are linked to Sir Thomas's involvement in the slave trade. Thus, although Sir Thomas is occasionally compassionate, he is usually represented as treating women like slaves, and, like many other men in these adaptations, he rapes women. Like Glyde in the adaptation of *The Woman in White* and Huntingdon in the adaptation of *The Tenant of Wilfell Hall*, he is also sexually dangerous.

In another sequence, Sir Thomas sends Fanny to Portsmouth with the expressed intention of making her remember what poverty is like so that she will understand why she does indeed need to "be sold off like a slave" and marry Henry Crawford. In its graphic depiction of the poverty Fanny faces in her Portsmouth home, this adaptation retains Austen's general emphasis on the extent to which economic necessity limited women's possibilities and shaped their feelings about men. When Henry tries to "buy" Fanny's affections by offering her family economic relief, he succeeds in confusing her. Her will weakened by the prospect of poverty, Fanny comes close to accepting Henry and the freedom from want that he offers.

Despite this adaptation's critique of the economic restrictions women faced, unlike in the novel, poverty seems a less formidable problem than the slavery and sexual aggression the film emphasizes. As in other adaptations, then, the way oppression is translated from the novel is important. Austen's Sir Thomas does the best he can for Fanny. He makes Fanny suffer not because he is evil or sexually abusive but because he holds to the conventional ideas of his time about women and class. Sir Thomas is a conventional man who means well when he tries to show Fanny what in his view are her best interests. It is the economic and class structures, and the ideologies that uphold them, working through Sir Thomas, that cause Fanny's suffering in the novel. However, because Rozema's Sir Thomas is so sexually threatening and cruel to his slaves, he is represented as an evil individual unconstrained, rather than shaped, by his society. He is represented not as a man who means well but can act only within a limited area of possibilities but as a man who has dangerous, abusive desires.

The postcolonial feminist interpretation of the novel makes Sir Thomas into a far more ominous character than he is in the novel. Like the telefilms of *The Tenant of Wildfell Hall* and *The Woman in White*, the *Mansfield Park* adaptation represents oppression in terms of sexual aggression and extreme male domination. This changes the critique in the novel. The film represents some men as evil and others as exempt from the conventions of their society. Thus, while Sir Thomas is represented as racist and sexist, Edmund is not. This film is therefore able to end with a less ambiguously happy domestic resolution than the novel. Eventually, Rozema's Fanny gets an erotically fulfilling partner who does not share his society's perspectives on women.

As in other adaptations made in the late 1990s, Fanny's erotic desires are represented within the context of sexual danger. In one episode, after Sir Thomas and Henry Crawford objectify her by discussing her physical appearance, Fanny flees their company and goes horseback riding in the rain. This scene is highly sexualized; close-ups focus on her pelvic area astride the horse and on her neck and head stretching upward toward the falling rain. In the wake of understanding her erotic allure to men, Fanny experiences sensuous pleasures independently of these men's proprietary gazes. Rozema's adaptation is unique in representing a woman's autoerotic pleasure as a liberated response to the oppressive structures of desire in her social environment.

In another scene, shot in soft orange lighting, Mary sensually undresses Fanny after she has gotten wet in the rain. Mary admires Fanny's "wonderful" body as she removes the sodden clothes. Although the conversation between the two women is about their shared male object of desire, Edmund (and Mary might also be assessing Fanny's worth for her brother), there is a homoerotic edge to the scene that cuts across the plot and the dialogue. Although Fanny's erotic awakening is triggered by men's admiration and by her own growing attraction to Edmund, her sexuality is not narrowly bound to or by male sexual objects and male desire as it is in other contemporary adaptations. Fanny's desire for Edmund, and sometimes for Henry Crawford, is thus situated in the context of transient moments of same-sex intimacy as well as moments of autonomous sensuous pleasure. In addition, Fanny's attraction to Henry Crawford is fed by economic fear and is represented as light and flirtatious in comparison to the deeper erotic feelings Fanny has for Edmund. Unlike in any of the other adaptations, here female desire is represented as shifting and complex, as fluid and autonomous, and sometimes not narrowly bound to desire by and for specific males. Thus, this adaptation made as the 1990s and this wave of adaptations drew to a close goes furthest and is the most explicit in its exploration of female sexual desire.

Rozema's *Mansfield Park* also depicts sexual desire as being accompanied by a need for intellectual and creative expression. Rozema merges Fanny and Jane Austen by depicting Fanny as a writer who struggles to obtain an appreciative audience for her talents. This adaptation differs from its predecessors in emphasizing the woman writer's intellectual life and aspirations. However, Fanny's intellectual recognition is represented as not very difficult to achieve. Fanny's writing is read to and admired and encouraged by Edmund. As in other adaptations, women are represented as more able to express themselves openly than they are in the novels, where women characters face immense cultural restrictions. More significantly, this depiction of creative empowerment is incorporated within the erotic trajectory of the narrative. At the end of the film Fanny publishes her work, but only after she is married; erotic and intellectual fulfillment merge. Even in the opening sequence, as the camera lightly glides over thickly textured papers that resemble lush sensuous fabrics, writing is obliquely eroticized. In contrast, for the real Jane Austen (who published despite never getting married) writing was not only a creative but also an economic activity. The film, despite its representation of women's poverty, locates women's aspirations for freedom within a predominantly erotic rather than economic discourse.

As in other contemporary adaptations, the film ends with a happy marriage. Whereas in Austen's novel Edmund is flawed, repressed, and often oppressive, in the film Fanny marries a relatively appealing character. In the final sequences of the film showing what happens to each of the characters, a voiceover repeats that each ending could have been "otherwise." Rozema's interesting postmodern twist at the end of her marriage plot highlights self-reflexively that this is a constructed conclusion. Nevertheless, despite its ontologically uncertain status, the ending has a triumphant feminist edge that the novel lacks. Edmund, though weak and vacillating, is far more sympathetic and handsome than he is in the novel, and, because he is contrasted with a far more villainous Sir Thomas, this marriage is represented as liberating and erotically fulfilling.

Adaptations such as these suggest that women can escape or reform dangerous men like Sir Thomas or Rochester, can break out of their asylums, and can marry ideal men. Unambiguous liberation is possible in these films, in ways it is not in the novels, because responsibility for the suffering these women experience is placed mostly on individual male characters who can be replaced with better ones. In the novels women are invisibly incarcerated by their culture; women characters are often unable to see, articulate, or completely escape the oppressive structures of their world. By representing the stifled lives of nineteenth-century women in terms of visible domestic abuse and male violence, the films are also able to represent empowered women who can see oppression clearly and escape it in idealized marriages.

These utopian endings have a complex timeframe. In Rozema's *Mansfield Park*, for example, Fanny Price is an assertive, active girl who is drastically different from the self-denying, oppressed, hesitantly assertive character in the Austen novel. When Fanny openly criticizes Sir Thomas's exploitation of slaves, not only does the film interpret Austen as being critical of the slave trade (something that is debated among Austen critics),[25] but it also enables Fanny to voice what no young girl indebted to her uncle for her keep could possibly have said at the beginning of the nineteenth century. The cinematic Fanny is openly rebellious and is as able to express herself as the 1990s television versions of Helen, Marian, and Jane do; these women are relatively more modern than their novelistic counterparts and can express contemporary feminist ideas.

In another scene in the *Mansfield Park* film, Mary Crawford criticizes the Bertrams' narrow morality by emphasizing that it is, after all, 1806. This line provokes laughter in cinema audiences, yet it reveals something important about the film's timeframes. By emphasizing, comically, the narrow conventions that oppressed and limited Fanny and Mary in 1806, the film reminds the amused audience that these oppressions belong to a past. The nostalgic mode of the heritage film works here to situate the limitations the female characters experience in the far away and long ago. Evil men like Sir Thomas are no longer allowed to rape slaves, market their nieces' physical attributes as choice commodities, or try to force women to marry men they do not love. The nineteenth century is represented as a time in which there were no social restrictions on the masculine abuse of women.

Concurrently, the films project empowered female characters, such as Fanny, into the nineteenth century so that they can criticize it from a contemporary perspective. Female characters who hold late twentieth-century views mock characters represented as adhering to the values of the "nineteenth century." As the films celebrate the characters who have more modern sensibilities, they condescend to the nineteenth century. By merging timeframes in this complex way, the films imply that the liberated women belong to the novels' futures, to the present. Thus, the feminist triumphalism that characterizes these adaptations actually points less toward a problematic past than toward an idealized present.

Historical films often represent history in terms that emphasize progress and suggest that "things have gotten better."[26] Even though oppressive experiences are translated into contemporary feminist terms of domestic violence and sexual abuse, these forms of oppression are largely represented as though they belong to a distant past, as though it was only in the nineteenth century that such things were allowed to happen. The women characters, though usually less formidable than in the novels, are able to express contemporary feminist views. Thus, when these women are liberated at the end and pair up with idealistically characterized male heroes such as Markham, Hartright, the reformed Rochester, and Edmund, this utopian ending is situated in a timeframe that points as much to an idealized present as to the past. Yet perhaps these films construct a utopian vision of the present precisely because the present is not so ideal.

In general, then, even though some feminists might mourn the way these adaptations empty the novels of the broader feminist social critique that has been identified by literary critics, such films did offer women viewers of the 1990s an erotic discourse resistant to much of mainstream culture. Although it is true that corporations such as Disney might prefer to produce seemingly feminist films that emphasize romance rather than films with contemporary ideological and economic critiques, it is also important to acknowledge the demands adaptations of British nineteenth-century novels did meet in terms of offering female viewers alternatives to *Terminator 2* or *Basic Instinct*. Indeed, perhaps the fact that so many of these 1990s films, unlike adaptations in earlier periods, go to such a great length to contrast men who are sexually invasive and dangerous with idealized men who exercise sexual restraint says something about the position of women vis-à-vis the culture at large. The films depict female characters who escape sexual threat and find safe erotically fulfilling spaces at the same time that the films themselves offer women viewers an erotic escape from the crass and sexually invasive dominant culture.

This turn to the domestic novel of the past reveals a need to find an alternative erotic discourse and an alternative world in which feminist triumph is unambiguous. By the 1990s, decades of feminism, as well as other social and economic forces, had changed the position of women drastically. A number of women occupied highly visible jobs in American government: secretary of state, attorney general, Supreme Court judge. More professional fields were open to women than had been the case decades earlier, and statistics show that a far greater percentage of women were receiving a higher education. A larger percentage of women were in the labor force than in earlier decades.[27]

However, third-wave feminists have emphasized that women had entered an extremely competitive economy. The second-wave feminists of the 1960s and 1970s had aspired to provide women with the option to work; by the 1990s, 80 percent of women in the United States had no economic choice other than to work. Women entering the workforce in the 1990s, like men, faced the prospect of unemployment, underemployment, and in some professional areas, such as academia, the growing reliance of employers on contingent labor. The generation of young women entering the job market in the 1990s, like men, faced the prospect of receiving comparatively low salaries, had to grapple with heavy debts incurred as a result of their education, and were increasingly anxious about their economic futures. All in all, claim third-wave feminists, although women were entering the labor force in unprecedented numbers, what had been such a desirable goal for second-wave feminists could no longer be seen as an ideal form of liberation in the context of the economy of the 1990s.[28]

Indeed, the growing participation of women in the workforce was accompanied by changes in women's lifestyles. In 1973, 57 percent of women in their twenties worked, but by 1993 this figure had risen to 73 percent.[29] By 1999, the number of these women who were not married had tripled, from 11 percent in 1975 to 30 percent in 1999.[30] With their growing economic participation in the labor market, women's personal lives had changed. Without the hindsight possible in relation to the 1930s and 1940s, it is difficult to assess how women felt about their increased participation in the workforce and whether changes in their personal lives reflected a greater sense of freedom or a feeling that women were paying a price in some areas of their lives for the gains they made in others.

In Britain a similar economic situation was evident in the 1990s. Although women represented a larger percentage of the workforce than men, their average salary was lower. Many women were engaged in part-time work that paid low salaries. In addition, to an even greater extent than women in the United States, women in Britain faced long-standing glass ceilings. In the medical profession, for example, only 22 percent of general practitioners were women, and in the legal field only 21 percent of solicitors were women.[31] Significantly, such labor conditions were also prevalent in the film and television industries that were producing film adaptations of British nineteenth-century novels. British media industries were increasingly hiring casual labor on the basis of short-term contracts. In surveys, women working in the British film and television industries expressed frustration with their unstable conditions of labor, the lack of maternity leave, the lack of viable day care, and the fact that women were paid the same salaries as men for doing twice as much work. Whereas two-thirds of the men in the industry were able to combine their careers with having children, only 30 percent of the women were able to have both children and a career.[32]

Whatever feminism had or had not achieved by the 1990s, its achievements were not unambiguous. A return to the domestic novel of the nineteenth century provided a clear benchmark against which to measure where women had been and how far they had come. If women's lives were not exactly easy now, for whatever reasons, they were certainly better than they had been 150 or so years earlier.

Perhaps these film adaptations of nineteenth-century novels were particularly popular in the 1990s because they preserved, in an altered form, the novels' atmosphere of feminine constriction and struggle and at the same time pointed toward a consoling unambiguous representation of feminist liberation. These films may have resonated with the contemporary woman viewer who, like Young's Jane Eyre, felt "restless" and "stifled." Women could identify with a cinema that represented visible forms of constraint that echoed the more amorphous incarcerations of their own lives. Easily visible clothed in the garments of the past, feelings of oppression and restriction caused by the often inexplicable complexities of modern life could be expressed in visible concrete forms and then assuaged by the suggestion that in the present women are relatively liberated. By providing the complex emotional experiences of women in the present with a point of identification in a constructed "oppressed past," these films point toward a utopian ideal of feminist triumph that consoled and concealed the harsher, more complex realities not only represented in the novels but also experienced, perhaps, in the lives of contemporary female audiences.

This new visual pleasure constructed for the 1990s female spectator combined eroticism with liberation in particularly alluring ways. These film adaptations developed and expressed the female erotic discourses that had always been submerged within the romantic plots of the novels and had always, in one way or another, existed in costume drama. Displacing the political feminist themes that the novels explored, these adaptations rejuvenated the marriage plot, represented it as feminist, and suggested that women could have it all. The cinema of the 1990s mined the British nineteenth-century novel for a female utopian fantasy of erotic fulfillment and feminist triumph. Providing audiences with a space in which to rest from the mainstream culture at large, they harked back to an erotic world that never was as they looked forward to an ideal liberated world that is not. Both nostalgic and utopian at once, these films sold well because in their translation of literary works from the past, they spoke to the deficiencies, anxieties, and dreams of the present.

6
Re-creating the Classics:
The Piano

Since its inception, the cinema has turned to the British nineteenth-century novel in search of narratives that would speak to twentieth-century audiences. Given the domestic themes of these novels, such adaptations always spoke to contemporary dreams and anxieties relating to women, marriage, and the home. In the 1930s and 1940s American adaptations used these narratives to construct traditional domestic ideals that had been challenged by social and cultural changes precipitated by the Depression and the Second World War. In Britain, adaptations of the 1930s and 1940s constructed images of women that furthered British cinema's larger goal of projecting an image of a unified nation successfully facing internal and external threats. Drawn more to writers such as Dickens and Eliot than the Brontës and Austen, British adaptations focused on Britain's social goals and marginalized women characters. Despite this exclusion, the adaptations reveal intense feelings about the relationship of women to British society. In the 1990s, British and American adaptations used the British domestic novel to address uncertainties about increasingly fluid gender identities, to assuage anxieties about feminism's uneven achievements, and to represent female sexuality in ways that were resistant to a mass culture increasingly catering to a male gaze. Whenever and wherever these adaptations were made, they made nineteenth-century novels conform to domestic ideals that were contemporary. However, British nineteenth-century novels resisted a seamless appropriation into the ideologies of the twentieth century. Every adaptation is ideologically uneven, unconsciously revealing the rifts that lie between the novels and the films.

Overall, adaptations made in Britain and America in the 1930s, 1940s, and 1990s represented the British nineteenth-century novel's portrayal of women in terms of contemporary domestic discourses. As the cinema negotiated the domestic novel's polyphonous representation of women's lives in the nineteenth century, it created novel women who differed substantially from their literary counterparts. By both translating and silencing different voices in their source texts, these adaptations appropriated nineteenth-century domestic fiction to create domestic plots that, in uncertain times, would project comforting images of women and their relationship to marriage, sexuality, and the home.

Among the many adaptations that were made in the twentieth century, *The Piano* (1993) stands out as unique. Although *The Piano* does not identify itself as an adaptation, it bears an important relationship to British nineteenth-century novels as well as to their cinematic adaptations. Although it is not a literal adaptation of a nineteenth-century domestic plot, Campion's work explores the themes of domestic fiction and employs its most familiar literary convention, the marriage plot. Despite drawing on the themes and plots of the British nineteenth-century novel, *The Piano* resists conventional modes of adaptation. Its complex relationship to the nineteenth-century novel and its adaptations makes *The Piano* a fitting intertext with which to conclude this review of the intertextual complexities of twentieth-century films adapted from British nineteenth-century novels.

Jane Campion has stated that she had planned to adapt *Wuthering Heights* before deciding to make *The Piano*, and she has identified Brontë's novel as the inspiration for her film.[1] In its depiction of a woman torn between two men and constricted by nineteenth-century culture, *The Piano* is rooted in the conventions of the nineteenth-century novel and is similar to *Jane Eyre* and especially *Wuthering Heights*. Campion has described *Wuthering Heights* as "a powerful poem about the romances of the soul."[2] Like the novel, the film posits a central female character whose soul is torn between two romantic choices that reflect larger psychic and cultural conflicts. Like the elder Cathy in *Wuthering Heights*, Ada is torn between a husband, Stuart, who is positioned within culture and George Baines, who lives outside culture, closer to nature. Like Linton, Stuart is, at least on the surface, polite, civilized, and good looking but devoid of imagination. Both men conform to the dominant cultural ideals of their time. In contrast, George Baines, like Heathcliff, resists dominant Western ideals. Baines lives in a little shack near a stable, reminiscent of the stable in which Heathcliff is made to live when Hindley wants to remind him of his excluded status. Even Jane Eyre's choice between the civilized St John and the less conformist, more naturally passionate Rochester is echoed in Ada's romantic dilemma. Like Jane and Cathy, Ada is torn between two men who also represent conflicting parts of herself.

Campion has been criticized for reproducing "a repertoire of colonial tropes" that marginalizes the Maoris and represents them as noble savages. As Dyson correctly points out, the Maoris "play 'nature' to the white characters' 'culture.'"[3] This problematic representation, however, is lifted out of the nineteenth-century novel, where "others" are used to represent the repressed inner forces of Western subjects and often function as metaphors for the oppression of women. Just as Charlotte Brontë has Jane make references to women in Eastern harems to emphasize her lack of power, so too Campion develops an analogy between the position of women and the position of colonized peoples.

The Brontës' symbolic use of imperial others travels into *The Piano*. In *Wuthering Heights*, it is because Heathcliff is a gypsy or Lascar, an imperial other, that he is able to stand outside British nineteenth-century culture. Brontë uses the appeal of Heathcliff's passions to expose deficiencies and absences in her own society. Since Heathcliff is an other who lives in Britain, he eventually learns enough about British cultural structures to be able to manipulate them to his advantage while retaining his non-British deeper passions. Baines, on the other hand, is British but learns from the Maoris, and later from Ada, to abandon his culture's imprisoning restrictions. Whereas Heathcliff represents the contortions an other goes through to live within British "civilization" and the losses this entails, Baines has left the metropolis physically and learns to give up the marks it has left on him internally. Baines becomes similar to the Maoris. Unlike Stuart, but like Heathcliff and especially the illiterate Hareton, Baines's working-class status makes him sufficiently marginal to make this journey possible. Like Hareton, Baines also, ultimately, makes a partial journey back to "civilization" when he finally moves from his shack to a small house near Nelson with Ada.

Campion develops the nature/culture theme so often identified in *Wuthering Heights* and uses the Maoris as figures in this binary opposition. In Campion's own words, "Civilization versus nature. That constitutes one of the greatest paradoxes of being human. To be cultivated and civilized on the one hand and on the other to have to deal with the worldly appetites and sexual drives and the romantic moments that derive from a completely different corner."[4] Although Campion obviously preserves the nature/culture binary, she also complicates it.

Campion reproduces the binary that William Wyler represented in his adaptation of *Wuthering Heights* to subvert her canonical precursor. After Ada's first sexual encounter with Baines, there is a shot of her standing at the edge of the forest that leads to his hut. From a close-up of Ada's highly wrought and elaborate hairdo the camera tracks backward, revealing the forest into which she is staring. Ada is torn between her attachment to culture, represented in her elaborate hairdo, and her sensuous attachment to Baines, figured by the forest. Like the heather in Wyler's adaptation of *Wuthering Heights*, the forest in *The Piano* represents the realm of natural passions, the place where Stuart's sexual passions get out of control, and the place where Ada's daughter rubs herself against trees. Ada is drawn to the natural forces she has discovered in her relationship with Baines. In this scene, the way in which Ada positions her arm across her back and the backward-tracking shot, as well as her hairdo, are reminiscent of a shot in Wyler's film that tracks backward out of Linton's window as it shows Catherine and Linton standing with their backs to the camera as he embraces her, resting his arm across her back. Tracking out of the window through which Cathy had first seen all the nice dresses she hoped Linton could buy her, Wyler's image emblematizes Cathy's imprisonment in the world of commodities she had desired. In *The Piano*, from an early shot of Ada, in a home that appears to imprison her, staring wistfully out of a window to the later explicit images of Stuart confining Ada to his home with wooden planks and locks, Campion also represents the home as a prison that separates her protagonist from her natural passions.

Despite their similar development of the nature/culture theme and their shared representation of Linton's/Stuart's homes as a type of prison, Wyler's and Campion's films have significant differences. Ada, unlike Wyler's Cathy, does not imprison herself in a marriage because of her desire to have "pretty things." Campion represents Ada/Catherine not as hungry for commodities but as a commodity herself. When Stuart first meets Ada on the beach, he is perplexed by her preference for her piano over her clothes and utensils. Campion emphasizes that Ada is not attached to material possessions.

Instead, Ada is a material possession. Unlike a classic Hollywood adaptation, such as *Pride and Prejudice* (1940), which opens with a shopping scene in which women are buying commodities, *The Piano* starts with the tale of a woman being bartered like a commodity. Ada is being sent to Stuart as the result of an exchange between men. After the exchange, in accordance with nineteenth-century British law, Ada is her husband's property and cannot own any property of her own. This is made clear when she arrives on the beach and is unable to keep her own piano because all her goods now belong to Stuart. When Ada stamps her foot and writes on a note that the piano "is mine," she is saying something that is not legally true, and Stuart follows the law. As has often been noted, the piano is also a metaphor for Ada herself. Like her piano,

Ada is owned property. The same type of wood that boxes up her piano is later used by Stuart to box Ada up in his house.

Stuart sees all possessions as equal and believes that everything has an exchange value. Just as Stuart cannot understand why the Maori would not want to sell a burial ground, he cannot understand Ada's attachment to her piano. He is unable to distinguish between a burial ground, Ada's piano, and clothing and utensils. In addition, he sees Ada in terms of his colonial will to master, possess, and own land, goods, and people. When Baines returns Ada's piano, Stuart cannot fathom why Baines would give it to him without requiring land in exchange. He also cannot understand that, as Baines states, the property is being returned to his wife and not himself. Stuart is unable to see his wife as an autonomous being who can own her own property. Stuart cannot see his marriage outside of his culture's notions of commercial and colonial exchange.

Baines is contrasted with Stuart. Although Baines starts out by attempting to buy Ada using the piano as barter, he eventually refuses this commercial exchange and lets her choose him of her own free will. In his refusal to turn her into a "whore," he resists a nineteenth-century culture that defined women as purchasable property. At one point, Baines tells one of the Maoris that he has left his wife in England because she has a "life of her own." Unlike Stuart, Baines is capable of seeing women as autonomous subjects. By portraying Ada as an object of exchange and critiquing this cultural model, Campion exposes and subverts Wyler's representation of *Wuthering Heights*. Whereas Wyler represents culture as a site in which women desire to buy goods, Campion represents culture as a site in which women are inscribed as goods. She deconstructs Wyler's insistence on women as active agents in a commodity culture and represents women as passive objects in an oppressive culture. Wyler critiques women for wanting to buy goods; Campion critiques the culture for turning women into goods.

Campion also revises another canonical precursor, the 1944 classic adaptation of *Jane Eyre*. *The Piano* inverts the classic film's positive characterization of Adèle, an idealization that enables a representation of Jane's sexuality as deeply tied to her maternal instincts. In Stevenson's 1944 adaptation, Adèle facilitates Jane's relationship with Rochester; Jane's sexual feelings are depicted as developing in parallel to and through her affection for Adèle. In *The Piano* women's relationships to children are represented very differently. Unlike Hollywood's sweet idealized illegitimate child Adèle, Ada's illegitimate daughter Flora is angry, possessive, jealous, and destructive. Motherhood and sexuality are in direct conflict. The child is jealous of her mother's sexual objects of desire because they are not integral to, but rather displace, maternal feelings. Thus, although many critics have identified *The Piano* as rooted in the nineteenth-century gothic novel, and some have interpreted it as an adaptation of *Wuthering Heights*, it is also important to remember that Jane Campion is as interested in the history of film as she is in literature. *The Piano* enters into a long tradition of film adaptations of the British nineteenth-century novel, and Campion attempts to reshape and redefine that tradition.

The Piano also bears an oppositional relationship to other adaptations made in the 1990s. Most 1990s adaptations give women expressive powers the novels show women to have lacked, but Campion explores the limits and paradoxes of female expression in a patriarchal culture. As mentioned in the previous chapter, the 1992 adaptation of *Wuthering Heights* starts and ends with shots of a woman wandering over the moors as a female voiceover narrates the story. Indirectly referencing Emily Brontë and Nelly, the adaptation erases the narrative frames the novel uses. Lockwood, who tells the story of Nelly, who tells the story of Catherine, is erased from an adaptation that gives women direct and unmediated access to cultural discourses. Ellis Bell has been forgotten. In the adaptations that followed *The Piano*, women characters, even those beset by male violence and abuse, are able to express feminist views and tell their story. Campion, in contrast, preserves the tendency of nineteenth-century novels to represent women as disempowered and silenced by creating a character who narrates the story but is also mute. *The Piano* thematizes, rather than elides, the problem of female expression in patriarchal cultures as it explores the relationship between language, art, and power.

Campion is interested in the woman artist. In an interview, Campion mentions Emily Brontë's silences: "It is incredible after all that such a story came out of this small woman, who had hardly seen anything of the world. Emily Brontë spoke barely a word when she went out, and she left her hometown Howarth very rarely."[5] Elsewhere Campion again says of Brontë that "she had a certain disdain for society and didn't like to speak in public. Charlotte took her out with her friends and she didn't say a word."[6] Campion's view of Brontë is echoed in Ada's characterization. Small and powerful, like Emily Brontë, Ada is silent but expressive through art. Fusing the character Cathy with her creator, Campion explores the nineteenth-century woman artist's relationship to the culture that both silenced her and gave her a voice.

Michael Davis has convincingly dismissed feminist critiques that see Ada's silence as an act of resistance.[7] Ada's muteness is a symbolic representation of her disempowered position in society. Her reliance on her piano, though, points to the fact that it was through art that some nineteenth-century women gained access to cultural discourses. In their haste to assess how feminist the film is, many critics have overlooked its central focus on the role of art for women. Cyndy Hendershot, for example, claims that "Ada's strained relationship with the symbolic is voluntary: she resigns speech in favor of signs."[8] It is important, however, that the signs Ada chooses are signs used in art forms. Ada minimizes her use of literal concrete language and instead communicates through the use of dramatic body language, sensuous piano playing, parables, and metaphors. For instance, when Ada describes Flora's father, she says of him, "I didn't need to speak. I could lay thoughts out in his mind like they were a sheet." Ada seeks a sensuous communion beyond words, something she finds with the illiterate Baines. Yet, even in her description of this desire, she uses a metaphor and reveals her reliance on the figurative language of art. Ada's story about Flora's father could be as creative as the one about the opera singer hit by lightning, the one Flora narrates and Campion animates. True communication, as opposed to what Flora, or Ada, calls the "rubbish" most people speak, is imaginative, sensuous, and beautiful. Although this language is sensuous and in that sense connected to nature, it is also deeply rooted in a Western culture that impinges on women's desires. As Campion notes, "There are symbolic signs of European culture, especially the piano which is a civilized instrument, that intrude on a world that is much more elementary and primitive."[9] Unlike Wyler's Cathy, who craves the commodities of her culture, or Brontë's Cathy, who craves its social benefits, Ada is tied to European culture because it gives her the keys to expressing her inner being even though it also intrudes on her more "elementary" passions. Ada is bound to her culture the way Brontë was.

In other words, the film suggests that it is not in silence that women find their resistance but in art. The same culture that confines women and silences them also gives them keys to self-expression. Although Emily Brontë might have been silent, her novel has transcended that silence. However, as art is rooted in a culture that constricts women, it exacts a heavy toll. Through art, women writers of the nineteenth century gave voice to the ways their society and culture silenced them – but, suggests Campion, at a price. Often drawing on French feminist ideas, as Michael Davis has suggested, Campion reveals that taking up the position of a speaking subject in a patriarchal symbolic order involves a considerable cost.[10]

The Piano avoids the kind of feminist triumphalism that characterizes most 1990s adaptations, a triumphalism many feminist critics have erroneously read into the film. Unlike other adaptations made just before and after, *The Piano* does not represent a world in which women can have it all. Sex, love, art, and power collide and conflict painfully and destructively.

By avoiding literal adaptation of a specific novel, *The Piano* is able to represent the themes of many nineteenth-century novels in a more archetypal way. Unlike in adaptations such as *The Tenant of Wildfell Hall* where individual flawed men are responsible for violence against women, agency for the violence enacted upon Ada is attributed as much to his culture as to Stuart. Campion invests male acts of violence with a mythic and symbolic layer of meaning that resists the limited representations of male violence used in other adaptations of the decade. Disturbingly graphic, Stuart's violence does not occur comfortably off screen. Starting with attempted rapes and climaxing when Stuart chops off Ada's finger with an axe, violence has a deeper resonance in *The Piano* than in subsequent films.

By making her male perpetrator less one-dimensionally evil than similar characters in other adaptations, Campion gives the violence a broader import. Stuart is not a womanizing drunken brute like Huntington in *The Tenant of Wildfell Hall*, someone who rapes slaves like Sir Thomas in *Mansfield Park*, or a man who sexually abuses little children like Glyde in *The Woman in White*. Unlike Huntingdon, Glyde, or Sir Thomas, Stuart is not an evil person. He is generally well meaning and acts kindly toward Ada, even waiting patiently, most of the time, for her to become more "affectionate." Stuart is a dull conventional man who lacks imagination. He has a very literal sense of the world that clashes with Ada's attachment to the world of imagination and art. When Stuart finds Ada playing the kitchen table as though it were a piano, he is alarmed and thinks her insane. He lacks the artistic imagination that would enable him to see a table metaphorically. His lack of imagination also makes it impossible for him to see outside of his culture's gender categories. He lacks the imaginative resources that enable Baines to transcend his cultural inscription.

Even when Stuart tries to rape Ada, it is as much a sign of his powerlessness, his castration, as it is of his power.[11] Unlike Huntingdon, Stuart tries to rape Ada only under the extreme circumstance of having witnessed her having sex with Baines. In fact, most of the time Stuart is sexually repressed, his sexual repression being yet another symptom of the ways in which he is unable to resist his culture's norms. The repression that confines Stuart as he tries to behave like a gentleman and conform to his culture's expectations for men of his class is what intensifies his violence when it finally erupts in a jealous rage. Like Linton, who has a cruel streak beneath his cultured exterior – exhibited in his attitude to his sister for instance – Stuart ultimately erupts in violence, but only in temporary bursts. He is not a brute or a villain all the time. Unlike the other abusers of 1990s adaptations, he is eventually able to "hear" Ada's voice. At the end of the film, he tells Baines that he could hear her will telling him to let her go. Stuart is disgusted with his more violent self and relieved to be able to part with Ada and the disruptive forces she has engendered in him. Although Stuart is certainly oppressive and violent, he is, like Ada, a victim of his culture. He is not, as in other adaptations of the decade, simply a male perpetrator; he is a conduit for the larger oppressive forces of Western culture.

The symbolic terms in which Ada's mutilation is represented accentuate these cultural dimensions. Ada's amputation is prefigured throughout the film. In the play about Bluebeard, he is shown about to chop off his wife's hand. Campion clearly situates male violence in the mythic subconscious of Western culture as it has been expressed in fables. She also evokes *Jane Eyre*'s many references to Rochester as Bluebeard, reinserting a subtext missing from the 1944 film. Campion provides her representation of male violence with psychic and cultural layers absent from adaptations made later in the decade.

Another foreshadowing of Ada's amputation is the three-legged dog who hovers around Stuart when he watches Baines and Ada have sex. Although it initially seems that the dog represents Stuart's phallic lack, it is later clear that it references Ada as well. These suggestions of castration symbolically associate sexuality with maiming and loss. Ada's mutilation is also prefigured by her own dismembering of her piano – consistently represented as her double – when she takes out a key on which she writes of her love to her illiterate lover. Ada's daughter does not take Baines the piano key; she takes him Ada's severed finger in its place. Ada's message of love is mutilated and transfigured. *The Piano* suggests that sexual desire, at least within patriarchal structures, is necessarily destructive and involves a loss of self. Ada's piano and then her hand lose their key and finger, their expressive capacities. When she finds sexual expression, Ada relinquishes artistic expression. Michael Davis argues that Ada needs to relinquish the piano because it binds her to a pre-Oedipal fantasy of power, to a maternal phallic omnipotence that Campion represents as destructive. He claims that to survive Ada must sever herself from the "deathly unconscious phantasy which underpins her relationship with this object."[12] Although this may be true on a deep psychological level, the loss of the piano is not represented positively in the film. The film's obvious love of art, expressed in its own cinematic artistry, as well as in the plot that valorizes the characters who have artistic imagination, suggests that the loss of the piano is a painful, not desirable, diminishing of Ada's self and her artistic powers.

Unlike other adaptations of the 1990s, this film emphasizes that within unequal power structures, art and love, free expression and romance, cannot co-exist. In striking contrast with subsequent adaptations, the end of the film refuses an optimistic closure in which women can have it all.

Like most British nineteenth-century novels, *The Piano* ends ambiguously. Closing with marriages that seem to provide their female characters with romantic fulfillment, the novels also undercut their conventional marriage plots. In *Wuthering Heights*, for example, the marriage of the second generation appears to be a balanced, civilized resolution of the troubles afflicting the older generation. Catherine and Hareton enter into a marriage that seems more egalitarian as a more powerful, younger Catherine educates Hareton and they build a cultivated home, symbolized by the gardens Catherine has Hareton plant. Catherine has a say over the shape her home will take. Nevertheless, the milder younger generation is far less compelling than the older generation hovering over the novel's conclusion. The forces of disruption Heathcliff represents are not really contained by the novel's tame ending. The alternative ending to the novel's traditional marriage plot, Heathcliff and Cathy walking the moors married in death, is eerily disturbing and disrupts the happier, more harmonious domestic resolution.

The Piano also subverts its own marriage plot. On the one hand, Baines is a highly idealized romantic partner who has some affinity with the new ideals of masculinity represented in other 1990s adaptations. *The Piano* goes even further than other films in constructing a male object of desire by undressing Baines completely for the female spectator. Other images are also sexually suggestive; the scene in which Baines attentively caresses the hole in Ada's stocking and the scene in which he buries his face under Ada's skirt suggest he is skilled at attending to women's sexual needs. In addition to being sexually desirable, like other male heroes of the 1990s he takes good care of children and places Ada at the center of his life even though he does not wish to possess her. Although he is as sexually potent and passionate as Heathcliff, he is in no way violent and renounces his possessive tendencies. Like other

1990s adaptations, *The Piano* has a female-oriented sexual narrative that constructs a desirable masculine ideal.

On one level, the ending of the film satisfies the viewer's longing for romantic closure as the idealized Baines finally lives with Ada in a neat little house. One critic, for example, claims that Ada experiences a "figurative rebirth," that she "enacts her own physical and spiritual baptism. The self that emerges is freer and more autonomous. Once she arrives in Nelson, we see Ada's self begin, with George's aid, its arduous but satisfying journey into self-determination, self-fulfillment, and self-revelation."[13] Interpretations such as these that emphasize Ada's eventual achievement of autonomy and fulfillment, her liberation, read the ending of the film as constructing a feminist marriage plot. On one level, such an interpretation is valid, but such an ending is also resisted by Campion.

After Ada allows herself to be trapped in the ropes of her piano and pulled by it to the depths of the ocean, her "will," as she says, chooses to live. However, Ada's resurfacing is shown in a series of discontinuous slow-motion shots. The editing makes this part of the film look like a sequence that commercial film editors would use to communicate a dream or a flashback. There is a suggestion that this "rebirth" is not as "real" as the rest of the narrative. Flora's cartwheels are shot not – as they are the first time she does them on the beach – at a normal speed but in the same slow, disjunctive way as Ada's resurfacing from the ocean. Her cartwheels, reminiscent of Adèle's in the 1944 *Jane Eyre*, seem dreamlike, more idealized than real. The "reality" of Ada's rebirth as a domestic woman, as a mother and wife, is put into question. In addition, the shot of Ada playing the piano with a silver finger whose clicking disrupts her music foregrounds her mutilation and reminds the viewer of her lost art. Before she was mute; now she is mutilated. In regaining her speaking voice, she has lost her music, her artistic voice. Although integrated to some extent in Nelson, she is still seen as a freak. In the next shot, Ada is shown walking outside with a black scarf that looks like a veil over her head. Her previous wedding, enacted only through the wearing of wedding clothes, is mirrored here. Baines catches her sensuously and lifts the black veil to kiss her. In this play on a wedding scene, the veil is black, signifying death. After the fatal marriage kiss, the film cuts to the ocean floor, which Ada calls, in the voiceover, her grave. Romantic fulfillment and artistic death are intertwined. The last shot of the film is not of the neat little house in Nelson but of the piano, with keys missing, in the depths of its ocean grave, with Ada, balloonlike, floating emptily above it still bound to her buried soul. The film ends, appropriately, on a note of silence as Ada recites a poem written by Thomas Hood.

> There is a silence where hath been no sound,
> There is a silence where no sound may be,
> In a cold grave – under the deep deep sea,

The final image of the film is not triumphal but dark and paradoxical. *The Piano* ends on a note of silence as Ada's music is displaced by Thomas Hood's poetry. Silenced yet heard, willful yet powerless, Ada embodies the contradictions of the female experience in the nineteenth, and perhaps the twentieth, centuries. By articulating the forced silences of women's lives, *The Piano* invokes what made the novels of the nineteenth century so alluring to the women of the twentieth century. Yet, just as Thomas Hood's words silence Ada's as they articulate her death, so too the adaptations of the twentieth century have articulated and silenced the voices of women from the past.

Notes

Introduction

1. "The Twenty Five Most Intriguing People of 1995," *People Weekly*, December 25, 1995.
2. John R. Harvey, *Victorian Novelists and Their Illustrators* (New York: New York University Press, 1970), 8.
3. Ibid., 33.
4. Kamilla Elliott, *Rethinking the Novel/Film Debate* (Cambridge: Cambridge University Press, 2003), 46.
5. Ibid., 3.
6. Sergei Eisenstein, "Dickens, Griffith and the Film Today," in *Film Form*, ed. and trans. Jay Leyda (New York: Harcourt Brace and Company, 1949), 195–256.
7. Elliott, *Novel/Film*, 96.
8. Ibid., 81.
9. Robert B. Ray, "The Field of Literature and Film," in *Film Adaptation*, ed. James Naremore (New Brunswick: Rutgers University Press, 2000), 44.
10. Ibid., 45–46.
11. Robert T. Self, "A Canon at Century's End" (paper presented at the annual Society for Cinema Studies Conference, Chicago, March 9–12, 2000).
12. James Naremore, ed., *Film Adaptation* (New Brunswick: Rutgers University Press, 2000), 10.
13. Deborah Cartmell and Imelda Whelehan, eds., *Adaptations: From Text to Screen, Screen to Text* (London: Routledge, 1999).
14. Michael Dunne, *Intertextual Encounters in American Fiction, Film, and Popular Culture* (Bowling Green: Bowling Green State University Popular Press, 2001).
15. Robert Stam, *Literature through Film: Realism, Magic and the Art of Adaptation* (Malden: Blackwell Publishing, 2005); Robert Stam and Alessandra Raengo, *A Companion to Literature and Film* (Malden: Blackwell Publishers, 2004); Robert Stam and Alessandra Raengo, *Literature and Film: A Guide to the Theory and Practice of Film Adaptation* (Malden: Blackwell Publishing, 2005).
16. Robert Giddings and Erica Sheen, eds., *The Classic Novel: From Page to Screen* (Manchester: Manchester University Press, 2000), 8.
17. Linda Troost and Sayre Greenfield, eds., *Jane Austen in Hollywood* (Lexington: Kentucky University Press, 1998).
18. Lisa Hopkins, *Screening the Gothic* (Austin: University of Texas Press, 2005).
19. Mary Poovey, *Uneven Developments: The Ideological Work of Gender in Mid-Victorian England* (Chicago: University of Chicago Press, 1988), 8–9.
20. Ibid., 64.
21. Ibid., 166.
22. Sarah S. Ellis, *The Daughters of England: Their Position in Society, Character and Responsibilities* (New York: D. Appleton and Company, 1842), 61–62.

23. Jeffrey L. Spear, *Dreams of an English Eden: Ruskin and His Tradition in Social Criticism* (New York: Columbia University Press, 1984), 172.

24. Caroline Norton, *A Letter to the Queen on Lord Chancellor Cranworth's Marriage and Divorce Bill* (London: Longman, Brown, Green and Longmans, 1855), 4–13, quoted in Poovey, *Uneven Developments*, 64.

25. Kate Ellis and E. Ann Kaplan, "Feminism in Brontë's Novel and Its Film Versions," in *The English Novel and the Movies*, ed. Michael Klein and Gillian Parker (New York: Frederick Unger, 1981), 83–94.

26. See, for example, Julian North, "Conservative Austen, Radical Austen: *Sense and Sensibility* from Text to Screen," in *Adaptations*, ed. Cartmell and Whelehan, 38–50.

27. Nancy Armstrong, *Desire and Domestic Fiction: A Political History of the Novel* (New York: Oxford University Press, 1987), 5–6.

28. Sue Harper, *Picturing the Past: The Rise and Fall of the British Costume Film* (London: British Film Institute, 1994), 179.

29. Pam Cook, *Fashioning the Nation: Costume and Identity in British Cinema* (London: British Film Institute, 1996), 3.

30. Stella Bruzzi, *Undressing Cinema: Clothing and Identity in the Movies* (London: Routledge, 1997), 38.

1 Consuming Women: *Pride and Prejudice* and *Wuthering Heights*

1. Warren I. Sussman, *Culture As History: The Transformation of American Society in the Twentieth Century* (New York: Pantheon, 1973), 2.

2. Stuart Ewan, *Captains of Consciousness* (New York: McGraw-Hill Book Company, 1976), 53.

3. Rita Barnard, *The Great Depression and the Culture of Abundance* (Cambridge: Cambridge University Press, 1995), 28.

4. For a full discussion of Hollywood glamour and its economic and social significance, see Sarah Berry, *Screen Style: Fashion and Femininity in 1930s Hollywood* (Minneapolis: University of Minnesota Press, 2000).

5. Mary Ann Doane, *The Desire to Desire: The Woman's Film of the 1940s* (Bloomington: Indiana University Press, 1987), 24.

6. Rachel Brownstein, "Out of the Drawing Room, onto the Lawn," in *Jane Austen in Hollywood*, ed. Linda Troost and Sayre Greenfield (Lexington: University Press of Kentucky, 1998), 14.

7. Brown, Ivor. Ed. *Four Plays of 1936*. London: H. Hamilton, 1936.

8. Robert Lawson-Peebles, "European Conflict and Hollywood's Reconstruction of English Fiction." *Yearbook of English Studies* 26 (1996): 1.

9. Ibid., 10–13.

10. Edward Copeland, *Women Writing about Money: Women's Fiction in England, 1790–1820* (Cambridge: Cambridge University Press, 1995), 89–90.

11. Ibid., 98.

12. James Thompson, "Jane Austen's Clothing," *Studies in Eighteenth Century Culture* 13 (1984): 219.

13. Copeland, *Women Writing*, 137.

14. Judith Lowder Newton, *Women, Power and Subversion: Social Strategies in British Fiction* (Athens: University of Georgia Press, 1981), 130; for further discussion, see also Claudia Johnson, *Jane Austen: Women, Politics and the Novel* (Chicago: University of Chicago Press, 1988).
15. Newton, *Women*,134.
16. Karen Newman, "Can This Marriage Be Saved: Jane Austen Makes Sense of an Ending," in *Sense and Sensibility and Pride and Prejudice*, ed. Robert Clark (New York: St. Martin's Press, 1994), 199.
17. Jane Austen, *Pride and Prejudice* (London: Penguin Books, 1985), 165–166.
18. Julia Prewitt Brown, *Jane Austen's Novels : Social Change and Literary Form* (Cambridge: Harvard University Press, 1979), 74.
19. *Pride and Prejudice*, dir. Robert Z. Leonard (MGM, 1940), shooting script, the New York Public Library for the Performing Arts, 110.
20. Sussman, *Culture As History*, xxi.
21. Stuart Ewan, *Captains of Consciousness* 155, 53.
22. Alice Kessler-Harris, *Out to Work: A History of Wage Earning Women in the United States* (Oxford: Oxford University Press, 1982), 251; Ruth Milkman, "Women's Work and the Economic Crisis: Some Lessons from the Great Depression," in *A Heritage of Her Own: Toward a New Social History of American Women* (New York: Simon and Schuster, 1979), 508.
23. Michael E. Parrish, *Anxious Decades: America in Prosperity and Depression, 1920–1941* (New York: W.W. Norton and Company, 1992), 401.
24. Winnifred D. Wandersee, *Women's Work and Family Values, 1920–1940* (Cambridge: Harvard University Press, 1981), 106.
25. William Henry Chafe, *The American Woman: Her Changing Social, Economic, and Political Roles, 1920–1970* (London: Oxford University Press, 1972), 62.
26. Kessler-Harris, *Out to Work*, 55.
27. Robert L. Daniel, *American Women in the 20th Century: The Festival of Life* (San Diego: Harcourt Brace Jovanovich, 1987), 92.
28. Kessler-Harris, *Out to Work*, 251.
29. Maria LaPlace, "Producing and Consuming the Woman's Film: Discursive Struggle in *Now, Voyager*," in *Home Is Where the Heart Is*, ed. Christine Gledhill (London: British Film Institute, 1994), 145.
30. Joseph Wiesenfarth, "The Garson-Olivier *Pride and Prejudice*: A Hollywood Story," in *Text und Tom im Film*, ed. Paul Goetsch and Dietrich Scheunemann (Tubingen: Gunter Narr Verlag Tubingen, 1997), 83–84.
31. Mary McComb, "Rate Your Date: Young Women and the Commodification of Depression Era Courtship," in *Delinquents and Debutantes: Twentieth Century American Girls' Cultures*, ed. Sherrie A. Inness (New York: New York University Press, 1998), 45.
32. Ibid., 49.
33. Lea Jacobs, *The Wages of Sin: Censorship and the Fallen Woman Film, 1928–1942* (Madison: University of Wisconsin Press, 1991), 133.
34. Ibid., 152.
35. George Bluestone, *Novels into Films* (Berkeley: University of California Press, 1973); John Harrington, "Wyler As Auteur," in *The English Novel and the Movies*, ed. Michael Klein and Gillian Parker (New York: Frederick Unger, 1981); Pamela Mills, "Wyler's Version of Brontë's Storms in *Wuthering Heights*," *Literature/Film Quarterly* 24 (1996).

36. Robert Jay Nash and Stanley Ralph Ross, *The Motion Picture Guide W–Z 1927–1984* (Chicago: Cinebooks, 1987), 3936.
37. Bluestone, *Novels into Films*, 99, 98.
38. Lawson-Peebles, "European Conflict," 6.
39. Ibid., 7.
40. *Wuthering Heights*, dir. William Wyler (United Artists, 1939), shooting script, the New York Public Library for the Performing Arts, 32–33.
41. Ibid., 51–55.
42. Nash and Ross, *Motion Picture Guide*, 3936.
43. Doane, *Desire to Desire*, 32–33.
44. *Wuthering Heights*, shooting script, 54–56.
45. David Cecil, *Early Victorian Novelists: Essays in Revaluation* (Indianapolis: Bobbs-Merrill, 1935); Dorothy Bendon Van Ghent, *The English Novel, Form and Function* (New York: Rinehart, 1953); H. M. Daleski, *The Divided Heroine: A Recurrent Pattern in Six English Novels* (New York: Homes and Meier, 1984).
46. Terry Eagleton, *Myths of Power: A Marxist Study of the Brontës* (London: Macmillan, 1975), 116–118.
47. See, for example, Carolyn Heilbrun, *Towards Androgyny: Aspects of Male and Female in Literature* (London: Gollanz, 1971), 79–82; Ellen Moers, *Literary Women* (London: The Women's Press, 1976); Sandra M. Gilbert and Susan Gubar, *The Madwoman in the Attic: The Woman Writer and the Nineteenth-Century Literary Imagination* (New Haven: Yale University Press, 1984).
48. Patsy Stoneman, "Catherine Earnshaw's Journey to Her Home among the Dead: Fresh Thoughts on *Wuthering Heights* and '"Epipsychidion"'," *Review of English Studies* 47 (1996): 530.
49. Ibid., 532.
50. *Wuthering Heights*, shooting script, 132–133.
51. For similar discussions see Naomi Jacobs, "Gender and Layered Narrative in *Wuthering Heights* and *The Tenant of Wildfell Hall*," *Journal of Narrative Technique* 16, no. 3 (1986): 204–219; Carol Senf, "Emily Brontë's Version of Feminist History – *Wuthering Heights*," *Essays in Literature* 12 (1985): 204–214. For a contrasting view see Anita Levy, "The History of Desire in *Wuthering Heights*," *Genre* 19, no. 4 (Winter 1986): 409–430.
52. Lyn Pykett, *The "Improper" Feminine: The Women's Sensation Novel and the New Woman Writing* (London: Routledge, 1992), 92.

2 Maternal Desire: *Jane Eyre*

1. Elizabeth Bowen, *English Novelists* (London: W. Collins, 1942), 141, 35.
2. Norman Collins, *The Facts of Fiction* (New York: E.P. Dutton, 1933), 181.
3. George Sampson, *Concise Cambridge History of English Literature* (Cambridge: Cambridge University Press, 1941), 181, 788.
4. Cecil, *Early Victorian Novelists* (see Chapter 1, n. 42).
5. Elizabeth Atkins, "Jane Eyre Transformed," *Literature/Film Quarterly* 21, no. 1 (1993): 54.

6. Kate Ellis and E. Ann Kaplan, "Feminism in Brontë's Novel," 84–85 (see Introduction, n. 24).

7. Jeffrey Sconce, "Narrative Authority and Social Narrativity: The Cinematic Reconstitution of Brontë's *Jane Eyre*," *Wide-Angle: A Film Quarterly of Theory, Criticism, and Practice* 10, no. 1 (1988): 52.

8. Natalie McNight, *Suffering Mothers in Mid-Victorian Novels* (New York: St. Martin's Press, 1997), 57.

9. Carolyn Dever, *Death and the Mother from Dickens to Freud: Victorian Fiction and the Anxiety of Origins* (New York: Cambridge University Press, 1998), 31.

10. Chafe, *American Woman*, 135 (see Chapter 1, n. 22).

11. Ibid., 136.

12. Ibid., 137.

13. Susan Hartmann, *The Home Front and Beyond: American Women in the 1940s* (Boston: Twayne, 1982), 77.

14. Maureen Honey, *Creating Rosie the Riveter: Class, Gender, and Propaganda during World War II* (Amherst: University of Massachusetts Press, 1984), 20–21.

15. Ibid.,19.

16. Chafe, *American Woman*, 79–80

17. Hartmann, *The Home Front*, 78.

18. Chafe, *American Woman*, 165.

19. Hartmann, *The Home Front*, 181.

20. Ibid., 82.

21. Chafe, *American Woman*, 165.

22. Honey, *Creating Rosie*, 6–7.

23. Ibid., 119.

24. Honey, *Creating Rosie*, 124–125

25. Ibid., 125.

26. Hartmann, *Home Front*, 125.

27. Honey, *Creating Rosie*, 137.

28. Atkins, "*Jane Eyre* Transformed," 55.

29. Honey, *Creating Rosie*, 124.

30. Sconce, "Narrative Authority," 52.

31. John Maynard, *Charlotte Bronte and Sexuality* (Cambridge: Cambridge University Press, 1984), 10–14.

32. Judith Mitchell, *The Stone and the Scorpion: The Female Subject of Desire in the Novels of Charlotte Brontë, George Eliot and Thomas Hardy* (Westport: Greenwood, 1944), 46–49.

33. Doane, *Desire to Desire*, 129, 137 (see Chapter 1, n. 4).

34. Ibid., 135.

35. Doris Weatherford, *American Women and World War II* (New York: Facts on File, 1990), 254–256.

36. Tania Modleski, *The Women Who Knew Too Much: Hitchcock and Feminist Theory* (New York: Routledge, 1988), 51–52.

37. Ibid., 46.

38. Gilbert and Gubar, *Madwoman in the Attic*, 339 (see Chapter 1, n. 44).

39. Doane, *Desire to Desire*, 135.

40. Sconce, "Narrative Authority", 56–57.
41. Charlotte Brontë, *Jane Eyre* (London: Penguin 1985), 141.

3   Recovering Victorian Ideals: *The Mill on the Floss*

1. Brian McFarlane, "A Literary Cinema? British Films and British Novels," in *All Our Yesterdays: 90 Years of British Cinema*, ed. Charles Barr (London: British Film Institute, 1986), 120–121.
2. Martin Pugh, *State and Society: British Political and Social History, 1870–1992* (London: Edward Arnold, 1994), 167–172.
3. Peter Miles and Malcom Smith, *Cinema, Literature and Society* (London: Croom Helm, 1987), 14–15.
4. Jane McDonnell, " 'Perfect Goodness' or 'the Wider Life': *The Mill on the Floss* As *Bildungsroman*," *Genre* 15, no. 4 (1982): 399–400.
5. Kristin Brady, *George Eliot* (New York: St. Martin's Press, 1992), 94.
6. Charlotte Goodman, "The Lost Brother, the Twin: Women Novelists and the Male Female Double Bildungsroman," *Novel* 17 (1983): 34.
7. Susan Fraiman, "*The Mill on the Floss*, the Critics, and the *Bildungsroman*," *PMLA* 108 (1993): 140.
8. Martin Pugh, *Women and the Women's Movement in Britain, 1914–1959* (London: Macmillan, 1992), 224.
9. Ibid., 212.
10. Jane Lewis, "In Search of Real Equality: Women between the Wars," in *Class, Culture and Social Change: A New View of the 1930s*, ed. Frank Gloversmith (Brighton: Harvester, 1980), 213.
11. Pugh, *Women*, 225–226.
12. Virginia Woolf, *Three Guineas* (San Diego: Harcourt Brace and Company, 1986), 30.
13. Edward Royle, *Modern Britain: A Social History 1750–1997* (London: Arnold, 1997), 387.
14. Woolf, *Three Guineas*, 51.
15. Fraiman, *Mill*, 140.
16. Marcia Landy, *British Genres: Cinema and Society, 1930–1960* (Princeton: Princeton University Press, 1991), 194.
17. Ibid., 195.
18. Raymond Durgnat, *A Mirror for England: British Movies from Austerity to Affluence* (New York: Praeger, 1971), 178.
19. Anthony Aldgate and Jeffrey Richards, *Best of British: Cinema and Society from 1930 to the Present* (London: I.B. Tauris, 199), 42.
20. Miles and Smith, *Cinema, Literature and Society*, 25.
21. For a summary of different perspectives on Maggie's sacrifice see Susan Fraiman, "*Mill*"; Sally Shuttleworth, ed., *The Mill on the Floss by George Eliot* (London: Routledge, 1991), 487–514.
22. George Eliot, *The Mill on the Floss* (New York: W.W. Norton and Company, 1994), 382.
23. Ibid., 417.
24. John Ruskin, "Of Queens' Gardens," in *Sesame and Lilies*, ed. J. W. Linn (Chicago: Scott, Foreman and Company, 1904), 88.

4   Twisted Femininities: *Great Expectations* and *Oliver Twist*

1. Stephen Watts, "Britain Makes Her Greatest Film," *Sunday Express*, December 15, 1946.
2. C. A. Lejeune, "Drawn by Cruikshank," *The Times*, June 27, 1948.
3. Antonia Lant, *Blackout: Reinventing Women for Cinema* (Princeton: Princeton University Press, 1991), 6.
4. Jeffrey Richards, *Films and British National Identity: From Dickens to Dad's Army* (Manchester: Manchester University Press, 1997), 133–134.
5. Ibid., 341.
6. Regina Barreca, "David Lean's *Great Expectations*," in *Dickens on Screen*, ed. John Glavin (Cambridge: Cambridge University Press, 2003), 43–44.
7. Richards, *Films*, 129.
8. Lesley A. Hall, *Sex, Gender and Social Change in Britain since 1880* (New York: St. Martin's, 2000), 146.
9. Jeffrey Weeks, *Sex, Politics and Society: The Regulation of Sexuality since 1800* (London: Longman, 1989), 240.
10. Catherine Waters, *Dickens and the Politics of the Family* (Cambridge: Cambridge University Press, 1997), 35.
11. Deborah Heller, "The Outcast As Villain and Victim: Jews in Dickens's *Oliver Twist* and *Our Mutual Friend*," in *Jewish Presences in English Literature*, ed. Derek Cohen and Deborah Heller (Montreal: McGill-Queen's University Press, 1990), 44–45.
12. Charles Dickens, *Oliver Twist* (London: Penguin, 1985), 186.
13. Ibid., 478–479.
14. Gail Turley Houston, *Consuming Fictions: Gender, Class and Hunger in Dickens' Novels* (New York: St. Martin's Press, 1997), 116–118.
15. Andrew Higson, *Waving the Flag: Constructing a National Cinema in Britain* (Oxford: Clarendon Press, 1995), 277.
16. Kevin Brownlow, *David Lean: A Biography* (New York: St. Martin's Press, 1996), 231.
17. Ibid., 245.
18. Tony Kushner, *The Persistence of Prejudice: Antisemitism in British Society During the Second World War* (Manchester: Manchester University Press, 1989), 119.
19. Anthony Slide, *"Banned in the USA": British Films in the United States and Their Censorship, 1933–1960* (London: I.B. Tauris), 113.
20. Kushner, *Persistence*, 117.
21. Paula Bartley and Barbara Gwinnett, "Prostitution," in *Women in Twentieth–Century Britain*, ed. Ina Zweiniger-Bargielowska (Harlow: Longman, 2001), 225.
22. Lant, *Blackout*, 79, 78.

5   Violence, Liberation, and Desire

1. Bruce M. Owen and Steven S. Wildman, *Video Economics* (Cambridge: Harvard University Press, 1992), 92.

2. Claire Monk, "The British Heritage-Film Debate Revisited," in *British Historical Cinema: The History, Heritage and Costume Film*, ed. Claire Monk and Amy Sargeant (London: Routledge, 2002), 177.
3. Claire Monk and Amy Sargeant, *British Historical Cinema: The History, Heritage and Costume Film* (London: Routledge, 2002), 1.
4. Julianne Pidduck, *Contemporary Costume Film: Space, Place and the Past* (London: British Film Institute, 2004), 8–9.
5. Terry A. Lugaila and Arlene F. Saluter, "Marital Status and Living Arrangements: March 1996" (Washington, DC: United States Department of Commerce, Economics and Statistics Administration, 1998).
6. For contrasting views see, for example, Barbara Dafoe Whitehead, *The Divorce Culture* (New York: Alfred A. Knopf, 1997); Kurz Demie, *For Richer, For Poorer: Mothers Confront Divorce* (New York: Routledge, 1995).
7. Martin Pugh, *Women and the Women's Movement in Britain, 1914–1999*, Second edition (Houndmills: Macmillan, 2000), 339–340.
8. Robert Bly, *Iron John: A Book about Men* (Reading: Addison-Wesley, 1990), 8.
9. Clarissa Pinkola Estes, *Women Who Run with the Wolves: Myths and Stories of the Wild Woman Archetype* (New York: Ballantine, 1992), 4.
10. Michael Korda, *Making the List: A Cultural History of the American Bestseller, 1900–1999: As Seen through the Annual Bestseller Lists of Publishers Weekly* (New York: Barnes & Noble, 2001), 201–219.
11. Janice Doane and Devon Hodges, *Nostalgia and Sexual Difference* (New York: Methuen, 1987), 142.
12. Devoney Looser, "Feminist Implications of the Silver Screen Austen," in *Jane Austen in Hollywood*, ed. Linda Troost and Sayre Greenfeild (Lexington: University of Kentucky Press, 1998), 159–162.
13. Kristin Flieger Samuelian, "Piracy Is Our Only Option: Postfeminist Intervention in *Sense and Sensibility*," in *Jane Austen in Hollywood*, ed. Troost and Greenfield, 148–149.
14. Pugh, *Women*, Second edition, 335.
15. Leslie Heywood and Jennifer Drake, eds., *Third Wave Agenda: Being Feminist: Doing Feminism* (Minneapolis: University of Minnesota Press, 1997), 3.
16. Christina Hoff Sommers, *Who Stole Feminism? How Women Have Betrayed Women* (New York: Simon and Schuster, 1994).
17. Kaite Roiphe, *The Morning After: Sex, Fear, and Feminism on Campus* (Boston: Little Brown and Company, 1993), 6.
18. Naomi Wolf, *Promiscuities* (New York: Random House, 1997), 223.
19. See, for example, Lisa Hopkins, "Mr. Darcy's Body: Privileging the Male Gaze," in *Jane Austen in Hollywood*, ed. Troost and Greenfield; Stella Bruzzi, *Undressing Cinema* (See Introduction, n. 29).
20. Elizabeth Langland, *Ann Bronte: The Other One* (Totowa: Barnes and Noble Books, 1989), 140.
21. Maria H. Frawley, *Anne Bronte* (New York: Twayne, 1996), 135.
22. Langland, *Ann Bronte*, 131.
23. *Jane Eyre*, dir. Robert Young (A & E Television Networks, 1997) (my transcription).
24. Arts and Entertainment Network, *Jane Eyre*, "Interview with Sally Head" http://www.aetv.com/scenes/janeeyre/index.html (no longer available).

25. See Edward Said, *Culture and Imperialism* (New York: Knopf, 1993); Johnson, *Jane Austen*, xvi–xvii (see Chapter 1, n. 12); Susan Fraiman, "Jane Austen and Edward Said: Gender, Culture and Imperialism," *Critical Inquiry* 21, no. 4 (1995): 805–821.
26. Robert A. Rosenstone, "Looking at the Past in a Postliterate Age," in *The Historical Film: History and Memory in Media*, ed. Marcia Landy (New Brunswick: Rutgers University Press, 2001), 55.
27. Marisa DiNatale and Stephanie Boras, "The Labor Force Experience of Women from Generation X," in *Monthly Labor Review* (Bureau of Labor Statistics, March, 2002), 3.
28. Michelle Sidler, "Living in Mcjobdom: Third Wave Feminism and Class Inequity," in *Third Wave Agenda: Being Feminist: Doing Feminism*, ed. Leslie Heywood and Jennifer Drake (Minneapolis: University of Minnesota, 1997), 27–28.
29. Ibid., 26.
30. DiNatale and Boras, "The Labor Force Experience of Women from Generation X."
31. Pugh, *Women*, Second edition, 342.
32. Charlotte Brunsdon, "Not Having It All: Women and Film in the 1990s," in *British Cinema of the 90s* ed. Robert Murphy (London: British Film Institute, 2000), 167.

6   Re-creating the Classics: *The Piano*

1. Marli Feldvoss, "Jane Campion: Making Friends by Directing Films," in *Jane Campion: Interviews*, ed. Virginia Wright Wexman (Jackson: University Press of Mississippi, 1999), 91.
2. Miro Bilbrough, "The Piano," in Wexman, *Interviews*, 114.
3. Lynda Dyson, "The Return of the Repressed? Whiteness, Femininity, and Colonialism in *The Piano*," *Screen* 36, no. 3 (1995): 267–268.
4. Feldvoss, "Jane Campion," 99.
5. Andreas Furler, "Structure Is Essential/Absolutely Crucial/One of the Most Important Things," in Wexman, *Interviews*, 91.
6. Thomas Bourguignon and Michel Ciment, "Interview with Jane Campion: More Barbarian Than Aesthete," in Wexman, *Interviews*, 110.
7. Michael Davis, "'Tied to That Maternal Thing': Death and Desire in Jane Campion's *The Piano*," *Gothic Studies* 4, no. 1 (2002): 63–64.
8. Cyndy Hendershot, "(Re)Visioning the Gothic: Jane Campion's *The Piano*," *Literature/Film Quarterly* 26, no. 2 (1998): 100.
9. Vincent Ostria and Thierry Jousse, "*The Piano*: Interview with Jane Campion," in Wexman, *Interviews*, 124.
10. Davis, "Tied," 64.
11. Diane Long Hoeveler, "Silence, Sex, and Feminism: An Examination of *The Piano*'s Unacknowledged Sources," *Literature/Film Quarterly* 26, no. 2 (1998): 112.
12. Davis, "Tied," 73.
13. Greg Bentley, "Mothers, Daughters, and (Absent) Fathers in Jane Campion's *The Piano*," *Literature/Film Quarterly* 30, no. 1 (2002): 56.

Bibliography

Aldgate, Anthony, and Jeffrey Richards. *Best of British: Cinema and Society from 1930 to the Present*. London: I.B. Tauris, 1999.

Armstrong, Nancy. *Desire and Domestic Fiction: A Political History of the Novel*. New York: Oxford University Press, 1987.

Atkins, Elizabeth. *"Jane Eyre* Transformed." *Literature/Film Quarterly* 21, no. 1 (1993): 54–60.

Austen, Jane. *Mansfield Park*. London: Penguin, 2003.

——. *Pride and Prejudice*. London: Penguin, 1985.

Barnard, Rita. *The Great Depression and the Culture of Abundance*. Cambridge: Cambridge University Press, 1995.

Barreca, Regina. "David Lean's *Great Expectations*." In *Dickens on Screen*, edited by John Glavin. Cambridge: Cambridge University Press, 2003.

Bartley, Paula, and Barbara Gwinnett. "Prostitution." In *Women in Twentieth-Century Britain*, edited by Ina Zweiniger-Bargielowska. Harlow: Longman, 2001.

Bentley, Greg. "Mothers, Daughters, and (Absent) Fathers in Jane Campion's *The Piano*." *Literature/Film Quarterly* 30, no. 1 (2002): 46–58.

Bilbrough, Miro. "The Piano." In *Jane Campion: Interviews*, edited by Virginia Wright Wexman. Jackson: University Press of Mississippi, 1999.

Bluestone, George. *Novels into Films*. Berkeley: University of California Press, 1973.

Bly, Robert. *Iron John: A Book about Men*. Reading: Addison-Wesley, 1990.

Bourguignon, Thomas, and Michel Ciment. "Interview with Jane Campion: More Barbarian Than Aesthete." In *Jane Campion: Interviews*, edited by Virginia Wright Wexman. Jackson: University Press of Mississippi, 1999.

Bowen, Elizabeth. *English Novelists*. London: W. Collins, 1942.

Braddon, Mary Elizabeth. *Lady Audley's Secret*. Oxford: Oxford University Press, 2003.

Brady, Kristin. *George Eliot*. New York: St. Martin's, 1992.

Brontë, Anne. *The Tenant of Wildfell Hall*. London: Penguin, 1996.

Brontë, Charlotte. *Jane Eyre*. London: Penguin, 1985.

Brontë, Emily. *Wuthering Heights*. London: Penguin, 1985.

Brownlow, Kevin. *David Lean: A Biography*. New York: St. Martin's, 1996.

Brownstein, Rachel. "Out of the Drawing Room, onto the Lawn." In *Jane Austen in Hollywood*, edited by Linda Troost and Sayre Greenfield. Lexington: University Press of Kentucky, 1998.

Brunsdon, Charlotte. "Not Having It All: Women and Film in the 1990s." In *British Cinema of the 90s*. ed. Robert Murphy. London: British Film Institute, 2000.

Bruzzi, Stella. *Undressing Cinema: Clothing and Identity in the Movies*. London: Routledge, 1997.

Cartmell, Deborah, I. Q. Hunter, Heidi Kaye, and Imelda Whelehan, eds. *Classics in Film and Fiction*. London: Pluto Press, 2000.

Cartmell, Deborah, and Imelda Whelehan, eds. *Adaptations: From Text to Screen, Screen to Text*. London: Routledge, 1999.

Cecil, David. *Early Victorian Novelists: Essays in Revaluation.* Indianapolis: Bobbs-Merrill, 1935.

Chafe, William Henry. *The American Woman: Her Changing Social, Economic, and Political Roles, 1920–1970.* London: Oxford University Press, 1972.

Collins, Norman. *The Facts of Fiction.* New York: E.P. Dutton, 1933.

Collins, Wilkie. *The Woman in White.* London: Penguin, 2003.

Cook, Pam. *Fashioning the Nation: Costume and Identity in British Cinema.* London: British Film Institute, 1996.

Copeland, Edward. *Women Writing about Money: Women's Fiction in England, 1790–1820.* Cambridge: Cambridge University Press, 1995.

Daleski, H. M. *The Divided Heroine: A Recurrent Pattern in Six English Novels.* New York: Homes and Meier, 1984.

Daniel, Robert L. *American Women in the 20th Century: The Festival of Life.* San Diego: Harcourt Brace Jovanovich, 1987.

Davis, Michael. "'Tied to That Maternal Thing': Death and Desire in Jane Campion's *The Piano.*" *Gothic Studies* 4, no. 1 (2002): 63–78.

Dever, Carolyn. *Death and the Mother from Dickens to Freud: Victorian Fiction and the Anxiety of Origins.* New York: Cambridge University Press, 1998.

Dickens, Charles. *Great Expectations.* London: Penguin, 2003.

———. *Oliver Twist.* London: Penguin, 1985.

DiNatale, Marisa, and Stephanie Boras. "The Labor Force Experience of Women from Generation X." In *Monthly Labor Review*: Bureau of Labor Statistics, Washington D.C. March 2002.

Doane, Janice, and Devon Hodges. *Nostalgia and Sexual Difference.* New York: Methuen, 1987.

Doane, Mary Ann. *The Desire to Desire: The Woman's Film of the 1940s.* Bloomington: Indiana University Press, 1987.

Dunne, Michael. *Intertextual Encounters in American Fiction, Film, and Popular Culture.* Bowling Green: Bowling Green University Popular Press, 2001.

Durgnat, Raymond. *A Mirror for England: British Movies from Austerity to Affluence.* New York: Praeger, 1971.

Dyson, Lynda. "The Return of the Repressed? Whiteness, Femininity, and Colonialism in *The Piano.*" *Screen* 36, no. 3 (1995): 267–276.

Eagleton, Terry. *Myths of Power: A Marxist Study of the Brontës.* London: Macmillan, 1975.

Eckert, Charles. "The Carol Lombard in Macy's Window." In *Movies and Mass Culture,* edited by John Belton. New Brunswick: Rutgers University Press, 1996.

Eisenstein, Sergei. "Dickens, Griffith and the Film Today." In *Film Form,* edited by Jay Leyda. New York: Harcourt Brace and Company, 1949.

Eliot, George. *The Mill on the Floss.* New York: W.W. Norton and Company, 1994.

Elliott, Kamilla. *Rethinking the Novel/Film Debate.* Cambridge: Cambridge University Press, 2003.

Ellis, Kate, and E. Ann Kaplan. "Feminism in Brontë's Novel and Its Film Versions." In *The English Novel and the Movies,* edited by Michael Klein and Gillian Parker. New York: Frederick Unger, 1981.

Ellis, Sarah S. *The Daughters of England: Their Position in Society, Character and Responsibilities.* New York: D. Appleton, 1842.

———. *The Wives of England, Their Relative Duties, Domestic Influence and Social Obligations.* London: Fisher, 1843.

Estes, Clarissa Pinkola. *Women Who Run with the Wolves: Myths and Stories of the Wild Woman Archetype.* New York: Ballantine, 1992.

Ewan, Stuart. *Captains of Consciousness.* New York: McGraw-Hill Book Company, 1976.

Feldvoss, Marli. "Jane Campion: Making Friends by Directing Films." In *Jane Campion: Interviews,* edited by Virginia Wright Wexman. Jackson: University Press of Mississippi, 1999.

Frawley, Maria H. *Anne Bronte.* New York: Twayne, 1996.

Furler, Andreas. "Structure Is Essential/Absolutely Crucial/One of the Most Important Things." In *Jane Campion: Interviews,* edited by Virginia Wright Wexman. Jackson: University Press of Mississippi, 1999.

Giddings, Robert, and Erica Sheen, eds. *The Classic Novel: From Page to Screen.* Manchester: Manchester University Press, 2000.

Gilbert, Sandra M., and Susan Gubar. *The Madwoman in the Attic: The Woman Writer and the Nineteenth-Century Literary Imagination.* New Haven: Yale University Press, 1984.

Goodman, Charlotte. "The Lost Brother, the Twin: Women Novelists and the Male Female Double Bildungsroman." *Novel* 17 (1983): 28–42.

Gordon, Suzy. "'I Clipped Your Wing, That's All': Auto-Erotism and the Female Spectator in *The Piano* Debate." *Screen* 37, no. 2 (1996): 193–205.

Hall, Lesley A. *Sex, Gender and Social Change in Britain since 1880.* New York: St. Martin's, 2000.

Harper, Sue. *Picturing the Past: The Rise and Fall of the British Costume Film.* London: British Film Institute, 1994.

Harrington, John. "Wyler as Auteur." In *The English Novel and the Movies,* edited by Michael Klein and Gillian Parker, 67–82. New York: Frederick Unger, 1981.

Hartmann, Susan. *The Home Front and Beyond: American Women in the 1940s.* Boston: Twayne, 1982.

Harvey, John R. *Victorian Novelists and Their Illustrators.* New York: New York University Press, 1970.

Heller, Deborah. "The Outcast As Villain and Victim: Jews in Dickens's *Oliver Twist* and *Our Mutual Friend.*" In *Jewish Presences in English Literature,* edited by Derek Cohen and Deborah Heller. Montreal: McGill-Queen's University Press, 1990.

Hendershot, Cyndy. "(Re)Visioning the Gothic: Jane Campion's *The Piano.*" *Literature/Film Quarterly* 26, no. 2 (1998): 97–108.

Heywood, Leslie, and Jennifer Drake, eds. *Third Wave Agenda: Being Feminist: Doing Feminism.* Minneapolis: University of Minnesota Press, 1997.

Higson, Andrew. *Waving the Flag: Constructing a National Cinema in Britain.* Oxford: Clarendon Press, 1995.

Hoeveler, Diane Long. "Silence, Sex, and Feminism: An Examination of *The Piano*'s Unacknowledged Sources." *Literature/Film Quarterly* 26, no. 2 (1998): 97–108.

Honey, Maureen. *Creating Rosie the Riveter: Class, Gender, and Propaganda during World War II.* Amherst: University of Massachusetts Press, 1984.

Hopkins, Lisa. "Mr. Darcy's Body: Privileging the Male Gaze." In *Jane Austen in Hollywood,* edited by Linda Troost and Sayre Greenfield. Lexington: Kentucky University Press, 1998.

———. *Screening the Gothic.* Austin: University of Texas Press, 2005.

Houston, Gail Turley. *Consuming Fictions: Gender, Class and Hunger in Dickens' Novels*. New York: St. Martin's Press, 1997.

Jacobs, Lea. *The Wages of Sin: Censorship and the Fallen Woman Film, 1928–1942*. Madison: University of Wisconsin Press, 1991.

Kessler-Harris, Alice. *Out to Work: A History of Wage Earning Women in the United States*. Oxford: Oxford University Press, 1982.

Kushner, Tony. *The Persistence of Prejudice: Antisemitism in British Society during the Second World War*. Manchester: Manchester University Press, 1989.

Landy, Marcia. *British Genres: Cinema and Society, 1930–1960*. Princeton: Princeton University Press, 1991.

Langland, Elizabeth. *Ann Bronte: The Other One*. Totowa: Barnes and Noble Books, 1989.

Lant, Antonia. *Blackout: Reinventing Women for Cinema*. Princeton: Princeton University Press, 1991.

LaPlace, Maria. "Producing and Consuming the Woman's Film: Discursive Struggle in *Now, Voyager*." In *Home Is Where the Heart Is*, edited by Christine Gledhill. London: British Film Institute, 1994.

Lawson-Peebles, Robert. "European Conflict and Hollywood's Reconstruction of English Fiction." *Yearbook of English Studies* 26 (1996): 1–13.

Lejeune, C. A. "Drawn by Cruikshank," *Times*, June 27, 1948.

Lewis, Jane. "In Search of Real Equality: Women between the Wars." In *Class, Culture and Social Change: A New View of the 1930s*, edited by Frank Gloversmith. Brighton: Harvester, 1980.

Looser, Devoney. "Feminist Implications of the Silver Screen Austen." In *Jane Austen in Hollywood*, edited by Linda Troost and Sayre Greenfield. Lexington: University of Kentucky Press, 1998.

Lugaila, Terry A., and Arlene F. Saluter. "Marital Status and Living Arrangements: March 1996." Washington, DC: United States Department of Commerce, Economics and Statistics Administration, 1998.

May, Leila Silvana. "The Strong-Arming of Desire: A Reconsideration of Nancy Armstrong's *Desire and Domestic Fiction*." *English Literary History*, no. 68 (2001): 267–285.

Maynard, John. *Charlotte Bronte and Sexuality*. Cambridge: Cambridge University Press, 1984.

McComb, Mary. "Rate Your Date: Young Women and the Commodification of Depression Era Courtship." In *Delinquents and Debutantes: Twentieth Century American Girls' Cultures*, edited by Sherrie A. Inness. New York: New York University Press, 1998.

McDonnell, Jane. "'Perfect Goodness' or 'the Wider Life': *The Mill on the Floss* As *Bildungsroman*." *Genre* 15, no. 4 (1982): 379–402.

McFarlane, Brian. "A Literary Cinema? British Films and British Novels." In *All Our Yesterdays: 90 Years of British Cinema*, edited by Charles Barr. London: British Film Institute, 1986.

McNight, Natalie. *Suffering Mothers in Mid-Victorian Novels*. New York: St. Martin's Press, 1997.

Miles, Peter, and Malcom Smith. *Cinema, Literature and Society*. London: Croom Helm, 1987.

Milkman, Ruth. "Women's Work and the Economic Crisis: Some Lessons from the Great Depression." In *A Heritage of Her Own: Toward a New Social History of American Women*. New York: Simon and Schuster, 1979.

Miller, D. A. "Cages aux folles: Sensation and Gender in Wilkie Collins's *The Woman in White*." *Representations* 14 (1986): 107–135.

Mills, Pamela. "Wyler's Version of Brontë's Storms in *Wuthering Heights*." *Literature/Film Quarterly* 24 (1996): 414–422.

Mitchell, Judith. *The Stone and the Scorpion: The Female Subject of Desire in the Novels of Charlotte Bronte, George Eliot and Thomas Hardy*. Westport: Greenwood, 1994.

Modleski, Tania. *The Women Who Knew Too Much: Hitchcock and Feminist Theory*. New York: Routledge, 1988.

Monk, Claire. "The British Heritage-Film Debate Revisited." In *British Historical Cinema: The History, Heritage and Costume Film*, edited by Claire Monk and Amy Sargeant. London: Routledge, 2002.

Monk, Claire, and Amy Sargeant. *British Historical Cinema: The History, Heritage and Costume Film*. London: Routledge, 2002.

Naremore, James, ed. *Film Adaptation*. New Brunswick: Rutgers University Press, 2000.

Nash, Robert Jay, and Stanley Ralph Ross. *The Motion Picture Guide W–Z 1927–1984*. Chicago: Cinebooks, 1987.

Newman, Karen. "Can This Marriage Be Saved: Jane Austen Makes Sense of an Ending." In *Sense and Sensibility and Pride and Prejudice*, edited by Robert Clark. New York: St. Martin's Press, 1994.

Newton, Judith Lowder. *Women, Power and Subversion: Social Strategies in British Fiction*. Athens: University of Georgia Press, 1981.

North, Julian. "Conservative Austen, Radical Austen." In *Adaptations: From Text to Screen, Screen to Text*, edited by Deborah Cartmell and Imelda Whelehan. London: Routledge, 1999.

Onega, Susana, and Christian Gutleben, eds. *Refracting the Canon in Contemporary British Literature and Film*. Amsterdam: Rodopi, 2004.

Ostria, Vincent, and Thierry Jousse. "*The Piano*: Interview with Jane Campion." In *Jane Campion: Interviews*, edited by Virginia Wright Wexman. Jackson: University Press of Mississippi, 1999.

Owen, Bruce M., and Steven S. Wildman. *Video Economics*. Cambridge: Harvard University Press, 1992.

Paglia, Camille. *Sex, Art and American Culture*. New York: Vintage, 1992.

Parrish, Michael E. *Anxious Decades: America in Prosperity and Depression, 1920–1941*. New York: W.W. Norton and Company, 1992.

Pidduck, Julianne. *Contemporary Costume Film: Space, Place and the Past*. London: British Film Institute, 2004.

Poovey, Mary. *Uneven Developments: The Ideological Work of Gender in Mid-Victorian England*. Chicago: University of Chicago Press, 1988.

Pugh, Martin. *State and Society: British Political and Social History, 1870–1992*. London: Edward Arnold, 1994.

———. *Women and the Women's Movement in Britain, 1914–1959*. London: Macmillan, 1992.

———. *Women and the Women's Movement in Britain, 1914–1999*. Second edition. Houndmills: Macmillan, 2000.

Pykett, Lyn. *The "Improper" Feminine: The Women's Sensation Novel and the New Woman Writing*. London: Routledge, 1992.

Ragussis, Michael. *Figures of Conversion: "The Jewish Question" and English National Identity*. Durham: Duke University Press, 1995.

Ray, Robert B. "The Field of Literature and Film." In *Film Adaptation*, edited by James Naremore. New Brunswick: Rutgers University Press, 2000.

Richards, Jeffrey. *Films and British National Identity: From Dickens to Dad's Army*. Manchester: Manchester University Press, 1997.

Roiphe, Kaite. *The Morning After: Sex, Fear, and Feminism on Campus*. Boston: Little Brown and Company, 1993.

Rosenstone, Robert A. "Looking at the Past in a Postliterate Age." In *The Historical Film: History and Memory in Media*, edited by Marcia Landy. New Brunswick: Rutgers University Press, 2001.

Royle, Edward. *Modern Britain: A Social History 1750–1997*. London: Arnold, 1997.

Ruskin, John. "Of Queens' Gardens." In *Sesame and Lilies*, edited by J. W. Linn. Chicago: Scott, Foreman and Company, 1904.

Sampson, George. *Concise Cambridge History of English Literature*. Cambridge: Cambridge University Press, 1941.

Samuelian, Kristin Flieger. "Piracy Is Our Only Option: Postfeminist Intervention in *Sense and Sensibility*." In *Jane Austen in Hollywood*, edited by Linda Troost and Sayre Greenfield. Lexington: Kentucky University Press, 1998.

Sconce, Jeffrey. "Narrative Authority and Social Narrativity: The Cinematic Reconstitution of Bronte's *Jane Eyre*." *Wide-Angle: A Film Quarterly of Theory, Criticism, and Practice* 10, no. 1 (1988): 46–61.

Sidler, Michelle. "Living in Mcjobdom: Third Wave Feminism and Class Inequity." In *Third Wave Agenda: Being Feminist: Doing Feminism*, edited by Leslie Heywood and Jennifer Drake. Minneapolis: University of Minnesota, 1997.

Slide, Anthony. *"Banned in the USA": British Films in the United States and Their Censorship, 1933–1960*. London: I.B. Tauris, 1998.

Sommers, Christina Hoff. *Who Stole Feminism? How Women Have Betrayed Women*. New York: Simon and Schuster, 1994.

Spear, Jeffrey L. *Dreams of an English Eden: Ruskin and His Tradition in Social Criticism*. New York: Columbia University Press, 1984.

Stam, Robert. *Literature through Film: Realism, Magic and the Art of Adaptation*. Malden: Blackwell Publishing, 2005.

Stam, Robert, and Alessandra Raengo. *A Companion to Literature and Film*. Malden: Blackwell Publishers, 2004.

———. *Literature and Film: A Guide to the Theory and Practice of Film Adaptation*. Malden: Blackwell Publishing, 2005.

Stoneman, Patsy. "Catherine Earnshaw's Journey to Her Home among the Dead: Fresh Thoughts on *Wuthering Heights* and 'Epipsychidion'." *Review of English Studies* 47 (1996): 521–533.

Sussman, Warren I. *Culture As History: The Transformation of American Society in the Twentieth Century*. New York: Pantheon, 1973.

Thompson, James. "Jane Austen's Clothing." *Studies in Eighteenth Century Culture* 13 (1984): 217–247.

Troost, Linda, and Sayre Greenfield, eds. *Jane Austen in Hollywood*. Lexington: Kentucky University Press, 1998.

"The Twenty Five Most Intriguing People of 1995." *People Weekly*, December 25, 1995.

Van Ghent, Dorothy Bendon. *The English Novel, Form and Function*. New York: Rinehart, 1953.

Wandersee, Winnifred D. *Women's Work and Family Values, 1920–1940.* Cambridge: Harvard University Press, 1981.

Waters, Catherine. *Dickens and the Politics of the Family.* Cambridge: Cambridge University Press, 1997.

Watts, Stephen. "Britain Makes Her Greatest Film." *Sunday Express*, December 15, 1946.

Weatherford, Doris. *American Women and World War II.* New York: Facts on File, 1990.

Weeks, Jeffrey. *Sex, Politics and Society: The Regulation of Sexuality since 1800.* London: Longman, 1989.

Wiesenfarth, Joseph. "The Garson-Olivier *Pride and Prejudice*: A Hollywood Story." In *Text und Tom im Film*, edited by Paul Goetsch and Dietrich Scheunemann. Tubingen: Gunter Narr Verlag Tubingen, 1997.

Wolf, Naomi. *Fire with Fire: The New Female Power and How It Will Change the 21st Century.* New York: Random House, 1993.

———. *Promiscuities.* New York: Random House, 1997.

Woolf, Virginia. *Three Guineas.* San Diego: Harcourt Brace and Company, 1986.

Index